food network kitchens
cookbook

Meredith® Press
Des Moines, Iowa

A note of thanks

This is Food Network Kitchens' first cookbook. And it happily coincides with Food Network's 10-year anniversary. We know that most people are totally unaware that there is an actual kitchen behind the many kitchens you see on Food Network's cooking shows. But there is.

It's a unique kitchen of talented food professionals who are passionate about food and who work alongside our amazing on-air chefs to keep things moving. They cook, taste, shop, prep, write recipes . . . and have a whole lot of fun along the way. Our goal here is to share what we've learned over the years with you.

Of course, none of this would have been possible without the support of our publisher, Meredith Books. Thanks to Jennifer Darling and Mick Schnepf for their guidance, Joline Rivera and Lisa Kingsley for their design and copy, Lynn Gimpel who put words to our food, Mark Ferri and Robert Jacobs for the delicious photos, and Francine Matalon-Degni for her thoughtful prop styling.

Very special thanks goes to our Food Network Kitchens development team headed up by Test Kitchen manager Katherine Alford, who has the ability to taste a recipe many times with equal enthusiasm—with the exception of split pea soup.

Food Network recipe testers Suki Hertz, Mory Thomas, and Santos Loo—with additional help from Todd Coleman, Wes Martin, Vivian Jao, Geraldini Cresci, Bianca Henry, Susanne Gruber, Cathy Young, Jeannie Chen—prepared, tweaked, and tasted recipes until we were all satisfied they were absolutely delicious. Thanks also to recipe editor Miriam Garron.

Food Network Kitchen stylists Krista Ruane, Leslie Orlandini, and chef Rob Bleifer styled these gorgeous food photos with help from staff stylists Jay Brooks, Bob Hoebee, and Andrea Steinberg.

Thanks also to department director Derek Flynn for his unflagging humor and good appetite, shopper Stacy Meyer, Lynn Kearney and her editorial team: Jill Novatt, Eileen McClash, and Harriet Siew. Also, Miguel Deleon, Athen Fleming, and David Martin for keeping on top of dishes and always knowing where everything is! Finally, thank you to Susan Maynard for keeping us all centered and on schedule.

I've had the unbelievable good fortune of being with Food Network Kitchens since the early days and I sincerely hope you'll enjoy this collection of our personal, all-time favorite foods; a lot of love comes with every recipe.

Susan

Susan Stockton, VP, Culinary Production

DEDICATION

This book is dedicated to every cook, author, celebrity chef, and home cook who has passed through the busy intersection that is Food Network Kitchens on their way to the studio. And to all the talented people who are the Food Network family.

Who's who at the Food Network Kitchens

Back row, left to right: Derek Flynn, Athen Fleming, Mory Thomas, Lynn Kearney, Santos Loo, Rob Bleifer, David Martin.
Middle row, left to right: Bob Hoebee, Susan Maynard, Andrea Steinberg, Krista Ruane, Susan Stockton, Eileen McClash, Katherine Alford, Jill Novatt. **Front row, left to right:** Jay Brooks, Suki Hertz, Miguel DeLeon, Vivian Jao, Harriet Siew.

Meredith₋ Press
An imprint of Meredith₋ Books

Food Network Kitchens Cookbook
Editor: Jennifer Dorland Darling
Senior Associate Design Director: Mick Schnepf
Contributing Editor: Lisa Kingsley
Graphic Designer: Joline Rivera, idesign&associates, inc.
Contributing Writer: Lynn Gimpel
Photographers: Mark Ferri, Robert Jacobs

Copy Chief: Terri Fredrickson
Copy and Production Editor: Victoria Forlini
Editorial Operations Manager: Karen Schirm
Managers, Book Production: Pam Kvitne, Marjorie J. Schenkelberg,
Rick von Holdt
Editorial & Design Assistants: Karen McFadden, Mary Lee Gavin

Meredith₋ Books
Editor in Chief: Linda Raglan Cunningham
Design Director: Matt Strelecki
Publisher: James D. Blume

Executive Director, Marketing: Jeffrey Myers
Executive Director, New Business Development: Todd M. Davis
Executive Director, Sales: Ken Zagor
Director, Operations: George A. Susral
Director, Production: Douglas M. Johnston
Business Director: Jim Leonard

Vice President and General Manager: Douglas J. Guendel

Meredith Publishing Group
President, Publishing Group: Stephen M. Lacy
Vice President-Publishing Director: Bob Mate

Meredith Corporation
Chairman and Chief Executive Officer: William T. Kerr

In Memoriam: E. T. Meredith III (1933–2003)

Food Network
A division of the E.W. Scripps Company
Vice President, Culinary Productions: Susan Stockton
Senior Writer, Content Development: Katherine Alford
Director, Culinary Production: Derek Flynn

contents

Pictured on front cover: Blue Cheese Steak Sandwiches (see recipe, page 84)

How to use this book

Like the gorgeous food we get to make every day, like the television shows we have a hand in producing, this book is a labor of love. Though we think it's beautiful enough to sit on your coffee table, we hope it will get butter-stained and dog-eared in your kitchen. **Here's what you'll find on every page:**

OUR FOOD: The food that went into *Food Network Kitchens Cookbook*—and what comes out of our kitchens—is best described as Modern American. It's inspired by the techniques and flavors of world cuisines—Asian, Latin, African, and European among them—but uses ingredients you can find in your local markets. What makes our recipes special, we think, is the twist we give them. We've included classics such as fried chicken, Cobb salad, and devil's food cake, but have made them fresher, fuller-flavored, or simply more fun.

SENSITIVITY TO YOUR SCHEDULE: Some of our recipes are all about getting dinner on the table on a weeknight; others are for puttering around and spending some leisure time in the kitchen on a weekend.

BASIC TECHNIQUE: As you leaf through the book trying to decide what to make next, be sure to check out the Essentials chapter that begins on page 266. You'll find shopping, cooking, and presentation tips that will make preparing the recipes in the rest of the book much easier—and the end result even more tantalizing to look at. If you see an ingredient or technique you're not familiar with, check Essentials for additional information—or simply for some good foundation that you can apply to all kinds of recipes. Before you bake, for example, look at page 277 for how we measure dry ingredients, cream our butter, and whip our egg whites.

HOW WE APPROACH EVERY RECIPE: There are a few very simple, almost effortless, things you can do to make your cooking better and easier. Make them—as we have—routine. Before you begin cooking, read the recipe from beginning to end so you know exactly what will be happening as you cook and you'll know just what to expect in terms of time. Use the best-quality ingredients you can find and have them all assembled so you don't have to do a harried last-minute run to the store. As you're gathering your ingredients, check your spices, baking powder and baking soda, and yeast for freshness. We use kosher salt for cooking (we love the burst of flavor it gives to foods and it's easy to handle), fine salt for baking, and always, always freshly ground pepper. Use the measured amounts of salt and pepper given in a recipe, but sample while you're cooking to suit your taste.

AN EYE FOR WHAT YOU WANT TO EAT: That's really what it all comes down to: your taste. We're confident that there's something for everyone in every chapter. From eye-opening breakfast foods to fabulous desserts, there's a terrific mix of comforting, familiar flavors and fun surprises. We know you can cook something from these pages that you, your family, and your friends will absolutely love. Our life's work may be to cook, but it's our passion too. There is nothing quite like the pleasure of good food and the satisfaction of having made it yourself.

The making of our kitchens

10 years behind the scenes | 11,000 cooking shows | 6 continents | 27 countries | 50 cuisines | 30,000 recipes tested & tasted | 214 combined years of culinary experience | 456 parties catered | 1,000 mixing bowls | 2,000 whisks, spoons & spatulas | 673 holiday turkeys | 6,000 quarts extra-virgin olive oil | 1,500 pounds Parmigiano-Reggiano | Enough chocolate to build an Eiffel Tower | A mountain of sea salt & freshly ground pepper, eggs & sugar, garlic & onions...never enough

5:45 A.M.
Early call. One of our Food Network chefs is on the *Today Show*, and food must be prepared and packed up for the short dash to Rockefeller Plaza.

7:00 A.M.
The daily mountain of produce, flowers, meat, and fish arrives and needs to be checked in. It must all be picture-perfect or it gets sent back.

8:00 A.M.
The on-set team of food stylists confers with the kitchen on the game plan for the taping of today's four cooking shows. Then they hurry to dress the set with some of that perfect produce that was just delivered and then rush to be on the soundstage to brief the guest chef at 8:30 a.m.

9:00 A.M.
The test kitchen is setting up to try out five new recipes for our cookbook while stylists work with our photographer to shoot five recipes that were tested and approved last week.

10:00 A.M.
Shoppers are in Chinatown for baby bok choy and at the farmer's market handpicking heirloom tomatoes for set still lifes that will be on-air this afternoon.

11:00 A.M.
Our editorial staff is researching the history of salt, sea urchins, and beets for an upcoming show script that will be sent to the kitchens for tomorrow's tapings. Later in the day, the recipes from today's shows will be proofed and loaded up to our Web site so viewers who were inspired by watching them being made can make them themselves.

12:00 NOON
Lunch is served! Check out the chicken-lemongrass soup from the test kitchen and let them know what you think.

Combine all these ingredients with a dash of wit, mix in a few bushels of passion, and you'll still only get a taste of what the Food Network Kitchens are about.

The Food Network Kitchens are the real-life kitchens behind every show you see on the air. Along with our terrific chefs and TV production crews, every show we broadcast requires the effort of dozens of food experts including shoppers, cooks and chefs, testers, tasters, stylists, bakers, and recipe developers. We even have professional food researchers who can come up with everything from the history of the string bean to the most classic recipe for pound cake.

A big part of our job is making sure the recipes you see on Food Network taste as good as they look. Slicing and dicing behind the scenes since 1993, the Food Network Kitchens staff tests every Food Network recipe before it goes on the air. We also create every dish in stages so our viewers can follow along every step of the way. You won't find any assembly lines in our kitchens, either. Each recipe is prepared individually, every time.

But the Food Network Kitchens also have a life of their own. We develop a lot of new recipes and take special delight in tweaking old-time favorites—such as macaroni and cheese—just enough to make them taste brand new. And since the best chefs and cooks in the country pass through our studio every day, we're always learning and trying new things.

We also hold cooking classes and throw parties. We play host to dozens of visiting cooking experts and members of the press—and believe us—we feed them well.

The secret ingredient to the success of Food Network Kitchens is simple. We love food. We love the taste of it. The scent of it. The look of it. We love the excitement of it and the surprise of it.

After 10 years of discovering how to pick the perfect produce or prepare the perfect platter of fried chicken; after all of our testing, testing and concocting behind the scenes and around the world, we're bringing the best of what we've learned in our kitchen into yours.

The recipes in this book are all our personal favorites. They are all fresh and new. Many were inspired by your requests for more comfort food, more quick and easy delights, more meatless dishes, more of everything. The flavors are big and bold with just the right amount of spice, and the cuisines are as diverse as America itself. Much like the recipes you've seen on Food Network, the recipes you'll find here were all developed to enchant and challenge you in just the right proportion.

So get cookin'. We'll be with you all the way.

1:00 P.M.
Cookie detail. We need 10 dozen tiny cookies for gift bags at tonight's event—and any event around here involves lots of good food.

3:00 P.M.
Tomorrow's shopping lists are reviewed and orders are placed. The mariachi band arrives early for the party—and they're hungry!

4:00 P.M.
Tasting begins on *Emeril Live's* latest recipe contest. This time it's chocolate. Pies, cookies, cakes, mole, truffles, puddings, soufflés. Who has the milk?

6:00 P.M.
Guests arrive and head straight for the kitchens to see what's cooking.

2:00 P.M.
Change gears. The kitchens are now in party mode making hors d'oeuvres for tonight's press dinner.

3:15 P.M.
Coffee break. Grab a cup of coffee and a slice of birthday cake!

5:00 P.M.
Wrapping up prep for tomorrow's shows. Carts are checked and food is wrapped before it's stored. Arrange hors d'oeuvres and set the tables for tonight's dinner.

morning foods

Whether it's a leisurely stack of cornmeal pancakes or a granola bar on the fly, breakfast sets up the day. Try any one of our morning food recipes and start your day with a smile.

red fruit salad

6 servings

2 red plums, such as Santa Rosa, pitted and quartered

2 cups strawberries, hulled and halved

8 ounces red cherries, halved and pitted

½ cup cranberry juice cocktail

⅓ cup honey

1 vanilla bean, split and scraped

3 coin-size pieces fresh ginger

1 cinnamon stick

1 star anise (optional)

1 cup raspberries

2 tablespoons chopped fresh mint

Crème fraîche or vanilla yogurt

1. Gently toss the plums, strawberries, and cherries together in a large bowl.

2. Stir together the cranberry juice, honey, vanilla bean pod and seeds, ginger, cinnamon, and star anise, if desired, in a small saucepan. Bring the mixture to a simmer, then stir into the fruit mixture. Set aside to cool. Remove vanilla bean pod, ginger, cinnamon stick, and star anise, if using.

3. Gently fold in the raspberries and mint. Serve in bowls topped with a dollop of crème fraîche or yogurt.

COOK'S NOTE Choose whole spices for poaching liquids or making syrups. They're more potent than ground spices and don't leave a dusty-looking residue behind.

1. To split a vanilla bean and release its intensely flavorful seeds, cut the pod lengthwise with the point of a small, sharp paring knife. 2. Scrape the seeds out of the pod with the broad cutting side of the knife. 3. Use both the pod and the seeds.

maple **granola-to-go**

12 servings

If your days start at dawn like ours do, these easy-to-make granola bars will make for a delicious power breakfast.

1½ cups rolled oats

1 cup mixed dried fruit, such as diced apricots, dates, and pears, or blueberries, cranberries, currants, and raisins

¼ cup toasted wheat germ

¼ cup green pumpkin seeds (pepitas)

¼ cup pecans, coarsely chopped

¼ cup whole unskinned almonds, coarsely chopped

2 tablespoons sesame seeds

2 tablespoons unsalted butter

½ cup maple syrup

2 teaspoons pure vanilla extract

2 large egg whites, lightly beaten

1. Preheat the oven to 225°F. Toss the oats, dried fruit, wheat germ, pumpkin seeds, pecans, almonds, and sesame seeds in a large bowl.

2. Melt the butter with 2 tablespoons of the maple syrup in a small saucepan over medium-low heat. Remove from the heat and stir in the vanilla extract. Pour the syrup mixture over the oat mixture and stir to coat evenly.

3. Spread the mixture on a baking sheet. Bake until golden brown, stirring occasionally, about 1½ hours. Remove the mixture from the oven, but leave the oven on.

4. Transfer the granola to a large bowl. Stir in the remaining 6 tablespoons maple syrup and the egg whites. Spray twelve ½-cup nonstick muffin cups with nonstick spray and firmly press about ⅓ cup of the mixture into each. Bake until set, about 45 minutes. Transfer the muffin tin to a rack and cool 15 minutes before unmolding. Store cooled granola up to 1 month at room temperature in a tightly sealed container.

SHOPSMART If you can't find green pumpkin seeds—also called pepitas—at your supermarket, look in a Latino market, or use sunflower or other peeled seeds.

turkey & sweet potato hash
4 servings

HASH

1½ cups coarsely chopped cooked and peeled sweet potatoes

2½ cups shredded cooked turkey

1 large egg white

½ cup queso fresco (see page 271) or farmer's cheese, crumbled (2 ounces)

¼ cup chicken broth, homemade (see page 278) or low-sodium canned

½ medium yellow onion, grated

3 tablespoons chopped fresh cilantro, plus whole leaves for garnish

2 teaspoons kosher salt

2 cloves garlic, minced

1 teaspoon minced chipotle chiles in adobo sauce (see page 273)

Freshly ground black pepper

3 tablespoons unsalted butter

1 teaspoon ground coriander

1 scallion, thinly sliced

Chipotle Cranberry Sauce (see recipe, below) (optional)

SAUCE

Makes ⅔ cup sauce

⅔ cup canned whole-berry cranberry sauce

½ teaspoon minced chipotle chiles in adobo sauce

¼ teaspoon freshly grated lime zest

½ teaspoon freshly squeezed lime juice

Kosher salt and freshly ground black pepper

1. Preheat the oven to 400°F. Mash 1 cup of the sweet potatoes in a large bowl. Stir in the remaining ½ cup sweet potatoes, the turkey, egg white, ¼ cup of the cheese, the chicken broth, onion, chopped cilantro, salt, garlic, chiles, and pepper.

2. Heat 2 tablespoons of the butter and ½ teaspoon of the coriander in an ovenproof 10-inch nonstick skillet over medium heat. Add the potato mixture and spread it evenly in the skillet, pressing lightly to form a solid cake. Cook, shaking the skillet occasionally, until the bottom is set, about 3 minutes.

3. Place a large plate over the skillet and invert so the hash falls onto the plate. Return the skillet to the heat and melt the remaining 1 tablespoon butter with the remaining ½ teaspoon coriander. Slide the hash back into the skillet cooked side up; if it breaks apart, simply reshape it into a solid cake. Cook, shaking the skillet occasionally, for 2 minutes.

4. Transfer the skillet to the oven and bake the hash until firm, about 10 minutes. Carefully invert or slide the hash onto a serving plate and scatter the remaining ¼ cup cheese, the cilantro leaves, and the scallion over the top. Serve with Chipotle Cranberry Sauce, if desired.

CHIPOTLE CRANBERRY SAUCE
Combine the cranberry sauce, chiles, lime zest, and lime juice in a small bowl. Season with salt and pepper.

breakfast crostini

4 to 6 servings

CROSTINI

- ¼ cup dried cherries
- ½ cup hot water
- 1 cup mascarpone cheese (see page 271)
- 2 tablespoons honey
- ¼ teaspoon ground cinnamon
- ¼ teaspoon freshly grated orange zest
- 4 ½-inch-thick slices pumpernickel bread

  Oven-Dried Plums (see recipe, below)
- 1 tablespoon whole unskinned almonds, chopped and toasted

PLUMS

- 4 ripe Santa Rosa or Italian plums, halved and pitted
- 1½ tablespoons sugar

  Pinch kosher salt

1. Position a rack in the upper part of the oven and preheat the broiler. Soak the cherries in the hot water until plumped, about 5 minutes. Drain, discard the liquid, and chop coarsely. Gently stir the cherries into the mascarpone along with the honey, cinnamon, and orange zest; do not overwork the mascarpone or it will get grainy.

2. Halve the bread slices and arrange them on a baking sheet. Broil, turning once, until lightly toasted on both sides, about 3 minutes total. Cool slightly.

3. Place a heaping tablespoon of the mascarpone mixture in the center of each slice of bread, gently press a plum half, skin side down, on top, and sprinkle with some almonds.

OVEN-DRIED PLUMS

1. Preheat the oven to 250°F. Line a baking sheet with parchment paper.

2. Toss the halved plums with the sugar and salt in a medium bowl. Arrange the plums, skin side down, on the prepared baking sheet and bake until almost dried but still slightly moist, about 2½ hours.

COOK'S NOTE In the fall when local plums hit the markets, we oven-dry big batches of them. We love how slow, low heat brings out their natural sweetness and concentrates their flavor. Try them with cheese, tossed in salads, or even with grilled pork or duck. They hold in the refrigerator for up to 5 days.

smoked salmon & cream cheese frittata 4 servings

Two classic luxury ingredients whipped up in a whole new way. This luscious and light blend of flavors takes only 20 minutes to prepare.

6 large eggs

2 tablespoons milk

2 tablespoons thinly sliced fresh chives

I tablespoon chopped fresh dill

I teaspoon kosher salt, plus more for greens

Freshly ground black pepper

2 ounces cream cheese, softened

2 ounces smoked salmon, roughly chopped

3 tablespoons extra-virgin olive oil

4 cups mesclun salad greens (about 3 ounces)

I teaspoon white wine vinegar

I. Position a rack in the center of the oven and preheat to 375°F. Whisk the eggs, milk, chives, dill, the I teaspoon salt, and pepper to taste in a bowl. Using 2 spoons or your fingers, break the cream cheese into bits. Fold the cream cheese and salmon into the egg mixture.

2. Heat I tablespoon of the olive oil in an ovenproof I0-inch nonstick skillet over medium-low heat. Pour the egg mixture into the skillet and stir gently to distribute the fillings in the pan. Cook until the bottom is set but not brown, about 2 minutes. Transfer the skillet to the oven and bake until the top is almost set but still moist, about 9 minutes. Remove from the oven, cover, and set aside for 5 minutes.

3. Season the greens with salt and pepper and toss with the remaining 2 tablespoons oil and the vinegar. Slip the frittata out of the pan onto a cutting board and cut into 4 wedges. Divide the salad and frittata among 4 plates.

SHOPSMART If a recipe calls for chopped smoked salmon, look for packages of smoked salmon trimmings at the deli counter. They're just as delicious as the paper-thin slices and often better priced.

cheese strata with ham & tomatoes

6 to 8 servings

12 large eggs

1½ cups milk

½ cup heavy cream

1 teaspoon kosher salt

¼ teaspoon freshly ground black pepper

Pinch freshly grated nutmeg

Pinch cayenne pepper

1 cup diced baked ham

1 cup Oven-Dried Tomatoes (see page 281), chopped

1 tablespoon minced fresh flat-leaf parsley

2 teaspoons thinly sliced fresh chives

2 cups shredded extra-sharp Cheddar cheese (about 8 ounces)

1 pound sourdough bread, crust trimmed, cut into 1-inch cubes

1 tablespoon unsalted butter, melted

1. Generously butter a 3-quart gratin dish or casserole. Whisk the eggs, milk, cream, salt, black pepper, nutmeg, and cayenne pepper in a large bowl. Toss the ham, tomatoes, parsley, and chives in a small bowl.

2. Scatter ½ cup of the cheese over the bottom of the prepared dish, followed by a third of the bread, and then half of the ham mixture. Repeat and top with a final layer of bread and the remaining 1 cup cheese.

3. Pour the egg mixture over the top and gently press down to make sure the top layer is evenly moistened. Drizzle the melted butter over the top. Cover the strata with plastic wrap and refrigerate for at least 1 hour or overnight.

4. Position a rack in the middle of the oven and preheat to 350°F. Bake the strata, uncovered, until it is golden brown and slightly puffed, about 45 minutes. Let the strata rest 10 minutes before serving.

COOK'S NOTE What's not to love about a strata? It's a cheesy, savory bread pudding that fits right into a laid-back cooking scheme. Stratas are a terrific brunch dish—they welcome improvisation and can be assembled in advance or on the spur of the moment.

Depending on which shows are taping that day, the ingredients that arrive are different every morning. **From Queen Anne cherries from Washington State, crayfish from Louisiana, and heirloom apples from the Hudson River Valley, our ingredients have only one thing in common:** They have to be perfect.

cornmeal pancakes with
blueberry-maple syrup 16 pancakes

PANCAKES

- ¾ cup all-purpose flour
- ½ cup cornmeal
- 3 tablespoons light brown sugar
- 1 teaspoon baking powder
- ¼ teaspoon fine salt
- ⅛ teaspoon baking soda
- ⅛ teaspoon freshly grated nutmeg
- 2 large eggs, separated and at room temperature
- 1 cup buttermilk, at room temperature
- ½ cup milk, at room temperature
- 3 tablespoons unsalted butter, melted
- ½ teaspoon pure vanilla extract

  Blueberry Maple Syrup (see recipe, below)

SYRUP

  Makes 1 cup

- 1 cup blueberries
- ¼ cup maple syrup
- 1 cinnamon stick
- 1 tablespoon unsalted butter
- 1 teaspoon lemon juice

1. Preheat the oven to 200°F. Set a wire rack on a baking sheet and place in the oven.

2. Whisk the flour, cornmeal, brown sugar, baking powder, salt, baking soda, and nutmeg in a large bowl. Whisk the egg yolks with the buttermilk, milk, melted butter, and vanilla extract in a large glass measuring cup. Whisk the buttermilk mixture into the flour mixture to make a thick batter—take care not to overmix or the pancakes will be dense. In another bowl whip the egg whites until they hold soft peaks. Use a rubber spatula to fold the whites into the batter.

3. Heat a large cast-iron or nonstick skillet over medium heat and coat the surface lightly with butter. Using about ¼ cup per pancake, pour the batter into the skillet, leaving space between pancakes. Cook until bubbles break the surface of the pancakes and the undersides are golden brown, about 2 minutes. Flip with a spatula and cook about 1 minute more. Keep the cooked pancakes warm in the oven while you cook the remaining batter. Serve the pancakes hot with warm Blueberry-Maple Syrup.

BLUEBERRY-MAPLE SYRUP

Toss the blueberries with the maple syrup in a small saucepan. Add the cinnamon stick and cook over high heat, stirring occasionally, until the mixture boils and the blueberries just start to pop, about 5 minutes. Remove from the heat, discard the cinnamon stick, and stir in the butter and lemon juice. Serve warm.

KNOW-HOW When folding whipped whites into a batter—be it for pancakes, soufflés, or cakes—don't add them all at once. Lighten the batter with about a third of the whites before delicately folding in the rest.

potato pancakes with pink applesauce 4 to 6 servings

PANCAKES

1   medium yellow onion

2   pounds waxy potatoes, such as red-skinned or Yukon gold (about 4 medium), peeled

2   tablespoons all-purpose flour

1   tablespoon chopped fresh thyme, plus sprigs for garnish

2   teaspoons kosher salt

⅛   teaspoon freshly grated nutmeg

    Freshly ground black pepper

1   large egg, lightly beaten

    Vegetable oil

    Pink Applesauce (see recipe, below)

    Crème fraîche or sour cream

APPLESAUCE

    Makes 3 to 4 cups

2½ pounds tart red apples, such as McIntosh

3   tablespoons sugar

3   tablespoons water

1   tablespoon freshly squeezed lemon juice

1. Preheat oven to 200°F. Set a wire rack on a baking sheet and place in oven. Grate onion on a box grater into a large bowl. Shred potatoes into the same bowl, shredding down the length of potato to form long strands. Toss potatoes with the onion as you work to keep them from discoloring. Put potato mixture in a clean dish towel and wring out excess liquid. Return mixture to bowl and toss it with flour, chopped thyme, salt, nutmeg, and pepper to taste. Stir in the egg.

2. Heat ¼ inch oil in a large cast-iron or other heavy skillet over medium heat. Using 2 heaping tablespoons per pancake, spread the batter in the skillet, pressing lightly to form thin 3-inch pancakes. To keep the pancakes crisp, don't overcrowd the pan. Cook until golden, 3 to 4 minutes per side, turning once. Keep the cooked pancakes warm in the oven while you cook the remaining batter. Serve the pancakes with Pink Applesauce and crème fraîche.

PINK APPLESAUCE

1. Cut the apples into chunks with their skins and seeds. (If you don't have a food mill, peel and seed the fruit; your applesauce just won't be pink.) Put the apples, sugar, water, and lemon juice in a large saucepan and bring to a boil over high heat. Lower the heat, cover, and simmer gently until the apples are very soft, about 15 minutes. Uncover the pan and cook, stirring frequently to prevent scorching, until the applesauce thickens, about 5 minutes.

2. Puree the mixture in a food mill or blender. Serve warm or refrigerate in a tightly sealed container for up to 1 week.

COOK'S NOTE Waxy potatoes are dense and hold their shape when cooked, making them perfect for potato salads—and potato pancakes.

breakfast **burritos**

4 servings

BURRITOS

- 8   large eggs
- ½   teaspoon kosher salt
- 4   10-inch flour tortillas
- 1   tablespoon extra-virgin olive oil
- ½   cup shredded Monterey Jack cheese (about 2 ounces)
- ½   Hass avocado, sliced (see page 272)
-     Salsa Verde Asada (see recipe, below)
- ¼   cup sour cream (optional)

SALSA

Makes about 1½ cups

- 1½   pounds tomatillos (about 20), husked and well washed
- 1   small onion, sliced and separated into rings
- 4   cloves garlic, unpeeled
- 1   to 2 chipotle chiles in adobo sauce, chopped (see page 273)
- 2   tablespoons chopped fresh cilantro
- 2   teaspoons kosher salt
- ⅛   teaspoon sugar

1. Whisk the eggs and salt together in a large bowl. Spread out a large piece of foil on a work surface. Heat a large skillet over high heat until very hot. Lay a tortilla in the skillet and cook, turning once, until slightly charred and puffy, about 15 seconds per side. Transfer to the foil and repeat with the remaining tortillas. Wrap the tortillas in the foil and set aside in a warm spot.

2. Heat the oil in the skillet until it just begins to smoke. Add the eggs and stir with a wooden spoon until large, firm curds form, about 2 minutes. Remove from the heat and stir in the cheese.

3. Unwrap the tortillas. Place ¼ of the eggs, ¼ of the avocado, and 1 tablespoon of the salsa in the center of a tortilla. Fold the edge of the tortilla closest to you over the filling, fold in the sides, and then roll the tortilla away from you to form a package. Repeat with the remaining tortillas. Serve with extra salsa and a dollop of sour cream, if desired.

SALSA VERDE ASADA (ROASTED TOMATILLO SALSA)

1. Position a rack in the upper part of the oven and preheat the broiler. Line a broiler pan with foil. Arrange the tomatillos, onion, and garlic on the prepared pan. Broil the vegetables until charred and soft, turning so they cook evenly, about 12 minutes. Cool.

2. Squeeze the garlic cloves out of their skins. Puree the garlic pulp, onion, and chiles in a blender until smooth. Add the tomatillos and their juices and pulse to make a chunky sauce. Add the cilantro, salt, and sugar and pulse just to combine. Transfer the salsa to a bowl and set aside at room temperature for 30 minutes so the flavors come together. If not serving immediately, refrigerate in a sealed container for up to 3 days.

These burritos are not just for the a.m. Their big, bold flavors make them a delicious option for lunch or dinner too.

baked eggs with **farmhouse cheddar & potatoes** 4 servings

3   tablespoons unsalted butter

1½ pounds red-skinned potatoes, diced

¼   cup chopped fresh flat-leaf parsley

2   large cloves garlic, minced

1   teaspoon kosher salt

    Freshly ground black pepper

8   large eggs

1   cup shredded extra-sharp farmhouse Cheddar (about 4 ounces) (see page 271)

1. Preheat the oven to 400°F. Melt the butter in a large, well-seasoned cast-iron skillet over medium heat. Add the potatoes and cook, stirring occasionally, until tender and brown, about 15 minutes. Stir in the parsley, garlic, salt, and pepper to taste and remove from the heat.

2. Push the potatoes aside to make 4 evenly spaced shallow nests and break 2 eggs into each. Bake until the egg whites are cooked and the yolks are still runny, about 10 minutes. Sprinkle the cheese over the eggs and continue baking until it just melts, about 1 minute more. Serve immediately.

STYLE A well-seasoned skillet is a thing of beauty, and we think it is equally at home on the table and on the stove. Serving this straight from the pan shows off the food with a wonderful rustic touch.

No matter how experienced a cook you are, you eventually come to believe that simple is best. Good ingredients make good food.

1. To fill and roll the strudel, spoon the pear mixture across the phyllo 1 inch from the edge closest to you. 2. Use the parchment to start rolling the phyllo tightly over the filling. 3. Lift the parchment with the strudel on it onto the baking sheet. 4. Bake the strudel on the parchment-lined baking sheet.

pear-cranberry **strudel**

6 servings

3 Bosc pears (about 1½ pounds), peeled, cored, and cut into 1-inch chunks

2 tablespoons freshly squeezed lemon juice

4 tablespoons granulated sugar

8 tablespoons unsalted butter

2 tablespoons dried cranberries

4 tablespoons plain dry bread crumbs

¼ teaspoon ground allspice

¼ teaspoon ground ginger

6 sheets phyllo dough

2 tablespoons finely chopped toasted almonds

Confectioners' sugar for dusting (optional)

Crème fraîche or whipped cream, for serving (optional)

STYLE Cut the strudel into thirds, then cut each one of the pieces in half on an angle. This way, you get beautiful portions that stand at attention, showing off the layers and the filling.

1. Position a rack in the center of the oven and preheat to 400°F. Toss pears with the lemon juice and 2 tablespoons of the granulated sugar. Melt butter in a small saucepan over medium-low heat. Set aside to cool, then skim the white foam off the surface and discard. Spoon the melted butter into a bowl, leaving behind the solids at the bottom of the saucepan.

2. Heat 2 tablespoons of the reserved butter in a medium nonstick skillet over medium-high heat. Add pear mixture and cook until pears start to give off juices. Add cranberries, cover, and reduce heat to medium-low. Cook until pears are crisp-tender, about 7 minutes. Remove from heat and stir in 2 tablespoons of the bread crumbs; cool the mixture slightly.

3. Combine remaining 2 tablespoons granulated sugar with allspice and ginger in a small bowl. Cut a piece of parchment paper slightly longer than the phyllo sheets and lay it with a long edge parallel to you. Set the stack of phyllo sheets beside it and cover with a clean kitchen towel. Transfer one sheet of phyllo to the parchment with a long edge facing you. Brush with some reserved butter and sprinkle with 1 teaspoon each of the nuts and sugar mixture. Repeat with each remaining phyllo, replacing the towel as you work. Sprinkle remaining 2 tablespoons bread crumbs over top sheet of phyllo.

4. Spoon the pear mixture across the phyllo about 1 inch from the edge closest to you to make a mound, with a 2-inch border at each end. Using the parchment to help you get started, roll the phyllo tightly over the filling to make a log, seam-side down. Lift the parchment with the strudel onto a baking sheet.

5. Bake until golden, about 30 minutes. Transfer on the baking sheet to a rack to cool. Trim ends with a serrated knife. Dust with confectioners' sugar and serve warm or at room temperature with crème fraîche or whipped cream, if desired.

bites

Looking for a savory little something to go with cocktails and conversation? These tasty morsels can start the party or be the party.

shrimp toast with thai basil & ginger 16 toasts

8 ½-inch-thick slices country-style white bread (not sourdough), crusts removed

8 ounces medium shrimp, peeled, deveined, and tails removed (see page 275)

1 large egg, lightly beaten

1 heaping tablespoon sliced fresh basil, preferably Thai (see Cook's Note, below)

1 tablespoon sugar

2 teaspoons fish sauce (see page 274)

2 teaspoons minced fresh lemongrass

1 teaspoon freshly grated peeled ginger

1 teaspoon grated lime zest

1 clove garlic, minced

Vegetable, soybean, or peanut oil, for deep frying

Black and/or white sesame seeds

Kosher salt

1. Cut the bread slices into triangles. Place shrimp in a food processor with the egg, basil, sugar, fish sauce, lemongrass, ginger, lime zest, and garlic. Pulse to make a coarse paste.

2. Heat about 2 inches of oil in a deep, heavy-bottomed pot until a deep-fry thermometer reads 350°F. Line a plate with paper towels.

3. While the oil heats, mound a tablespoon of the shrimp mixture onto each piece of bread and sprinkle with sesame seeds. Fry the toasts in batches, turning once, until golden, about 2 minutes. Transfer cooked toasts to the prepared plate to drain. When you have fried all the toasts, transfer them to a serving platter and sprinkle with salt. Serve immediately.

Here's our uptown version of a Chinatown classic.

COOK'S NOTE Thai basils are spicier than sweet-scented Italian varieties. We love any one of the three types found in Asian markets—citrusy lemon, pungent holy, and anisey Thai. If you can't find Thai basil, use Italian with a bit of fresh mint as a substitute.

crab cakes

12 small cakes

Crab cakes are enjoyed with enthusiasm up and down the Eastern Shore at beachside crab shacks and white-linen establishments alike.

1   pound lump crabmeat

4   tablespoons unsalted butter

¼   cup finely chopped onion

1   rib celery, minced

1   clove garlic, minced

1½ teaspoons kosher salt

1   large egg

¼   cup heavy cream

¼   teaspoon grated lemon zest

2   tablespoons freshly squeezed lemon juice

1   tablespoon whole-grain mustard

2   teaspoons finely chopped fresh flat-leaf parsley

2   teaspoons finely chopped fresh dill

¾   teaspoon hot pepper sauce

Freshly ground black pepper

⅓   cup cracker meal, plus additional for coating

1   tablespoon vegetable oil

Spicy Red Pepper Sauce (see page 278) or Remoulade (see page 128)

1. Spread the crabmeat on a pan and carefully pick out and discard any bits of shell. Transfer the meat to a bowl. Line a baking sheet with waxed or parchment paper.

2. Melt 1 tablespoon of the butter in a small skillet over medium heat. Add the onion, celery, garlic, and ½ teaspoon of the salt and cook until soft, about 5 minutes; cool. Stir the mixture gently into the crab, keeping the crabmeat in lumps.

3. Lightly beat the egg with the cream, lemon zest, lemon juice, mustard, parsley, dill, hot sauce, the remaining 1 teaspoon salt, and pepper to taste. Again working with a light hand, toss the egg mixture with the crab. Stir in the ⅓ cup cracker meal. Shape the mixture into 1½-inch patties. Place them on the prepared baking sheet, cover, and refrigerate for 1 hour.

4. Preheat the oven to 200°F and place another baking sheet inside. Cover the bottom of a pie tin or rimmed plate with cracker meal and lightly pat the crab cakes in the meal to coat both sides. Heat a large skillet over medium heat and add the remaining 3 tablespoons butter and the oil. Cook the crab cakes in batches, turning once, until golden, about 2 minutes per side. Keep cooked cakes warm in the oven. Serve with Spicy Red Pepper Sauce or Remoulade.

COOK'S NOTE Make these into four large cakes and they make a lovely main course, served with some crisp coleslaw.

corn fritters with charred tomato salsa about 30 fritters

FRITTERS

1¾	cups all-purpose flour
2	teaspoons chili powder
1½	teaspoons baking powder
1	teaspoon ground cumin
1	teaspoon fine salt, plus additional for sprinkling on hot fritters
⅛	teaspoon ground anise seeds (optional)
12	ounces lager-style beer
4½	cups fresh corn kernels (about 5 ears corn)
2	scallions (white and green parts), thinly sliced
	Vegetable oil for deep-frying
	Charred Tomato Salsa (see recipe, right)

SALSA

Makes about 1 cup

2	ripe medium tomatoes
2	tablespoons extra-virgin olive oil
1	jalapeño, stemmed and minced
1	scallion (white and green parts) chopped
1	clove garlic, minced
2	teaspoons chopped fresh cilantro
1½	teaspoons kosher salt

1. Whisk 1½ cups of the flour, the chili powder, baking powder, cumin, the 1 teaspoon salt, and anise seeds, if desired, in a large bowl. Add beer and whisk to make a smooth batter. Toss corn kernels and scallions with remaining ¼ cup flour, and stir into the batter.

2. Heat about 2 inches of oil in a large, heavy-bottomed pot over medium heat until a deep-fry thermometer reads 365°F. Line a large plate with paper towels.

3. Working in batches, add heaping tablespoons of the batter to the oil and fry, turning once, until golden brown and crispy, about 5 minutes per batch. Use a slotted spoon to transfer the cooked fritters to the paper towels to drain. Sprinkle the fritters with salt and serve immediately with the salsa.

CHARRED TOMATO SALSA

1. Position an oven rack in the upper part of the oven and preheat the broiler. Line a broiler pan with foil. Place the tomatoes on the prepared pan and broil, turning as needed, until the skins blacken and split, 15 to 20 minutes. Wrap up the tomatoes in the foil and cool.

2. Core the tomatoes. In a small food processor pulse the tomatoes, skins and all, with the oil, jalapeño, scallion, and garlic to make a chunky sauce. Transfer the sauce to a bowl and stir in the cilantro and salt. The salsa sets up a bit if prepared ahead and chilled; stir to loosen it up before serving.

In the Food Network Kitchens, "fried" stands for "fabulous" or, in this case, the crunchiest, most scrumptious fritters you've ever had.

KNOW-HOW Before spooning up the batter, coat the measuring spoon with a little nonstick spray; the batter will slip off the spoon easily. To ensure your fritters don't absorb too much oil, let the oil return to 365°F after each batch.

vietnamese-style beef
in grape leaves 16 pieces

STUFFED GRAPE LEAVES

- 1 tablespoon peanut or vegetable oil, plus additional for grilling
- ½ small onion, chopped
- 1 clove garlic, minced
- 8 ounces ground beef
- 2 tablespoons salted cashews, chopped
- 2 tablespoons finely minced fresh lemongrass
- 1½ teaspoons sugar
- 1½ teaspoons fish sauce (see page 274)
- ½ teaspoon chile paste, such as *sambal oelek* (see page 274)
- ½ teaspoon kosher salt
- 16 jarred, brined grape leaves, rinsed, drained, and patted dry
- 8 short skewers

  Vietnamese Dipping Sauce (see recipe, below)

SAUCE

  Makes 1 cup

- ⅓ cup water
- ⅓ cup freshly squeezed lime juice
- 2 tablespoons fish sauce
- 3 tablespoons sugar
- 1 tablespoon finely grated carrot
- 1 teaspoon chile paste, such as *sambal oelek*
- 1 clove garlic, minced

1. Heat the oil in a small skillet over medium heat. Add the onion and garlic and cook until soft, about 2 minutes. Cool slightly. Put the ground beef in a large bowl and stir in the onion mixture, cashews, lemongrass, sugar, fish sauce, chile paste, and salt.

2. Lay a grape leaf, stem side up, on your work surface with the tip of the leaf pointing away from you; snip off the little stem piece. Place a heaping tablespoon of the beef mixture in the center of the leaf. Fold the bottom of the leaf over the filling, fold in the sides, and then roll the leaf up to make a tight package. Repeat with the remaining leaves and filling.

3. Thread 2 rolls lengthwise onto each skewer. Preheat a grill pan or outdoor grill to medium. Lightly brush the grill pan with oil and grill the packages for 2 minutes on each side; the grill marks should be quite distinct, and if the leaves char and even fray a bit, that's fine. Serve warm or at room temperature with Vietnamese Dipping Sauce.

VIETNAMESE DIPPING SAUCE
Whisk the water with the lime juice, fish sauce, and sugar in a small bowl until the sugar is dissolved. Stir in the carrot, chile paste, and garlic. If not using immediately, refrigerate the sauce in a sealed container for up to 2 days. Serve at room temperature. Stir right before using.

COOK'S NOTE If you're using bamboo skewers, be sure to soak them in water for about an hour before threading them so they don't burn on the grill.

Just when we think we've seen it all, something surprising shows up in our kitchen, like Greek-style stuffed grape leaves going Asian.

Grate a lemon and breathe deeply. Like all of our great Food Network Kitchens recipes, the preparation of this one is as much fun as the result.

crostini with spinach, pine nuts & aged goat cheese 6 servings

18 ½-inch-thick baguette slices

¼ cup extra-virgin olive oil

2 cloves garlic, peeled, 1 left whole and 1 minced

2 tablespoons pine nuts

Pinch crushed red pepper flakes

8 ounces fresh spinach, preferably small leaves

Kosher salt

½ teaspoon freshly grated lemon zest

3 ounces aged goat cheese

1. Preheat the oven to 400°F. Brush both sides of the bread slices with some of the olive oil and place on a baking sheet. Bake until golden, about 7 minutes, turning once about halfway through. While the toasts are hot, rub both sides with the whole garlic clove, placing them back on the baking sheet as you work. Leave the oven on.

2. Toss the pine nuts in a dry skillet over medium heat until their bellies get golden, about 3 minutes. Set aside in a bowl.

3. Add the remaining olive oil, the minced garlic, and the red pepper flakes to the same skillet and cook until fragrant, stirring frequently, about 1 minute. Add the spinach in batches, seasoning with salt as you go, and pushing it to the sides of the skillet as it wilts before adding the next handful. When all the spinach is cooked, remove the pan from the heat and stir in the lemon zest and pine nuts. Drain the mixture in a colander and chop it very roughly.

4. Put about a tablespoon of the spinach mixture on each toast, crumble some goat cheese over the spinach, and bake just until cheese starts to melt, 3 to 5 minutes. Serve warm.

COOK'S NOTE We love aged goat cheese—it's tangy, earthy, and deeply flavorful. Crumble it over salads or enjoy it with fresh or dried fruit.

cajun chicken lollipops

12 pops

12   chicken wing first joints,
     (also called "drumettes"),
     about 2 pounds

1   cup hot pepper sauce

    Vegetable oil for deep frying

8   tablespoons unsalted butter

2   teaspoons plus 2 tablespoons Cajun
    seasoning, store-bought or
    homemade (see page 280)

¾   cup all-purpose flour

COOK'S NOTE Exposure
to some metals (aluminum,
copper, and cast iron among
them) can cause acidic foods
such as lemon juice, tomatoes,
and vinegar to undergo a
chemical reaction that gives
them a metallic taste. When
cooking with acidic foods, use
nonreactive materials such as
stainless steel, glass, or ceramic.

1. Stand a drumette on its wide end and, holding the narrow bone at the top, use a paring knife to push and scrape the skin and meat downward to expose the bone and make a plump "lollipop" of chicken at the bottom. Repeat with the remaining drumettes. Toss the lollipops in ½ cup of the hot pepper sauce in a nonreactive bowl (see Cook's Note, left) and refrigerate for 1 hour.

2. Heat about 3 inches of oil in a deep, heavy-bottomed pot over medium heat until a deep-fry thermometer registers 375°F. While the oil heats, melt the butter with the remaining ½ cup hot sauce and 2 teaspoons of the Cajun seasoning. Stir to blend well and set the mixture aside in a warm spot.

3. Line a large plate with paper towels. Whisk flour with the remaining 2 tablespoons Cajun seasoning. Working in small batches, toss lollipops in seasoned flour until completely coated. Fry until golden brown, about 7 minutes. Drain on prepared plate.

4. When all the lollipops are cooked, put them in a large bowl and toss with the warm spiced butter. Serve lollipops warm or at room temperature.

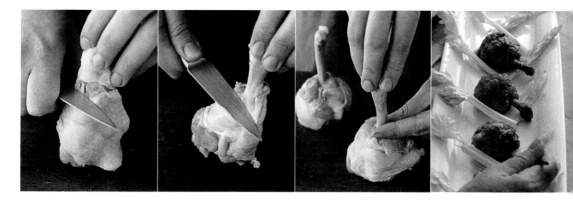

Get in touch with your inner food stylist.

Use color, shape, arrangement, and garnishing as artistic tools. Be inventive by letting the authenticity of the food shine through. Color is great, but a big white plate is like a little black dress—always in style.

French Lentil & Roasted Beet Salad, page 72.

In the Food Network Kitchens, timing is everything. So, put any or all of these yummy nibbles on your party production schedule. Then sit back, relax, and enjoy your own show.

really onion dip
4 cups

3 medium onions, 2 unpeeled, 1 peeled

1 cup extra-virgin olive oil

2 cups mayonnaise

½ cup sour cream

1 tablespoon white wine vinegar

2 teaspoons kosher salt

2 scallions (white and green parts), minced

Freshly ground black pepper

Hot pepper sauce

Potato chips, for serving

1. Preheat oven to 425°F. Rub unpeeled onions with a bit of the olive oil; roast until soft, about 45 minutes. Cool and peel.

2. Finely dice the peeled raw onion. Heat a large skillet over medium-high heat; add remaining oil and heat until quite hot. Add diced onion and cook, stirring occasionally, until edges begin to brown, about 5 minutes. Turn to medium-low and cook until onion is golden brown, about 18 minutes. Scrape onion, oil, and juices into a sieve over a bowl. Drain onions and spread on a paper towel-lined plate. Cool the strained oil.

3. Puree roasted onions in a food processor. Add mayonnaise, sour cream, vinegar, and salt; pulse until smooth. With the motor running, drizzle in ¼ cup of the flavored reserved oil. Transfer to a serving bowl. Stir in scallions, pepper, and hot sauce to taste. Refrigerate at least 3 hours. Scatter the fried onions over the top just before serving with potato chips.

sweet & spicy mixed nuts
2 cups

1 large egg white

3 tablespoons dark brown sugar

1 tablespoon kosher salt

2 teaspoons dried oregano

¾ teaspoon ground coriander

½ teaspoon ground cumin

¼ heaping teaspoon cayenne pepper

Pinch ground cloves

2 cups unsalted mixed nuts

1. Preheat the oven to 250° F. Line a baking sheet with aluminum foil or parchment paper.

2. Whisk the egg white, brown sugar, salt, oregano, coriander, cumin, cayenne, and cloves in a medium bowl until thoroughly blended and slightly foamy. Add nuts and toss to coat evenly. Spread nuts on the prepared baking sheet and roast, stirring every 15 minutes, for 45 minutes. Nuts will be fragrant and slightly darker but still a bit moist (they crisp as they cool). Cool completely on pan and serve at room temperature. Store in an airtight container for up to 5 days.

cheddar pennies
8 dozen small crackers

1½ cups all-purpose flour

¼ teaspoon fine salt

Pinch hot paprika

8 tablespoons unsalted butter, softened

4 ounces grated extra-sharp farmhouse Cheddar cheese (1 cup)

2 teaspoons Dijon mustard

Toppings: caraway, fennel, or other whole seeds; fresh dill, thyme, or rosemary; coarse salt; cracked black pepper; black onion seeds

1. Whisk flour, salt, and paprika in a small bowl. With an electric mixer, beat butter, cheese, and mustard until smooth. Beat in flour mixture until dough comes together. Divide dough into thirds and roll each piece into a log 1 inch across and 9 inches long. Wrap the logs in plastic wrap and refrigerate for at least 1 hour, or freeze for up to 2 months.

2. Preheat oven to 425°F. Line 2 baking sheets with parchment paper. Slice logs into ¼-inch-thick coins; place on baking sheets 1 inch apart. Press on toppings and bake until golden brown, 8 to 10 minutes. Cool on pans on wire racks.

Want to understand the meaning of "inflation"? Try our spice-laden variation on this old Cheddar classic and watch pennies turn a priceless golden brown.

broiled peaches
8 bites

2 ripe medium peaches, quartered and pitted

1 tablespoon extra-virgin olive oil, plus additional for drizzling

½ teaspoon fresh thyme

Kosher salt and freshly ground black pepper

2 ounces soft blue cheese, such as Gorgonzola or Saga blue, thinly sliced (see page 271)

¼ cup fresh mint, roughly torn

4 thin slices prosciutto (about 2 ounces), halved lengthwise

1 tablespoon balsamic vinegar

1. Position a rack in the middle of the oven and preheat broiler to high. Line a small baking sheet with aluminum foil. Gently toss the peaches in a bowl with the 1 tablespoon olive oil and thyme. Season with salt and pepper to taste and toss again.

2. Arrange the peaches cut side down on the prepared baking sheet. Broil until the skins are slightly charred, about 5 minutes. Turn skin side down and broil until the flesh is lightly browned, about 5 minutes more. Drizzle the peaches lightly with olive oil and cool slightly.

3. With the peaches still skin side down, lay a piece of cheese on each and sprinkle with mint. Wrap a strip of prosciutto around each peach quarter and arrange them on a platter. Drizzle the balsamic vinegar and grind some fresh black pepper over the peaches and serve.

41

chicken & mushroom quesadillas 4 servings

1 large boneless, skinless chicken breast (about 8 ounces)

Kosher salt and freshly ground black pepper

4 tablespoons vegetable oil or lard

3 tablespoons unsalted butter

5 ounces white mushrooms, sliced (about 3 cups)

1 teaspoon kosher salt

½ teaspoon ground cumin

½ medium onion, finely chopped

3 cloves garlic, minced

½ pickled jalapeño, minced, plus 1 tablespoon of the jar juices

1 19-ounce can black beans, rinsed and drained

2 8-inch flour tortillas

2 cups grated white Cheddar cheese (about 8 ounces)

Avocado slices (optional), sour cream, and salsa, for serving

1. Season the chicken breast with salt and pepper to taste. Heat a 10-inch skillet over medium heat; add 1 tablespoon of the oil or lard. Cook the chicken until nicely browned on both sides and firm when you press it gently with your fingertip, about 10 minutes total. Cool the chicken slightly and then tear into bite-size pieces.

2. Melt 1 tablespoon of the butter in the same skillet over medium heat. Add the mushrooms, ½ teaspoon of the salt, the cumin, and some black pepper and cook, stirring occasionally, until the mushrooms are dry, about 4 minutes. Transfer mushrooms to a small bowl.

3. Add the remaining 3 tablespoons oil or lard to the skillet, along with the onion, garlic, jalapeño and the jar juices, and the remaining ½ teaspoon salt. Cook until the onion is translucent, about 5 minutes. Add the beans and mash them into the onion mixture until the mixture is almost smooth but still dotted with bits of bean. Set aside.

4. Now build the quesadillas: Lay the tortillas on your work surface and spread ¼ of the beans on half of each one. Follow the beans with ¼ of the cheese, half of the chicken, half of the mushrooms, and finally the rest of the cheese. (You will have about half the beans left over; you can refrigerate them for up to 2 days.) Fold the tortillas over to encase the filling.

5. In a clean skillet fry each quesadilla in 1 tablespoon of the remaining butter until blistered and golden on both sides, about 4 minutes total. Cut into wedges with a pizza wheel or serrated knife. Serve with the avocado slices, if desired, sour cream, and salsa.

No wonder parties wind up in the kitchen (ours do too). It's where the action is—and you can sample straight from the pan.

seared scallops with bacon, tarragon & lemon 16 bites

1   1-ounce slice bacon, cut crosswise into thin pieces

8   1-inch sea scallops, foot removed, if necessary, and patted dry

    Kosher salt and freshly ground black pepper

1   tablespoon unsalted butter

¼   cup dry white vermouth

2   tablespoons freshly squeezed lemon juice

2   tablespoons water

1   tablespoon chopped fresh tarragon

1   tablespoon chopped fresh flat-leaf parsley

1. Cook the bacon in a medium skillet over medium heat until crisp but not dry and drain on a piece of paper towel. Leave 1 tablespoon of the drippings in the pan (there probably won't be much more than that, but discard any extra if there is).

2. Season the scallops with salt and pepper to taste. Increase the heat under the skillet to medium-high, add the butter, and sear the scallops until brown and glossy, about 1½ minutes per side. Transfer the scallops to a plate and set aside.

3. Remove from heat and add the vermouth and lemon juice to the skillet. Now return the skillet to the heat and stir with a wooden spoon to scrape up the brown bits on the bottom of the pan. Bring the sauce to a simmer and cook until reduced by half. Stir in the water.

4. While the sauce reduces, slice the scallops in half vertically. Slip them into the reduced sauce with the tarragon, parsley, and bacon bits and give the skillet a swirl to bring everything together. Taste and season with salt and pepper, if desired. Divide the scallops with their sauce among small plates or Asian soup spoons and serve immediately.

STYLE We also love to serve these scallops as an hors d'oeuvre nestled in broad-bottomed Chinese soup spoons. When a series of spoons is placed on a platter, they look both elegant and inviting.

soups, salads & sandwiches

Pair them up or serve them solo—this casual trio is all about simplicity and flavor. Terrific for family food or company fare.

soups

thai-style chicken noodle soup

6 servings

Vegetable oil

6 cloves garlic, thinly sliced crosswise

5 ounces rice stick noodles

7 cups chicken broth, homemade (see page 278) or low-sodium canned

¼ cup fish sauce (see page 274)

3 scallions (white and green parts), thinly sliced on an angle

1 small carrot, peeled and thinly sliced

One-inch piece ginger, unpeeled and thinly sliced into coins

1 teaspoon sugar

2 cups shredded roasted chicken, preferably dark meat

⅓ cup roughly chopped fresh dill fronds (stems and leaves)

⅓ cup roughly chopped fresh cilantro

⅓ cup torn fresh basil

⅓ cup roughly chopped fresh mint

Lime wedges

1. Heat about ½ inch of oil in a small, heavy-bottomed skillet over medium-low heat until just warm. Add the garlic and fry, stirring occasionally, until fragrant and golden, about 15 minutes. Scoop the garlic from the oil with a slotted spoon, drain, and cool on a piece of paper towel. While the garlic cooks, soak the noodles in a large bowl of warm water to soften, about 10 minutes. Drain.

2. Put the chicken broth, fish sauce, scallions, carrot, ginger, and sugar in a soup pot and bring to a simmer, uncovered, over medium-high heat. Add the noodles and chicken and simmer until noodles are the desired doneness. Stir in the dill, cilantro, basil, and mint. Ladle the soup into warm bowls and sprinkle with some of the reserved crisped garlic. Serve with lime wedges to squeeze over soup.

KNOW-HOW Reserve the fragrant garlic oil for use in salad dressings or marinades or for drizzling over grilled meat, fish, or bread.

corn chowder with summer herb salad 6 servings

CHOWDER

- 8 ears fresh corn, preferably white, shucked
- 6 tablespoons unsalted butter
- 8 scallions, white parts chopped, green reserved for Herb Salad
- 6 cloves garlic
- 1 tablespoon kosher salt
- 2 teaspoons sugar
- Freshly ground black pepper
- 3 sprigs fresh parsley
- 3 sprigs fresh thyme
- 1 bay leaf
- 6 cups water
- Summer Herb Salad (see recipe, below)

SALAD

Makes about 2 cups

- ½ cup torn fresh basil
- ½ cup roughly chopped fresh dill fronds (stems and leaves)
- ⅓ cup chopped scallion greens
- 3 tablespoons torn tarragon
- 1 tablespoon extra-virgin olive oil
- 1 teaspoon kosher salt
- Freshly ground black pepper
- 1 large ripe tomato, cored and roughly chopped

1. Shear the corn kernels from the cobs with a knife. Put about ⅔ of the kernels in a large bowl. Set aside the remaining kernels for adding to the soup before serving. Working over the large bowl, run a knife along the cobs to press out the milky liquid. Snap or cut 3 of the cobs in half; discard the remaining cobs.

2. Melt the butter in a soup pot over medium-low heat. Add the scallion whites, garlic, salt, sugar, and pepper to taste. Cook, covered, stirring occasionally, until the vegetables are soft and fragrant, about 12 minutes. Add the larger amount of corn kernels, with their milk, and cook, covered, stirring occasionally, until the corn is tender, about 10 minutes. Tie the parsley, thyme, and bay leaf together with kitchen twine and add to the soup along with the reserved cobs and water. Bring mixture to a boil, reduce the heat, and simmer, uncovered, until slightly thickened, about 30 minutes. Remove the herb bundle and cobs and discard.

3. Puree the soup in batches in a blender (or in the pot with an immersion blender) until creamy. Return the puree to the pot, add the reserved corn kernels, and simmer over medium heat, uncovered, until the whole corn kernels are just tender, about 5 minutes. Taste and adjust the salt and pepper. Divide the chowder among soup bowls and mound a generous portion of the salad in the center of each bowl. Pass any remaining herb salad at the table.

SUMMER HERB SALAD

In a large bowl combine the basil, dill, scallion greens, tarragon, oil, salt, and pepper to taste. Add the tomato and toss to combine. Serve immediately.

We always try to cook what's in season: strawberries in spring, corn in summer, pumpkins in fall. Try this delectable corn chowder on a summer night and you'll taste why.

cauliflower soup with grilled curried shrimp 4 servings

SOUP

- 3 tablespoons unsalted butter
- 1 medium onion, roughly chopped
- 2 cloves garlic, minced
- 3 teaspoons kosher salt, plus additional for seasoning
- 1 teaspoon finely grated peeled ginger
- 1 head cauliflower (about 1½ pounds), cut into florets
- 2 teaspoons ground coriander
- ½ teaspoon ground turmeric
- 6½ cups water

  Freshly ground black pepper

SHRIMP

- 20 medium shrimp, peeled and deveined (see page 275)
- 1 tablespoon unsalted butter, melted
- 1 tablespoon curry powder

  Kosher salt

  Lime wedges and fresh cilantro sprigs, for garnish

1. For the soup: Melt the butter in a large soup pot over medium heat. Add the onion, garlic, 1 teaspoon of the salt, and the ginger and cook until tender, about 8 minutes. Add the cauliflower, coriander, turmeric, and the remaining 2 teaspoons salt and cook, stirring occasionally, another 5 minutes. Add the water. Bring the mixture to a boil, reduce the heat, and simmer, uncovered, until the cauliflower is very tender, about 20 minutes. Puree the soup in small batches in a blender (keep the lid cracked to allow steam to escape), or in the pot with an immersion blender, until smooth. Taste and season with salt and pepper as needed; keep the soup hot while you prepare the shrimp.

2. For the shrimp: Heat a stovetop grill pan over medium-high heat. Toss the shrimp with the melted butter. Add the curry powder and salt to taste and toss again. Grill the shrimp until translucent, about 1½ minutes on each side.

3. To serve, place 5 shrimp in each of 4 soup bowls, then ladle soup over the shrimp. Garnish each serving with a wedge of lime and a cilantro sprig.

STYLE Food stylists know that odd numbers make for a more pleasing presentation than even numbers. In this case, five shrimp add up to a soup that looks as good as it tastes.

manhattan whole clam chowder

4 to 6 servings

1½ tablespoons olive oil

3 ounces diced pancetta (about ½ cup) (see Cook's Note, page 189)

1½ celery ribs with leaves, thinly sliced

1 medium onion, chopped

¼ teaspoon crushed red pepper flakes

¼ cup minced garlic

¼ cup tomato paste

2 cups bottled clam juice

2 cups chicken broth, homemade (see page 278) or low-sodium canned

6 small red-skinned potatoes, quartered

1 tablespoon fresh thyme

1 bay leaf

1 28-ounce can whole peeled tomatoes (with liquid), roughly chopped

¼ teaspoon Worcestershire sauce

Freshly ground black pepper

36 littleneck clams, scrubbed

2 tablespoons chopped fresh flat-leaf parsley

Crusty bread, for serving (optional)

1. Heat the oil in a large soup pot over medium heat. Add the pancetta and cook until just brown. Add the celery, onion, and red pepper flakes and cook, stirring occasionally, until soft, about 10 minutes. Add the garlic and cook, stirring frequently, until fragrant, about 2 minutes. Stir in the tomato paste and cook for 2 minutes more.

2. Increase the heat and add the clam juice, chicken broth, potatoes, thyme, and bay leaf. Bring the soup to a boil, lower the heat, and simmer, uncovered, until the potatoes are tender, about 15 minutes.

3. Stir in the tomatoes and their juices, the Worcestershire sauce, and black pepper to taste and simmer for 5 minutes. Add the clams, cover, and simmer until the clams open, about 8 minutes. (Discard any unopened clams.) Remove the bay leaf. Divide the soup among warm bowls and sprinkle each serving with some of the parsley. Serve immediately with crusty bread, if desired.

SHOPSMART Littlenecks are small, hard clams that run about 1½ inches across. As for all clams and mussels, buy those that are firmly closed (or that shut when tapped) and are free of any strong aromas. When you come home from the market, take the clams out of their bag and put them in a colander. Cover the clams with a damp towel and set the colander in a bowl of ice in the refrigerator. If storing for a day or more, pour off the melted ice and add fresh as needed.

One spoonful of this mouthwatering broth of spices overflowing with fresh whole clams and you'll never settle for chopped clam chowder again—red or white.

Ready for the swapout!

The magic of cooking in TV time is every recipe must be prepared and presented in less than 30 minutes—whether it's a 20-pound turkey, a 3-tiered cake or a 12-hour BBQ. For it to look seamless, the kitchen must prepare each dish to key stages, multiple times. That's a lot of gumbo!

white bean & escarole soup

4 to 6 servings

Two winter-night delights—heavy on comfort and high on flavor. You'll find both these creamy soups hearty, satisfying, and oh-so-easy to make.

2 tablespoons extra-virgin olive oil, plus additional for drizzling

2 ounces pancetta, chopped (about ⅓ cup) (see Cook's Note, page 189)

1 small onion, chopped

4 cloves garlic, minced

1 small sprig fresh rosemary

¼ teaspoon crushed red pepper flakes

1 head escarole (about 1 pound), coarsely chopped

5 cups chicken broth, homemade (see page 278) or low-sodium canned

2 15-ounce cans Great Northern or cannellini beans, rinsed and drained

1 cup chopped canned plum tomatoes

Kosher salt and freshly ground black pepper

Chunk of Parmesan cheese

1. Heat 2 tablespoons of the olive oil in a soup pot over medium heat. Add the pancetta and cook until brown, about 5 minutes. Transfer pancetta to a plate with a slotted spoon. Add the onion to the pot and cook, stirring occasionally, until soft and golden, about 10 minutes. Add the garlic, rosemary, and red pepper and cook until onion is translucent, about 3 minutes.

2. Stir in the escarole and cook until just wilted, about 2 minutes. Add the chicken broth, beans, and tomatoes and bring to a gentle simmer. Cover and cook for 10 to 15 minutes, stirring once or twice, until the broth has been slightly thickened by the starch from the beans and the escarole is deep green. Stir in the reserved pancetta, taste, and season with salt and pepper to taste. Ladle the soup into warm bowls. Drizzle some olive oil and grate a good soup spoon or so of Parmesan cheese over each serving.

STYLE We love to ladle hot soup into very warm bowls (just heat them a little in your oven). So little effort for such a big difference.

wild mushroom soup

4 to 6 servings

7 cups water

½ ounce dried porcini mushrooms (about ⅔ cup)

6 slices bacon

2 tablespoons unsalted butter

3 leeks (white and light green part only), sliced and well rinsed

3 teaspoons kosher salt

1 pound mixed wild mushrooms, such as shiitake, cremini, or portobello, cleaned, trimmed, and sliced

Freshly ground black pepper

¼ cup Madeira or cognac

3 sprigs fresh flat-leaf parsley

3 sprigs fresh thyme

1 bay leaf

½ cup crème fraîche, plus additional for garnish

KNOW-HOW Strain the soaking liquid for dried mushrooms through a clean paper towel or cheesecloth placed in a fine sieve to remove any grit. Use the liquid to flavor soups, sauces, or broth for risotto.

1. Bring 1 cup of the water to a boil in a small saucepan and add the dried porcini. Set aside to soften, about 20 minutes. Scoop the mushrooms from the liquid and chop coarsely. Reserve the mushrooms in a small bowl. Ladle ⅔ cup of the soaking liquid into a measuring cup, taking care to leave any grit at the bottom of the saucepan.

2. Line a plate with paper towels. Cook the bacon in a soup pot over medium heat until crisp, about 5 minutes. Transfer the bacon to the plate. Add the butter, leeks, and 1½ teaspoons of the salt to the drippings in the pot and cook, stirring occasionally, until the leeks are soft, about 10 minutes. Add the fresh and reserved soaked mushrooms, pepper to taste, and the remaining 1½ teaspoons salt. Increase the heat to high and cook, stirring occasionally, until the mushrooms are wilted, about 5 minutes. Add the Madeira or cognac and cook, uncovered, until the mixture is almost dry. Add the remaining 6 cups of water and the reserved mushroom soaking liquid and bring to a simmer. Tie the parsley, thyme sprigs, and bay leaf together with a piece of clean kitchen string and toss in the pot. Cover, reduce heat if necessary, and simmer until the mushrooms are tender, about 30 minutes.

3. Scoop out about 2 cups of the mushrooms with a slotted spoon and puree in a blender with 1 cup of the broth and the ½ cup crème fraîche until very smooth. Stir puree into soup. Taste and add salt and pepper, if desired. Remove herb bundle. Ladle soup into warm bowls. Spoon a bit of crème fraîche and crumble some bacon over each serving.

watermelon curry
with grilled shrimp 4 to 6 servings

Wonderfully exotic, this cool fruit curry really hits the spot on a summer day.

CURRY

5   pounds watermelon

1   3-inch-long piece peeled
    fresh ginger

4   cloves garlic

3   tablespoons water

2   tablespoons Madras-style curry
    powder (see page 274)

2   teaspoons kosher salt

    Pinch cayenne pepper

3   tablespoons vegetable oil

1   3-inch-long cinnamon stick

1   teaspoon sugar

½   cup chopped fresh mint

2   teaspoons freshly squeezed lime
    juice

SHRIMP

1   pound medium-large shrimp,
    shelled and deveined (see page
    275)

2   tablespoons unsalted butter, melted

    Kosher salt and freshly ground
    black pepper

    Half of a lime

    Grilled Indian flat bread or
    pappadam (Indian lentil crackers),
    for serving (optional)

1. For the curry: Remove the rind from the watermelon; cut the flesh into I-inch chunks and remove the seeds. Puree 2 cups of the chunks. Set aside the remaining chunks and the puree separately.

2. If you have a mini-food processor, blend the ginger, garlic, water, curry powder, salt, and cayenne pepper to a paste. To make the spice paste by hand: Finely grate ginger into a small bowl. Smash the garlic cloves, sprinkle with the salt, and, with the side of a large knife, mash and smear the mixture to a coarse paste. Stir the paste and the water, curry powder, and cayenne into the ginger.

3. Heat the oil in a large skillet over medium-high heat. Add the cinnamon stick and cook until it unfurls, about 30 seconds. Add the ginger-garlic paste and cook, stirring constantly, until it is quite fragrant and lightly browned, about 3 minutes. Add the reserved watermelon puree and the sugar, reduce the heat, and simmer until thick, about 5 minutes. Stir in the reserved watermelon chunks and simmer for 2 minutes more. Transfer the curry to a bowl and cool. Stir in the mint and lime juice and refrigerate, covered, until thoroughly chilled. (You can prepare the curried watermelon a day ahead and refrigerate. If you do, add the chopped mint and lime juice right before serving.)

4. For the shrimp: Heat a grill to medium-hot or a grill pan over medium heat. Toss the shrimp with the butter in a large bowl; season with salt and pepper to taste. Grill the shrimp, turning once, until just cooked through, about 4 minutes. Transfer the shrimp to a plate or bowl and squeeze the lime over them.

5. To serve, ladle the curried watermelon into serving bowls and arrange the shrimp in the centers. Serve with grilled Indian flat bread or crispy pappadam, if desired.

garlic & herb soup with croutons
4 to 6 servings

We order ropes and ropes of garlic for our productions. If you love garlic as much as we do, this is the soup for you.

SOUP

- 4 medium heads garlic
- 8 cups water
- ½ bay leaf
- 3 teaspoons kosher salt
- ½ cup chopped fresh flat-leaf parsley
- ¼ cup chopped fresh basil
- ¼ cup extra-virgin olive oil

  Freshly ground black pepper

CROUTONS

- 2 tablespoons extra-virgin olive oil
- 1½ cups crustless cubed sourdough bread
- 2 cloves garlic, minced
- 2 tablespoons freshly grated Parmesan or Parmigiano-Reggiano cheese (see page 271)
- 2 tablespoons minced fresh flat-leaf parsley

  Kosher salt

COOK'S NOTE An immersion blender is a hand-held stick blender that you simply run through a pot of soup to puree it. We love it for blending soups, sauces, and smoothies.

I. For the soup: Put the garlic heads on their pointy ends and press them with the heel of your hand so that they split open. Discard the loose, papery outer skin and separate the cloves, leaving them in their skins. Set aside 3 medium cloves and put the rest in a soup pot with the water, bay leaf, and 2 teaspoons of the salt. Bring to a simmer over medium heat and cook, uncovered, until the garlic cloves are squishy-soft all the way through, about 20 minutes. Remove the bay leaf from the broth. Scoop the garlic cloves from the broth and cool slightly; when they are cool enough to handle, squeeze them out of their skins back into the pot. While the soup simmers, peel and mince the 3 reserved garlic cloves. Mix the minced garlic, parsley, basil, olive oil, the remaining I teaspoon salt, and some pepper in a bowl and set aside.

2. For the croutons: Heat I tablespoon of the olive oil in a large skillet over medium heat. Add the bread cubes and cook, tossing occasionally, until lightly toasted, about 5 minutes. Transfer to a bowl. Add the remaining I tablespoon oil and the minced garlic to the skillet and cook until golden brown, about I minute, stirring frequently. Take care the garlic doesn't get too brown or it will be bitter. Toss the toasted garlic, the cheese, and the parsley with the warm bread. Taste a crouton and add more salt as desired.

3. Puree the soup in batches in a blender, or puree it in the pot with an immersion blender. Over low heat, stir in the herb mixture and the croutons and simmer for I minute. The croutons will soften slightly and thicken the soup a bit. Ladle the soup into warm serving bowls and serve immediately.

pistou

6 servings

SOUP

¾ cup dried cannellini beans

1 whole clove

½ medium onion

1 medium carrot, peeled

1 bay leaf

2 teaspoons kosher salt

2 tablespoons extra-virgin olive oil

1 medium onion, chopped

1 medium carrot, peeled and sliced

½ fennel bulb, cored and chopped

4 cloves garlic, smashed

1 tablespoon kosher salt

1 15-ounce can whole tomatoes

6 red-skinned potatoes, quartered

1 tablespoon chopped fresh thyme

1 cup diced butternut squash (see Know-How, page 109)

¼ cup small pasta, such as ditalini

1 strip lemon zest

PESTO

Makes about ⅔ cup

2 cups loosely packed basil leaves

2 tablespoons toasted pine nuts

2 tablespoons freshly grated Parmigiano-Reggiano cheese

¼ teaspoon minced garlic

½ teaspoon kosher salt

¼ cup plus 1 tablespoon extra-virgin olive oil

1. Put the beans in a medium pot of cold water, bring to a boil, and boil for 5 minutes. Remove from the heat, cover, and soak for 1 hour. Drain. Stick the clove in the onion half and add it to the bean pot with the whole carrot, the bay leaf, 2 teaspoons salt, and 8 cups of cold water. Bring to a boil, reduce the heat, and simmer, covered, until tender, about 1 hour. Set the beans and their liquid aside. Remove the onion and bay leaf.

2. Heat the olive oil in a large soup pot over medium heat. Add the chopped onion, sliced carrot, fennel, garlic, and 1 tablespoon salt. Cook, stirring occasionally, until the vegetables are tender, about 10 minutes. Add the beans and their liquid, the tomatoes and their juice, the potatoes, thyme, and 2 cups water and cook until the potatoes are crisp-tender. Add squash, pasta, and lemon zest and cook until the squash is tender, about 20 minutes. Ladle the soup into warm bowls and garnish each with a healthy spoonful of Basil Pesto.

BASIL PESTO

In a food processor, combine the basil, pine nuts, cheese, garlic, and salt and puree. With the motor running, drizzle in the olive oil until incorporated. If not using right away, refrigerate with a piece of plastic wrap pressed to the surface of the pesto to prevent discoloration for up to 3 days.

COOK'S NOTE Pistou is a Provençal vegetable soup finished with a flourish of basil pesto. If you can't find cannellini beans, dried Great Northern work just fine.

salads

summer chopped salad with ranch dressing 4 servings

SALAD

8 ounces small red-skinned potatoes, halved

   Kosher salt

1 cup fresh corn kernels (from 2 ears of corn)

1 cup chopped fresh green or wax beans

1 cup small broccoli florets

1 cup cherry tomatoes, halved

1 Kirby cucumber with peel, chopped

   Ranch Dressing (see recipe, below)

   Freshly ground black pepper

4 cups torn mixed greens, such as arugula, romaine, and watercress

1 cup sprouts, such as alfalfa, broccoli, radish, or pea (optional)

DRESSING

   Makes about 1⅓ cups

1 clove garlic

½ teaspoon kosher salt

1 cup mayonnaise

⅓ cup buttermilk

2 tablespoons minced fresh flat-leaf parsley

2 tablespoons minced fresh chives

1 scallion (white and green parts), thinly sliced

1 teaspoon white wine vinegar

   Freshly ground black pepper

1. Put the potatoes in a small saucepan with enough cold water to cover and season with salt. Bring to a boil and then simmer, uncovered, until just tender, about 5 minutes. Drain and put in a large bowl.

2. Bring a medium pot of water to a boil and salt it generously. Fill a medium bowl with ice water and salt it as well. Add the corn, beans, and broccoli to the boiling water and cook until crisp-tender, about 2 minutes. Use a slotted spoon or strainer to scoop out the vegetables and plunge them immediately into the ice water. Drain the vegetables, pat them dry, and add to the bowl of potatoes along with the tomatoes and cucumber. Toss the salad with ½ cup of the dressing. Taste, and add more salt and pepper, if desired. (The salad may be prepared up to this point 2 hours ahead and refrigerated.)

3. When ready to serve, toss the salad with the greens and the sprouts, if desired, and with a bit more dressing if you like your salad on the well-dressed side. Pass the remaining dressing at the table.

RANCH DRESSING

Smash the garlic clove, sprinkle with the salt, and, with the side of a large knife, mash and smear the mixture to a coarse paste. Scrape the paste into a small bowl, add the remaining ingredients, and whisk well to make a creamy dressing. Use immediately or refrigerate in a tightly sealed container for up to 3 days.

KNOW-HOW Immersing vegetables in boiling salted water and then plunging them into ice water is called blanching and refreshing. Having the water at a full rolling boil before adding the vegetables, as well as cooking uncovered, is the key to keeping green vegetables vibrant.

Forget bottles and jars. Our homemade 1-2-3 ranch dressing turns this American classic into the real deal.

celery & soppressata salad with lemon

4 servings

¼ medium red onion, very thinly sliced

1 pound celery (about half a bunch), with leaves

3 ounces soppressata salami, in a chunk or sliced (see ShopSmart, below)

6 fresh basil leaves, torn into small pieces

2 teaspoons finely grated lemon zest

2 tablespoons freshly squeezed lemon juice

½ teaspoon kosher salt

Freshly ground black pepper

⅓ cup extra-virgin olive oil

1- to 2-ounce wedge Parmigiano-Reggiano cheese (see page 271)

1. To mellow the raw bite of the onion, soak the slices in cold water for 10 minutes, then drain, pat dry, and put them in a serving bowl.

2. Peel the tough, stringy fibers from the celery ribs. Slice the celery and some of the inner leaves very thinly on an angle. If you have a chunk of soppressata, dice it; if slices, cut them into thin strips. Toss the celery, soppressata, basil, lemon zest, and lemon juice with the onion. Season with salt and a generous grinding of pepper. Toss the salad with the olive oil.

3. Divide the salad among 4 serving plates. Use a vegetable peeler to shave large, thin pieces of Parmigiano-Reggiano over each serving and serve immediately.

An antipasto platter takes a tossing and a salad is born.

SHOPSMART There is a whole world of Italian cured meats and salamis to choose from, and soppressata—a dry-cured pork salami—is one of our favorites. If you can't find it, feel free to substitute another hard slicing salami. Not sure what to buy? Don't be shy about asking for tastes at the deli counter. It's one of the rewards of shopping.

asian-style apple-jicama slaw 4 servings

¼ cup rice vinegar

3 tablespoons freshly squeezed lime juice

2 teaspoons fish sauce (see page 274)

2 teaspoons sugar

¼ teaspoon kosher salt

1 medium jicama (about 1 pound), peeled

1 crisp red apple, with skin (Fuji is a good choice)

2 ounces fresh pea shoots, roughly chopped (optional)

2 scallions (white and green parts), thinly sliced

3 tablespoons chopped fresh mint or cilantro

Lime wedges

1. Stir the vinegar with the lime juice, fish sauce, sugar, and salt in a serving bowl. Using a hand-held mandoline or a knife, cut the jicama into long matchstick-size strips. Repeat with the apple, giving it a quarter turn as you reach the core on each side.

2. Toss the jicama, apple, pea shoots, if desired, scallions, and mint or cilantro with the dressing. Set aside for at least 15 minutes or up to 1 hour to let the flavors develop. Serve with lime wedges for squeezing over individual servings.

COOK'S NOTE Cutting vegetables into a uniform, thin matchstick is called a julienne. It's a great way to sharpen your knife skills, but if you want consistency and speed, use a mandoline. This affordable hand-held tool is a godsend for slicing, grating, and julienning like a pro.

hearts of romaine with blue cheese & bacon 4 servings

SALAD

- 8 strips good-quality bacon
- 1 large egg
- 2 hearts romaine lettuce

    Kosher salt and freshly ground black pepper

    Blue Cheese Dressing (see recipe, below)

DRESSING

    Makes 2 cups

- 1 cup mayonnaise
- 1 cup crumbled blue cheese (about 4 ounces)
- ½ cup buttermilk
- 1 shallot, peeled
- 1 tablespoon freshly grated lemon zest
- ½ teaspoon Worcestershire sauce
- ½ teaspoon kosher salt
- ¼ teaspoon celery seeds
- 2 tablespoons minced fresh flat-leaf parsley

    Freshly ground black pepper

KNOW-HOW This is the method we use whenever we hard-cook eggs. Because they are not actually boiled, the egg's yolk doesn't turn drab green or develop a strong taste.

1. Preheat the oven to 375°F. Lay the bacon strips on a roasting rack and bake in the oven until crisp, about 20 minutes. (To make bacon curls: Wrap each slice of raw bacon around a metal skewer in a barber-pole fashion and lay the skewers on the roasting rack.) Pat dry with a paper towel. When cool enough to handle, break into pieces or in half, if using curls.

2. Put the egg in a small saucepan with enough cold water to cover. Bring to a boil, cover, and remove from the heat. Set aside for 10 minutes. Drain the egg and roll it between your palm and the counter to crack the shell, then peel under cool running water. Rub the egg through a fine-mesh strainer and set aside.

3. Remove the large outer leaves from the romaine hearts and rinse. Chop these leaves into bite-size pieces and spin dry. (Use an extremely sharp knife to minimize bruising the edges.) Halve the hearts through the cores to make 4 wedges. Rinse under cold running water and shake to air dry.

4. Divide the wedges among 4 plates. Mound some of the chopped romaine on top and season with salt and pepper to taste. Spoon about ¼ cup of Blue Cheese Dressing over each salad and top with some of the sieved egg and bacon. Pass the remaining dressing at the table.

BLUE CHEESE DRESSING

Pulse the mayonnaise, blue cheese, buttermilk, shallot, lemon zest, Worcestershire sauce, salt, and celery seeds in a food processor to make a chunky but pourable sauce. Stir in the parsley and season with plenty of pepper. Use immediately or refrigerate in a tightly sealed container for up to 3 days.

Combine the enhanced flavor of romaine with smidgens of bacon and our irresistible blue cheese dressing, and that old-fashioned wedge of lettuce becomes a slice of heaven.

picnic three-bean salad

4 to 6 servings

½ small red onion, finely chopped

1 15¼-ounce can kidney beans, rinsed and drained

8 ounces green beans

8 ounces wax beans

⅓ cup cider vinegar

¼ cup sugar

¼ cup vegetable oil

½ teaspoon kosher salt, plus additional for seasoning

Freshly ground black pepper

2 tablespoons minced fresh flat-leaf parsley

1. To mellow the bite of the raw onion, soak it in cold water for 10 minutes, then drain it well, pat dry, and put it in a serving bowl. Stir in the kidney beans.

2. Fill a bowl with ice water. Bring a saucepan of water to a boil and salt it generously. Add the green and wax beans and cook until crisp-tender, 4 to 5 minutes. Drain the beans and plunge them into the ice water to stop the cooking and set their color. Drain the beans well, pat dry, and toss them with the kidney beans and onion.

3. Bring the vinegar, sugar, oil, and the ½ teaspoon salt to a boil in a small saucepan and immediately pour over the beans. Marinate the beans at room temperature for 1 hour, tossing several times.

4. Just before serving, taste the beans, season with salt and pepper to taste, and stir in the parsley.

This three-bean salad is a four-star recipe that will add colorful crunch to any spread anywhere— from picnic blanket to kitchen table.

STYLE Pack your picnic foods—such as slices of cake, cups of chilled soups, or salads—in individual portions. It makes serving the food effortless and gives company the freedom to eat at whatever pace they choose.

Get fresh.
Lovely greens catch your eye at the farmer's market? Take them home and dress them in something delicious.

vinaigrette

extra-virgin olive oil

balsamic vinegar

radicchio

Dijon mustard

freshly ground
black pepper

fresh lemon

mixed greens

shallot

kosher salt

garlic

COOK'S NOTE A simple green salad can
be a triumph. Salads can be easily improvised and
have endless variations. Combine lettuces to balance their
qualities, pairing mild, crisp lettuces, for instance, with peppery,
textured greens. Simple vinaigrettes start with salt and pepper
blended with 1 part vinegar or freshly squeezed citrus juice. Then
3 or 4 parts of a tasty extra-virgin olive oil are slowly whisked in to
make a smooth dressing. Adding mustard before whisking in oil
gives the dressing a kick while keeping it creamy. For riffs on the
same basic theme, add flavorings such as minced garlic, shallots,
herbs, and spices—or use nut oils such as walnut or hazelnut oil
instead of olive oil.

71

french lentil & roasted beet salad 6 servings

Everywhere we travel, we taste, we test, we shop, we eat. Here are two American salads inspired by Mediterranean cuisines.

SALAD

- 1 pound beets (about 3 medium), red, gold, striped, or a mixture
- 1 tablespoon olive oil
- 1 cup de Puy lentils (small, slate-green lentils from France)
- 1 sprig fresh rosemary, plus 2 teaspoons chopped leaves
- 1 bay leaf
- 2 large cloves garlic, peeled and smashed
- ½ onion, studded with a whole clove
- ½ teaspoon kosher salt, plus additional for seasoning

  Sherry Vinegar and Mustard Dressing (see recipe, below)
- ¼ cup minced fresh flat-leaf parsley

  Freshly ground black pepper
- 6 cups mixed greens
- 6 ounces aged goat cheese

DRESSING

Makes ½ cup

- 3 tablespoons aged sherry wine vinegar
- 2 tablespoons whole-grain mustard
- 1 teaspoon kosher salt

  Freshly ground black pepper
- ⅓ cup extra-virgin olive oil
- 2 shallots, minced

1. Preheat the oven to 400°F. Trim all but 1 inch of the beet stems. Put the beets on a large piece of aluminum foil, drizzle with olive oil, and seal the foil to make a tight package. Put the package in a small roasting pan. Roast the beets until easily pierced with a knife, about 1 hour. When the beets are cool enough to handle, peel them—the skins should slide right off with a bit of pressure from your fingers. If they don't, use a paring knife to scrape off any bits that stick. Dice the beets and set aside.

2. While you roast the beets, spread the lentils on a pan and pick out any pebbles or other foreign matter; rinse and drain. Put the lentils in a saucepan with cold water to cover by about 2 inches. Tie the sprig of rosemary and the bay leaf together with a piece of kitchen twine and add to the pan along with the smashed garlic, onion half, and ½ teaspoon salt. Bring to a boil over high heat; reduce the heat and simmer, uncovered, until the lentils are tender, about 25 minutes. Strain the lentils and discard herbs and onion.

3. Put the warm lentils in a bowl and stir in half the dressing. Cool the lentils completely, then add the beets, parsley, and chopped rosemary. Season to taste with salt and pepper. Lightly dress the greens with a bit of the dressing and divide among 6 plates. Spoon some of the lentil salad onto the greens, crumble goat cheese over each serving, and drizzle with some of the remaining vinaigrette.

SHERRY VINEGAR AND MUSTARD DRESSING

Whisk the vinegar with the mustard, 1 teaspoon salt, and pepper to taste in a small bowl. Gradually whisk in the olive oil, starting with a few drops and then adding the rest in a steady stream to make a smooth, slightly thick vinaigrette. Stir in the shallots. Use immediately or refrigerate in a tightly sealed container for up to 3 days.

greek rice & herb salad

4 to 6 servings

RICE

2 teaspoons extra-virgin olive oil

1½ cups long-grain rice, not converted

2¼ cups water

1 teaspoon kosher salt

SALAD

⅓ cup extra-virgin olive oil

5 tablespoons freshly squeezed lemon juice

2 teaspoons kosher salt

¼ teaspoon ground allspice

2 ripe medium tomatoes

1 Kirby cucumber with peel, seeded and finely diced

2 scallions (white and green parts), thinly sliced

¼ cup minced fresh flat-leaf parsley

¼ cup minced fresh dill

¼ cup minced fresh mint

½ teaspoon finely grated lemon zest

Freshly ground black pepper

Hot pepper sauce

1½ cups coarsely crumbled feta cheese (about 6 ounces)

Lemon wedges

1. For the rice: Heat the oil in a medium saucepan over medium heat. Add the rice and cook, stirring, until slightly toasted and golden, about 1½ minutes. Stir in the water and salt, bring to a boil, cover, reduce the heat, and simmer for 18 minutes. Then let the rice rest off the heat for 5 minutes—please don't lift the lid to give a peek or stir or the rice will not cook evenly. Put the rice in a large serving bowl, fluff and separate the grains with a fork, and cool to room temperature. (Don't refrigerate the rice or it will get grainy.)

2. For the salad: Whisk the oil, lemon juice, salt, and allspice in a small bowl. Toss the dressing with the cooled rice. Halve the tomatoes crosswise to expose their seeds. Use your fingertip to pop the seeds out of the flesh and discard. Cut the tomatoes into fine dice. Add the tomatoes, cucumber, scallions, parsley, dill, mint, and lemon zest to the rice mixture and toss again. Season with pepper and hot pepper sauce to taste. Scatter the feta cheese across the top and serve, passing the lemon wedges.

COOK'S NOTE Kirby cucumbers aren't just for pickling; they are great in salads, too. We love them for a variety of reasons: They aren't waxed so you don't need to peel them, they are sweeter than your standard cucumber, and one is just the right size for adding crunch to a salad.

grilled plum salad with aged gouda & pecans 4 servings

DRESSING

2   tablespoons sherry vinegar

1   teaspoon honey

¾   teaspoon kosher salt

Freshly ground black pepper

3   tablespoons extra-virgin olive oil

SALAD

4   ripe plums (about 1 pound), pitted and quartered

1   teaspoon extra-virgin olive oil

Kosher salt and freshly ground black pepper

3   cups torn escarole leaves (about ½ head)

1   bunch watercress, washed, dried, and stems trimmed (about 3 cups)

4   ounces aged Gouda cheese, thinly sliced

¼   cup pecan halves, toasted

1. For the dressing: Whisk the vinegar, honey, ¾ teaspoon salt, and pepper to taste in a large bowl. Gradually whisk in oil, starting with a few drops and adding the rest in a steady stream to make a smooth, slightly thick vinaigrette. Set aside.

2. For the salad: Heat a grill pan over medium-high heat. Brush the plums with olive oil and sprinkle with salt and pepper to taste. Grill the plums until slightly soft, about 1 minute per side. To get distinct grill marks, resist the temptation to move the fruit around on the pan as it cooks. Cut the plum wedges in half crosswise and toss with the dressing. Set the plums aside to marinate in the dressing for 15 minutes. (The salad can be prepared up to this point 1 hour before serving.)

3. Right before serving, toss the greens with the plums and dressing. Divide the salad among 4 serving plates and scatter the cheese and pecans over the tops.

SHOPSMART Almost universally, the longer a cheese is aged, the sharper and more complex its flavor. Aged Gouda has a Cheddar-like quality.

grilled asparagus with tomato & mozzarella salad 4 to 6 servings

2   bunches medium asparagus (about 2 pounds), peeled and woody stems trimmed

2   tablespoons extra-virgin olive oil

2   cups grape or cherry tomatoes, halved

8   ounces fresh mozzarella cheese, cut into ½-inch cubes

2   tablespoons chopped fresh flat-leaf parsley

1   teaspoon finely grated lemon zest

1   tablespoon freshly squeezed lemon juice

1   teaspoon kosher salt

¼   teaspoon crushed red pepper flakes

Freshly ground black pepper

1. Arrange the asparagus in a microwave-safe dish, cover with plastic wrap, and microwave on high until crisp-tender, about 2 minutes. (If you don't have a microwave, you can steam the asparagus instead.) Brush asparagus with 1 tablespoon of the olive oil and set aside.

2. Toss tomatoes and mozzarella cheese in a large bowl with the remaining 1 tablespoon olive oil, the parsley, lemon zest and juice, salt, red pepper flakes, and black pepper to taste.

3. Heat a grill pan over medium heat. Grill asparagus, turning occasionally, until tender and lightly charred, about 5 minutes. Cut asparagus in half crosswise and arrange the upper portions, spoke-like, tips out, on a serving dish. Cut the lower portions into ½-inch pieces and toss with the tomato and cheese mixture. Mound the salad in the center of the tips and serve.

KNOW-HOW Peeling asparagus? Yes, but just the lower part of a thick stalk to make more of the spear edible. We peel before we snap off the fibrous end.

crab louis

4 servings

DRESSING

- 2 ripe medium tomatoes
- 1 tablespoon extra-virgin olive oil
- ¾ teaspoon kosher salt
- ½ cup mayonnaise
- 2 tablespoons minced piquillo pepper (see page 273) or jarred roasted sweet red pepper
- 1 tablespoon minced red onion
- 1 teaspoon chipotle hot sauce

  Freshly ground black pepper

SALAD

- 1 pound jumbo lump crabmeat
- ¼ cup peeled, diced jicama
- 1 teaspoon extra-virgin olive oil
- 1 lemon, halved

  Kosher salt

- 1 ripe Hass avocado
- 2 ripe tomatoes
- 1 head Boston lettuce, leaves separated
- ¼ cup fresh whole cilantro leaves

1. For the dressing: Halve the tomatoes crosswise to expose their seeds. Use your fingertip to pop the seeds out of the flesh and discard. Working over a small, shallow saucepan, grate the cut side of each tomato half against the large teeth of a box grater; discard the skins. Add the olive oil and ½ teaspoon of the salt and simmer over medium heat, stirring frequently, until thickened and reduced to about ⅓ cup, about 15 minutes. Set aside to cool.

2. Stir cooked tomatoes, mayonnaise, piquillo or red pepper, onion, hot sauce, remaining ¼ teaspoon salt, and black pepper to taste in a small bowl until combined. Refrigerate, covered, until ready to serve. (Dressing can be made up to 1 day ahead.)

3. For the salad: Spread the crabmeat on a pan and carefully pick out and discard any bits of shell. Place the crab and the jicama in a large bowl. Drizzle with the olive oil and some lemon juice, sprinkle with salt to taste, and use a rubber spatula or wooden spoon to very gently fold the ingredients together. Fold in ½ cup of the dressing.

4. Halve, seed, peel, and slice the avocado into thin wedges (see page 272). Squeeze a bit of lemon juice over the avocado to keep the flesh from discoloring. Core the tomatoes and cut into wedges. Divide the lettuce leaves among 4 chilled plates and arrange the avocado and tomatoes attractively on top. Spoon some crab salad on each and drizzle with some of the dressing. Scatter cilantro leaves over each salad and serve, passing the remaining dressing.

Some believe this "King of Salads" was named after King Louis XIV, who was known for his enormous appetite. One thing's for sure. Our version of this succulent dish is fit for a king.

southwestern cobb salad with chili-rubbed steak 6 servings

DRESSING

- 2 cloves garlic
- ½ teaspoon kosher salt
- ⅓ cup mayonnaise
- ⅓ cup buttermilk
- 1 tablespoon chipotle hot sauce
- 3 tablespoons minced fresh cilantro
- 1 scallion (white and green parts), very thinly sliced
- 1 teaspoon finely grated orange zest

STEAK

- Kosher salt
- 1 tri-tip steak or other sirloin steak (about 1¾ pounds)
- 2 tablespoons chili powder
- 1 tablespoon extra-virgin olive oil

SALAD

- 1 ripe Hass avocado
- 1 head romaine lettuce, torn into pieces
- 3 ripe medium tomatoes, diced
- 1 orange, cut into segments (see page 272)
- ½ medium jicama, peeled and diced (about 2 cups)
- 4 ounces Cotija (see page 271) or feta cheese, crumbled (about 1 cup)
- Kosher salt and freshly ground black pepper

1. For the dressing: Smash the garlic cloves, sprinkle with the salt, and, with the flat side of a large knife, mash and smear the mixture to a coarse paste. Scrape the paste into a small bowl, add the mayonnaise, buttermilk, hot sauce, cilantro, scallion, and orange zest, and whisk well to make a creamy dressing. Set aside.

2. For the steak: Position a rack and broiler pan about 6 inches from the heat element and preheat the broiler to high. Season steak with salt to taste. Stir the chili powder into the oil in a small bowl and rub the spiced oil on both sides of the steak. Carefully lay the steak on the hot pan and broil, turning once, 8 to 10 minutes per side for medium- rare. Transfer the steak to a cutting board and let rest 5 minutes before cutting into bite-size cubes.

3. For salad: Halve, seed, peel, and dice the avocado (see page 272). Put the romaine into a large salad bowl. Arrange the steak, avocado, tomatoes, orange, jicama, and cheese over the lettuce in wide stripes and season with salt and pepper to taste.

4. At the table, pour about 3 tablespoons of dressing over the salad and toss well. Pass the remaining dressing. Serve the salad with warm corn or flour tortillas, if desired.

COOK'S NOTE Don't rush to slice meat directly after it's cooked, but let it rest—5 minutes for a steak and up to 30 minutes for a large roast. This allows the juices to distribute throughout, and you avoid a bull's-eye of rare meat in the center of the cut.

leslie's ham salad

4 servings

1	small red onion, minced
1	pound cooked ham, cut into large pieces
2	ribs celery, quartered
6	cornichon or gherkin pickles
1	pickled jalapeño, seeded and stemmed
2	scallions (white and green parts), minced
⅓	cup mayonnaise
2	tablespoons Dijon mustard
¼	teaspoon freshly ground black pepper
1	bunch watercress, washed, dried, and stems trimmed (about 3 cups)
1	bunch arugula, washed, dried, and stems trimmed (about 2 cups)
4	to 8 slices rustic sourdough bread, toasted or grilled

1. To mellow the minced onion, soak it in cold water for 10 minutes, then drain it well, pat dry, and put it in a serving bowl. Pulse the ham in a food processor until chunky and add it to the red onion. Pulse the celery, pickles, and jalapeño in the processor until chopped and add to the ham.

2. Add the scallions to the ham mixture along with the mayonnaise, mustard, and pepper. Refrigerate the salad, covered, until thoroughly chilled, about 1 hour.

3. Toss the watercress and arugula together and divide among 4 plates. Divide the ham salad evenly on the greens and serve with the toasts.

COOK'S NOTE This is just the thing to make with leftover holiday ham. (We don't recommend deli ham as a stand-in.) Our favorite smoked ham is neither too salty nor watery. Better hams still have a bone and most of their skin intact.

Whenever we get a great ham from one of our shows, our sous-chef, Leslie, makes this classic spiced up with pickled jalapeño and served on fresh, peppery greens.

sandwiches

patty melts

4 servings

8 ounces ground sirloin

8 ounces ground chuck

½ teaspoon kosher salt, plus additional for seasoning

Freshly ground black pepper

3 tablespoons vegetable oil

2 medium onions, thinly sliced

2 to 3 tablespoons unsalted butter, softened

8 slices rye bread

8 slices Swiss or American cheese (about 3 ounces)

1. Break both meats by hand into small pieces onto a large piece of waxed or parchment paper. Sprinkle the ½ teaspoon salt and some pepper over the meat. Bring the meat together by hand, avoiding kneading it, and don't worry if it seems loosely knit. (This light touch keeps the meat from getting tough.) Divide into 4 portions, then into balls by gently tossing from hand to hand; finally, press each one into an oval patty somewhat larger than the slices of bread.

2. Heat 1 tablespoon of the oil in a large cast-iron skillet over medium heat. Add the onions, season with some salt and pepper, and cook until golden, about 7 minutes. Put in a bowl. Wipe out the skillet and add another 1 tablespoon of oil. Cook the patties in batches in the remaining oil until well browned, about 1 to 3 minutes per side for medium burgers.

3. Butter each bread slice on one side. Lay the bread, butter side down, on the counter. Divide the onions among 4 bread slices and top with a slice of cheese, a patty, another slice of cheese, and a slice of bread, butter side up. Heat the cast-iron skillet over medium heat. Cook the sandwiches, in batches if needed, turning once, until the bread is lightly browned and the cheese has melted, 1 to 2 minutes per side. Halve the melts and serve.

One of the rewards of being on location is savoring local foods—whether it's a Philly cheese steak, an Iowa corn dog, or this classic Jersey patty melt.

blue **cheese steak**
sandwiches 6 servings

SANDWICHES

- 6 crusty rolls, such as Portuguese, split
- ⅓ cup Dijon mustard
- 1½ pounds grilled medium-rare steak, thinly sliced

  Kosher salt and freshly ground black pepper

- 12 ounces Saga blue cheese, cut into 12 slices (see page 271)

  Roasted Shallots (see recipe, below), roughly chopped

- 4 cups loosely packed watercress, washed and dried

ROASTED SHALLOTS

- 8 shallots, unpeeled
- ¼ cup extra-virgin olive oil
- 1 tablespoon kosher salt, plus additional for seasoning

  Freshly ground black pepper

1. Preheat the broiler. Spread the rolls out on a pan and toast on both sides.

2. Slather the bottom half of each roll with some of the mustard and top with slices of the steak, overlapping the slices slightly. Season to taste with salt and pepper. Cover each portion of meat with 2 slices of cheese. Broil until the cheese is lightly browned and melted, about 1 minute.

3. Transfer the open-faced sandwiches to the work surface. Top each sandwich with some of the roasted shallots and watercress. Slather the tops with the remaining mustard and cover the sandwiches. Slice in half and serve.

ROASTED SHALLOTS

1. Preheat the oven to 400°F. Toss the shallots with olive oil, 1 tablespoon salt, and pepper to taste in a large bowl. Spread out on an aluminum foil-lined baking sheet. Bake until the shallots are very tender, about 40 minutes. Set aside to cool.

2. Slice off the tips of the shallots and discard. Gently squeeze the shallots from their skins and season with additional salt and pepper to taste.

STYLE Don't hide your wooden cutting boards in the kitchen. A well-worn board or a pizza paddle can be the perfect backdrop for a spread of sandwiches, tarts, or cheeses.

panini with bresaola, **endive & provolone** 4 servings

Press a few strips of Italian air-dried beef into a slice or two of provolone and some endive, and you'll forget all about those grilled cheese sandwiches your mother used to make.

1 tablespoon unsalted butter

1 Belgian endive, separated into leaves

½ teaspoon sugar

1 teaspoon balsamic vinegar

4 ciabatta rolls

4 slices aged provolone cheese (about 4 ounces)

8 thin slices bresaola (Italian air-dried beef) (about 2 ounces)

Extra-virgin olive oil

1. Melt the butter in a large skillet over medium heat. Add the endive leaves, rounded side down, and cook until slightly wilted and brown. Turn the leaves, press gently with a spatula, and cook until pliable, about 3 minutes. Sprinkle with sugar, add the vinegar, turn the endive to coat, and cook until lightly glazed, about 1 minute. Cool.

2. Heat a sandwich press or waffle iron to medium-high. Slice the rounded tops off the rolls and halve horizontally. Lay a slice of provolone on the bottom half of each roll, followed by ¼ of the bresaola and endive, and finally the top of the roll. Brush both sides of the panini lightly with olive oil—take care not to soak the bread or the panini will be greasy. Cook each panino in the press until the cheese melts and the bread browns, about 4 minutes. Serve.

COOK'S NOTE Ciabatta, which means "slipper" in Italian, is a broad, chewy bread with a thin, crisp crust. It makes great panini, but if you can't find it, feel free to use another rustic bread. Good bread goes stale in the refrigerator. Store it either in an old-fashioned bread box or well wrapped in the freezer.

miso chicken sandwiches
with **ginger** mayonnaise 4 servings

CHICKEN

- ¼ cup light miso (see Cook's Note, below)
- ¼ cup dark sesame oil
- ¼ cup soy sauce
- 1 tablespoon finely grated peeled fresh ginger
- 4 boneless, skinless chicken breast halves, pounded very thin (about 1 pound total)

MAYONNAISE

- ½ cup mayonnaise
- 2 teaspoons rice vinegar
- 2 teaspoons soy sauce
- 2 teaspoons finely grated peeled fresh ginger
- 1 teaspoon Asian chili sauce or hot pepper sauce
- ½ teaspoon dark sesame oil

SANDWICHES

- 8 slices multigrain sliced sandwich bread
- 1 Hass avocado, halved, seeded, peeled, and thinly sliced (see page 272)
- ½ medium cucumber, thinly sliced
- 1 cup sprouts, such as alfalfa, broccoli, or radish

1. For the chicken: Heat the broiler and line a broiler pan with aluminum foil, or prepare an outdoor grill. Stir the miso, sesame oil, soy sauce, and ginger together in a bowl and brush both sides of the chicken with the mixture. Broil on the prepared pan, 6 inches from the heat, or grill, turning once, until cooked through, about 2 minutes per side.

2. For the flavored mayonnaise: Whisk the mayonnaise with the vinegar, soy sauce, ginger, chili sauce or hot pepper sauce, and sesame oil in a small bowl.

3. To assemble the sandwiches: Halve each chicken breast on an angle. Spread 4 slices of bread with the flavored mayonnaise and top with the chicken, avocado and cucumber slices, sprouts, and remaining bread slices. Cut sandwiches in half and serve.

COOK'S NOTE We love the distinctive taste miso (fermented soy paste) adds to soups, sauces, and marinades. There are different types of miso, ranging from yellow to deep brown. If you are new to this intensely flavored Japanese condiment, start with a mellower, lighter-colored one.

Like a good chicken sandwich with mayo? Try our intensely delicious East-West variation and experience the difference between good and great.

extra-virgin olive oil

celery

black olives

cauliflower

pimiento

green olives

carrots

dried oregano

flat-leaf parsley

dried thyme

muffuletta 4 servings

OLIVE SALAD

- ½ cup extra-virgin olive oil
- 3 tablespoons water
- 1 small carrot, peeled and thinly sliced
- 1 small rib celery, thinly sliced
- ½ cup small cauliflower florets
- ½ teaspoon dried thyme
- ½ teaspoon dried oregano
- ¾ cup pitted large green olives, such as Manzanilla, finely chopped
- ¼ cup pitted black olives, such as kalamata, finely chopped
- 2 tablespoons chopped jarred pimiento
- ½ teaspoon kosher salt
- 1 tablespoon chopped fresh flat-leaf parsley

SANDWICHES

- 1 6-inch round Italian bread with sesame seeds
- 2 tablespoons extra-virgin olive oil
- 6 ounces sliced provolone cheese
- 6 ounces sliced mortadella
- 4 ounces sliced soppressata (see ShopSmart, page 65), sweet or hot

1. To make the olive salad: Put the oil, water, carrot, celery, cauliflower, thyme, and oregano in a medium saucepan. Bring to a boil over medium heat, cover, reduce the heat to medium-low, and then simmer until the vegetables are crisp-tender, about 6 minutes. Transfer the mixture to a bowl and stir in the olives, pimiento, and salt. Cool, then add the parsley.

2. To assemble the sandwich: Slice the bread in half horizontally, then pull out some of the inside from each half to make a pocket. Brush the inside of the top half with olive oil. Pack the bottom half with the olive salad. Layer the cheese and meats over the salad and top with the remaining bread. Wrap the muffuletta very tightly with plastic wrap. Place the sandwich in a broad, shallow container and weight it with something heavy (we use a cast-iron skillet) for at least 1 hour at room temperature. Cut muffuletta into quarters and serve with plenty of napkins.

COOK'S NOTE Olive salad is what separates a muffuletta from any other hero, but don't confine its use to this sandwich. It pairs up well with grilled fish, chicken, or steak. Make a double batch and keep it on hand to round out a quick dinner.

A New Orleans favorite, this incredibly indulgent sandwich can be found almost nowhere else but The Big Easy. Now you can bring it home where it belongs.

salmon burgers

4 servings

1¼ pounds skinless salmon fillets, very cold

1 large egg

1 shallot, minced

2 tablespoons chopped fresh flat-leaf parsley

1 tablespoon chopped fresh dill

2 teaspoons whole-grain mustard

2 teaspoons kosher salt, plus additional for grilling

1 teaspoon finely grated lemon zest

Olive oil, for grilling

Freshly ground black pepper

4 hamburger buns or English muffins

Tomato slices (optional)

Tartar sauce, mustard, or other condiments of your choice

KNOW-HOW Forming the patties is easier if the mixture is cold, and dipping your hands in cold water keeps it from sticking. As with all burgers, don't overwork the mixture or they will be tough.

1. Cut the salmon into 1-inch cubes and put in the freezer for 5 minutes. Process the egg, shallot, parsley, dill, mustard, salt, and lemon zest in a food processor until fairly smooth. Add half of the chilled salmon and pulse to make a chunky paste. Add the remaining salmon and pulse 10 times to make a rough-textured mixture. Wet your hands with cool water and shape the mixture into 4 patties, each about ³/4 inch thick. Place each patty on a square of waxed or parchment paper and refrigerate, lightly covered, for 30 minutes.

2. Heat a stovetop grill pan or outdoor grill to medium-high heat. Brush the tops of the patties with olive oil and season with salt and pepper. Pick each patty up by its paper and turn it oil-side down onto the pan or grill; the paper should peel right off. Cook the patties without pressing, and don't move them until you see distinct grill marks, about 3 minutes. Brush the tops lightly with olive oil and season to taste with salt and pepper. Flip the patties and cook until they give just a bit when you press them with your fingertip, about 1½ minutes. Transfer the burgers to a platter, cover loosely with foil, and let rest for 2 minutes. Toast the buns or English muffins until golden. Serve the burgers on the toasted buns with tomato, if desired, tartar sauce, mustard, or your favorite condiment.

grilled portobello, scallion & manchego sandwiches 6 servings

DRESSING

2 teaspoons pimenton (see Cook's Note, below)

3 drained jarred piquillo peppers (see page 273)

1/4 cup mayonnaise

2 teaspoons sherry wine vinegar

2 teaspoons honey

1 teaspoon kosher salt

Freshly ground black pepper

VEGETABLES

4 medium portobello mushrooms (about 1 pound), stemmed

1/4 cup extra-virgin olive oil

Kosher salt and freshly ground black pepper

8 scallions (white and green parts), trimmed

SANDWICHES

8 1/2-inch-thick slices country-style bread

1 clove garlic, peeled

4 ounces manchego cheese, cut into 1/8-inch-thick slices (see page 271)

1. For the dressing: Toast the pimenton in a small skillet over medium heat, stirring frequently, until fragrant, about 4 minutes. Puree the pimenton, piquillo peppers, mayonnaise, vinegar, honey, 1 teaspoon salt, and pepper to taste in a blender until smooth. Transfer the mixture to a bowl, cover, and refrigerate. (The dressing may be made a day ahead.)

2. For the vegetables: Preheat an outdoor grill or stovetop grill pan to medium-high heat. Brush both sides of the mushrooms with some of the olive oil and season with salt and pepper. Grill the mushrooms, turning once, until tender and somewhat charred, about 5 minutes. Brush the scallions with some of the oil, season with salt and pepper to taste, and grill, turning occasionally, until soft and slightly charred, about 8 minutes. Transfer to a cutting board and roughly chop.

3. To assemble the sandwiches: Grill the bread on both sides until lightly toasted. Rub the garlic and slather the dressing on one side of each piece of toast. Layer scallions, mushrooms, and cheese on 4 toasts, and top with the remaining bread. Press down slightly and cut in half; serve.

COOK'S NOTE Hot Off the Grill turned us on to the bold flavors of Spanish ingredients, and this sandwich uses three of our favorites—pimenton, piquillo peppers, and manchego cheese. Pimenton, a smoked paprika available both sweet and hot, is a fantastically easy way to add depth of flavor to a dish. Sprinkle pimenton on mashed potatoes for a thoroughly modern makeover of a comfort classic.

lobster rolls

4 servings

An East Coast specialty, one bite of these luxurious lobster rolls and you can almost smell the salt air.

¹/₄ cup mayonnaise

1 tablespoon freshly squeezed lemon juice

2 teaspoons Dijon mustard

1 small rib celery, peeled and minced

1 tablespoon minced fresh chives

2 teaspoons minced fresh flat-leaf parsley

¹/₂ teaspoon kosher salt

Freshly ground black pepper

2 teaspoons minced fresh tarragon or basil (optional)

2 cups diced cooked lobster meat (about 14 ounces) (see note, right)

2 teaspoons unsalted butter

4 hot dog rolls, preferably New England-style (top-split, with pale sides)

COOK'S NOTE It goes without saying that a great lobster roll should be full of nuggets of fresh lobster. But passionate fans of this enduring New England sandwich—and we count ourselves among that crowd—feel strongly about the bun as well. The plain roll in contrast to the lavish lobster is what makes this summer sandwich so sublime.

1. Mix the mayonnaise, lemon juice, mustard, celery, chives, parsley, salt, and pepper to taste in a large bowl. Using a rubber spatula, fold in first the tarragon or basil, if desired, and then the lobster until just combined. Refrigerate, covered, for at least 1 and up to 24 hours.

2. When ready to serve, melt the butter in a large skillet over medium-high heat. Toast the sides of the rolls in the hot butter, two at a time, until golden, about 30 seconds per side. Split the rolls open, mound the lobster salad inside, and serve immediately.

Lobster note: To dispatch a live lobster humanely before it's dropped into boiling water, hold a sharp chef's knife over the lobster's head, right where there's an "x" in the shell. Push the point of the knife rapidly all of the way down to the cutting board, then quickly push the length of the blade forward onto the board. Drop the lobster into a very large pot of boiling water and cook for 6 to 8 minutes, or until the shell is completely red. Remove the lobster from the pot and let cool. To remove the meat, twist off the tail from the body. Remove the claws by twisting them off. Pull off the flippers at the end of the tail and push the meat out through the front end of the shell with your fingers. Bend the lower, smaller pincer on the claw side to side and pull it away from the claw. With the back of a chef's knife, crack the top side of the claw. Open the claw and pull out the meat. With kitchen shears, cut open the smaller pincer and arm sections and remove the meat from those also.

the main dish

Worknights or weekends, dinner should always be an end-of-the-day reward. So forget take-out and cook up one of these prize recipes instead.

noodles, beans & grains

SHOW #3
NOODLES, GRAINS
BEANS

chicken ragù with farfalle

4 to 6 servings

2   tablespoons extra-virgin olive oil

4   whole chicken legs (about 2 pounds)

2   teaspoons kosher salt, plus additional for seasoning

    Freshly ground black pepper

1   medium red onion, diced

1   large carrot, peeled and diced

1   rib celery, diced

1   clove garlic, minced

1/2 cup dry white wine

4   canned plum tomatoes, chopped

1   tablespoon tomato paste

1   teaspoon dried thyme

1   teaspoon dried sage

1   teaspoon dried rosemary

2   sprigs fresh flat-leaf parsley, plus 2 tablespoons chopped

    About 1 1/2 cups chicken broth, homemade (see page 278), or low-sodium canned

1   pound farfalle pasta (bow ties)

2   tablespoons freshly grated Pecorino Romano cheese, plus more for serving (see page 271)

1. Heat a large skillet over medium heat, add the olive oil, and heat until shimmering. Season the chicken with some salt and pepper to taste, and cook until brown on all sides, about 20 minutes. Remove the chicken to a platter. Add the onion, carrot, celery, and the 2 teaspoons salt to the skillet and cook, stirring occasionally, until the vegetables begin to soften, about 5 minutes. Add the garlic and cook until the vegetables are just tender, about 5 minutes more. Add the wine, tomatoes, tomato paste, thyme, sage, rosemary, and the parsley sprigs. Cook, stirring occasionally, until the tomatoes break down and mixture is saucy, about 5 minutes.

2. Slip the chicken with any juices into the tomato sauce. Add enough chicken broth to cover about 2/3 of the chicken. Simmer the ragù with the lid slightly ajar until the meat pulls easily from the bone, turning the chicken halfway through, about 30 minutes. Remove the chicken and when cool enough to handle, pull the meat from the bones, discarding the skin and bones. Skim off any fat that has collected on the top of the sauce and stir in the chicken. (The dish can be prepared up to this point 1 day ahead and refrigerated in a tightly sealed container.)

3. When ready to serve, heat the ragù over low heat. Bring a large pot of cold water to a boil over high heat and salt it generously. Add the farfalle and cook, stirring occasionally, until al dente, about 10 minutes. Ladle out about 1 cup of cooking water and set aside. Drain the pasta, add it to the ragù, and toss over low heat, adding about 1/4 cup of the reserved pasta-cooking liquid at a time until the sauce coats the farfalle. Add the chopped parsley and the Pecorino Romano cheese and toss again. Serve in warm bowls with additional cheese.

linguine with mussels, herbs & wine 4 servings

12 ounces linguine

8 tablespoons unsalted butter

4 shallots, thinly sliced

4 cloves garlic, chopped

1 1/2 teaspoons kosher salt

1/2 teaspoon crushed red pepper flakes

3/4 cup dry white vermouth

1/4 cup water

3/4 cup chopped fresh flat-leaf parsley

2 tablespoons chopped fresh tarragon

2 teaspoons chopped fresh thyme

1 1/2 pounds farm-raised mussels (about 4 dozen)

1. Bring a large pot of cold water to a boil over high heat and salt it generously. Add the linguine and cook, stirring occasionally, until al dente, about 8 minutes. Drain.

2. While the linguine cooks, melt the butter in a large skillet. Add the shallots, garlic, salt, and red pepper flakes and cook, stirring occasionally, until the shallots are soft, about 8 minutes. Stir in the vermouth, water, parsley, tarragon, and thyme and bring to a boil. Add the mussels, cover, and steam, giving the pot a good shake every minute or so, until mussels open, about 5 minutes. Discard any mussels that remain shut.

3. Divide the pasta among 4 large, warm serving bowls. Spoon the mussels over the pasta and pour some of the broth over the tops.

KNOW-HOW Rinse the mussels in several changes of cold water and give them a scrub if they are muddy. Discard any raw mussels that don't close when tapped. Tug off any beard—the small, dark tuft that sticks out from the shell—before steaming. When possible, cook mussels the day you buy them.

tubetti with crab, fennel & lemon 4 to 6 servings

1 pound lump crabmeat

3 tablespoons extra-virgin olive oil, plus additional for drizzling

4 scallions (white and green parts), thinly sliced

1 rib celery, finely diced

½ medium fennel bulb, finely diced (about 1¼ cups)

1½ teaspoons kosher salt, plus additional for seasoning

2 tablespoons chopped fresh flat-leaf parsley

½ teaspoon finely grated lemon zest

Pinch crushed red pepper flakes

Freshly ground black pepper

1 pound tubetti pasta

2 tablespoons freshly squeezed lemon juice

2 heads Bibb or 1 head Boston lettuce, leaves separated

2 ripe medium tomatoes, cut into wedges

Extra-virgin olive oil

Lemon wedges, for serving

1. Spread the crabmeat on a pan and carefully pick out and discard any bits of shell. Heat the 3 tablespoons oil in a large skillet over medium heat. Add the scallions, celery, fennel, and the 1½ teaspoons salt and cook, stirring occasionally, until vegetables are softened and fragrant, about 8 minutes. Add the crab and cook just until heated through, tossing gently to keep the crabmeat in lumps, about 2 minutes. Transfer the crab mixture to a large bowl and very gently fold in the parsley, lemon zest, red pepper flakes, and black pepper to taste. Cover and refrigerate the crab mixture for about 1 hour to allow the flavors to come together.

2. Bring a large pot of cold water to a boil over high heat and salt it generously. Add the pasta and cook, stirring occasionally, until al dente, about 9 minutes. Ladle out ¼ cup of the cooking water, set aside, and drain the pasta. Gently toss the pasta, the reserved pasta cooking liquid, and the lemon juice with the crab mixture. Cool to room temperature.

3. Divide the lettuce leaves and tomato wedges among individual plates. Season with salt and pepper to taste and drizzle with olive oil. Spoon the pasta mixture over the salads, place a lemon wedge on each, and serve immediately.

three-meat ragù for pasta
4 quarts

- ¼ cup extra-virgin olive oil
- ½ teaspoon crushed red pepper flakes
- 1 large onion, chopped
- 1 large carrot, peeled and chopped
- 4 28-ounce cans whole peeled tomatoes
- 6 cloves garlic, minced
- ¼ cup Italian tomato paste
- 1 tablespoon sugar, plus a pinch if needed
- 3 teaspoons kosher salt, plus additional for seasoning
- Freshly ground black pepper
- 4 ounces ground beef chuck
- 4 ounces ground pork
- 4 ounces ground veal
- 2 teaspoons dried rosemary or savory, crumbled
- 2 teaspoons dried thyme
- 2 teaspoons dried oregano
- 2 teaspoons fennel seeds, cracked
- 2 bay leaves
- 1 3-inch piece of Parmigiano-Reggiano cheese rind (optional) (see Know-How, right), plus ½ to 1 cup freshly grated Parmigiano-Reggiano cheese (4 ounces)

1. In a large soup pot or Dutch oven, heat the olive oil over medium heat. Stir in the red pepper flakes and cook for 15 seconds. Add the onion and carrot and cook, stirring occasionally, until onion is golden brown, 10 to 15 minutes. While vegetables are cooking, pour tomatoes and their juices into a large bowl and crush the tomatoes with your hands.

2. Stir the garlic into the onion mixture and cook until fragrant, about 1 minute. Stir in tomato paste and cook until brick red, about 1 minute. Add all the crushed tomatoes, the 1 tablespoon sugar, 1 teaspoon of the salt, and pepper to taste. Bring to a simmer. Set the pot lid slightly ajar and reduce heat to low.

3. Heat a large skillet over medium-high heat. Add the beef, pork, veal, rosemary, thyme, oregano, and fennel seeds. Season with the remaining 2 teaspoons salt and some pepper to taste. Break up the meat with a wooden spoon and cook until it loses its rosy color, about 5 minutes. Stir the meat into the sauce with the bay leaves and the cheese rind, if desired. Simmer the sauce, partially covered, stirring occasionally, for 1½ hours. (If sauce gets too thick, add some water.) Taste and season with salt, pepper, and sugar, if desired. Just before serving, remove the bay leaves and cheese rind and stir in the grated cheese.

KNOW-HOW Every piece of Parmigiano-Reggiano is pure gold, including the rind. Toss the rind into sauces, soups, and stews as they cook to impart its fabulous flavor.

Freeze this beautiful sauce in 3- to 4-cup portions. When you're world-weary, thaw it, heat it up, and toss it with a pound of cooked pasta.

shiitake & sun-dried tomato lasagna 4 to 6 servings

SAUCE

16	sun-dried tomatoes
2	pounds fresh shiitake mushrooms
4	tablespoons unsalted butter
4	tablespoons extra-virgin olive oil
3	teaspoons kosher salt
	Freshly ground black pepper
2	shallots, thinly sliced
4	cloves garlic, minced
1	tablespoon tomato paste
3½	cups canned whole tomatoes
3	sprigs fresh thyme
3	sprigs fresh oregano
1	sprig fresh rosemary
1	bay leaf
6	fresh flat-leaf parsley stems and 3 tablespoons chopped

LASAGNA

12	dry lasagna noodles
½	cup freshly grated Parmesan cheese
½	cup freshly grated Pecorino Romano cheese (2 ounces) (see page 271)
1	recipe Béchamel Sauce (see page 280)

1. For the mushroom and tomato sauce: Put the sun-dried tomatoes in a bowl and add boiling water to cover. Set aside until soft, about 20 minutes, and then drain and quarter. Stem and quarter mushrooms. Melt 1 tablespoon of the butter with 1 tablespoon of the olive oil in a soup pot or Dutch oven over medium-high heat. Add half of the mushrooms and cook, stirring occasionally, until well browned and soft, about 10 minutes. Repeat with another 1 tablespoon each of butter and oil and other half of mushrooms. When all the mushrooms are cooked, put them in a bowl and toss with 1½ teaspoons of the salt and pepper to taste.

2. Reduce heat to medium and melt remaining 2 tablespoons butter with remaining 2 tablespoons olive oil. Add shallots, remaining 1½ teaspoons salt, and some pepper and cook, stirring, until shallots are golden brown, about 10 minutes. Add garlic and cook, stirring, until lightly browned. Add sun-dried tomatoes and tomato paste and cook, stirring, until paste is brick red, about 3 minutes. Crush tomatoes through your fingers into the pot. Stir in tomato juices and mushrooms and bring to a boil. Tie thyme, oregano, rosemary, bay leaf, and parsley stems together with a piece of clean kitchen string and add to the pot. Reduce heat and simmer sauce, stirring occasionally, until thick, about 10 minutes. Remove from heat and stir in chopped parsley. Discard herb bundle.

3. Cook lasagna noodles according to package directions.

4. Preheat the oven to 350°F. Butter a 9x13-inch casserole. Mix Parmesan and Pecorino cheeses in a small bowl. Cover bottom of prepared dish with ⅓ of the noodles. Top with ¼ of the cheese, ⅓ of the mushroom-tomato sauce, and ⅓ of the béchamel. Repeat twice, and top with the remaining cheese. Bake, uncovered, until hot and bubbly, about 45 minutes. Let lasagna stand for 10 minutes before slicing.

Make this tangy vegetarian lasagna on Friday and serve it up Saturday night—if you can wait that long, that is.

mac & cheese with red peppers & tomatoes *8 servings*

Familiar as a childhood memory with just enough of a twist to make them seem brand new, both of these recipes are as comforting as a roaring fire.

1	pound ziti or penne pasta
4	tablespoons unsalted butter
1	clove garlic, smashed
2½	cups fresh bread crumbs, preferably from sourdough bread
1	tablespoon finely chopped fresh flat-leaf parsley
1	tablespoon finely chopped fresh thyme
6	ounces shredded sharp white Cheddar cheese (about 2 cups)
4	ounces shredded fontina cheese (about 1⅓ cups)
3	ounces shredded smoked Gouda cheese (about 1 cup)
1	recipe hot Béchamel Sauce, (see page 280)
10	Oven-Dried Tomato halves (see page 281)
1	roasted red pepper, seeded and diced (see page 273)
1	teaspoon kosher salt
	Freshly ground black pepper

1. Preheat the oven to 400°F. Lightly butter a 9x13-inch gratin or casserole dish. Bring a large pot of cold water to a boil over high heat; salt it generously. Add the pasta and boil, stirring occasionally, until it is just barely al dente (it will finish cooking in the sauce), about 8 minutes. Drain the pasta, put it in a large bowl, and cool slightly.

2. While the pasta cooks, melt the butter with the garlic clove in a medium skillet over medium heat. Add the bread crumbs, parsley, and thyme and toss to coat the bread crumbs thoroughly with the butter. Remove the garlic clove and set the crumbs aside.

3. Toss the pasta with the cheeses. Fold in the béchamel sauce, then the tomatoes, red pepper, salt, and pepper. Transfer the mixture to the prepared baking dish and scatter the bread crumbs over the top. Bake until the sauce bubbles and the crumbs crisp and brown, 25 to 30 minutes. Let rest for 10 minutes before serving.

wild mushroom stroganoff

6 servings

2½ cups water

¼ ounce dried morel mushrooms

8 tablespoons unsalted butter

8 ounces button mushrooms, stemmed, caps left whole

8 ounces cremini mushrooms, stemmed, caps left whole

8 ounces shiitake mushrooms, stemmed, caps left whole

8 ounces oyster mushrooms, gently torn into medium pieces

3 teaspoons chopped fresh thyme

Freshly ground black pepper

4½ teaspoons kosher salt

1 medium onion, cut in 1½-inch dice

5 cloves garlic, chopped

1 tablespoon tomato paste

2 tablespoons all-purpose flour

⅔ cup sour cream (not low-fat)

2 teaspoons Dijon mustard

2 teaspoons fresh-squeezed lemon juice

1 recipe Parslied Egg Noodles (see page 279)

2 tablespoons chopped fresh flat-leaf parsley

1. Bring water to a boil in a saucepan, add morels, and set aside until soft, about 20 minutes. Scoop morels from liquid, squeeze out water, and set aside. Reserve 2¼ cups liquid.

2. Melt 2 tablespoons of the butter in a large skillet over medium-high heat. When the butter stops foaming, add half the fresh mushrooms, 1½ teaspoons of the thyme, and a generous amount of pepper. Let the mushrooms sizzle for a few minutes without stirring. Stir them once they brown and then cook, stirring only occasionally, until the mushrooms are a deep, rich brown and very fragrant, about 10 minutes. Transfer to a bowl and cook the remaining mushrooms, using 2 more tablespoons butter, remaining 1½ teaspoons thyme, and some pepper. When all mushrooms are cooked and in the bowl, toss with 2 teaspoons of the salt and set aside.

3. Reduce heat to medium and add remaining 4 tablespoons butter to the skillet. Add onion, 1 teaspoon of the salt, some pepper, and cook, stirring, until browned, about 15 minutes. Add garlic and cook, stirring, until lightly browned, about 2 minutes. Add tomato paste and cook, stirring, about 1 minute.

4. Sprinkle flour over onion mixture and cook, stirring, for 1 minute. Increase heat to high and add morels and their reserved soaking liquid. Whisking constantly, bring mixture to a boil, then reduce heat and simmer for 5 minutes, whisking frequently. Pull pan off the heat and whisk in sour cream, mustard, lemon juice, remaining 1½ teaspoons salt, and some pepper. Stir in cooked mushrooms and set sauce aside.

5. Prepare Parslied Egg Noodles.

6. Reheat the mushroom sauce over medium heat until hot (don't let it boil) and stir in the parsley. Divide noodles among serving plates and top with the mushrooms. Grind a generous amount of pepper over each serving and serve immediately.

Cook like a pro: plan ahead.

Mise en place may sound chef-y, but all it really means is "putting in place." Have all of your ingredients ready up to the point of cooking, and there's no stopping you.

seven-vegetable couscous

4 to 6 servings

STEW

- 3 cloves garlic, smashed
- 2 small turnips, peeled and quartered
- 1 medium yellow onion, quartered lengthwise, root end intact
- 1 large carrot, peeled and cut into 2-inch chunks
- ½ fennel bulb, thickly sliced lengthwise, root end intact
- ⅓ cup golden raisins
- 1 tablespoon peeled, chopped fresh ginger
- 1 tablespoon kosher salt
- 2 teaspoons each ground cumin, paprika, and sugar
- 1½ teaspoons ground turmeric
- ⅛ teaspoon ground cloves
- 1 cinnamon stick, snapped in half
- 1 pound butternut squash
- 4 sprigs fresh flat-leaf parsley
- 1 zucchini, cut into 2-inch rounds
- 1 15½-ounce can chickpeas, rinsed and drained
- 1 cup canned whole peeled tomatoes

COUSCOUS

- 1 tablespoon unsalted butter
- 1 teaspoon kosher salt
- 1½ cups uncooked couscous
- ½ cup sliced almonds, toasted

  Harissa (see page 274) (optional)

1. For the stew: Put the garlic, turnips, onion, carrot, fennel, raisins, ginger, salt, cumin, paprika, sugar, turmeric, cloves, and cinnamon in a large soup pot with a tight-fitting lid. Add 2 cups cold water and bring to a boil over high heat; cover, reduce the heat, and simmer until the vegetables are somewhat soft, about 10 minutes. Halve and seed the butternut squash and cut it into wedges. Tie parsley sprigs together with kitchen string. Add squash, zucchini, chickpeas, and parsley sprigs to the pot. Using your fingers and working over the pot, tear the tomatoes into big pieces and add them to the pot with their juices. Simmer the stew, covered, until it is slightly thick and fragrant and the vegetables are fork-tender but not mushy, about 15 minutes. (You can test the vegetables a bit sooner, remove them as soon as they are tender, and return them to the pot when you are ready to serve. All the vegetables should be tender enough to cut with the side of a fork but should still hold their shape.) Remove cinnamon sticks.

2. For the couscous: Bring 2 cups cold water to a boil with the butter and salt in a small saucepan. Stir in the couscous, pull the saucepan off the heat, cover, and set aside until the water has been absorbed and the couscous is plump, about 5 minutes. Transfer to a bowl and fluff with a fork.

3. To serve, spread the couscous over a large serving platter and, using a slotted spoon, mound the vegetables in the center. Pour some of the broth over the vegetables and sprinkle with the almonds. Pass the remaining broth and the harissa, if desired, at the table.

KNOW-HOW To peel or not to peel winter squash, that is the question. We don't. Peeling is a pain, and most squash skin, once cooked, is delicious. Just give them a good scrubbing, and if they're waxed, scrape it off.

Thailand's most famous noodle dish is often most people's introduction to Thai food. A little sweet, a little hot, and very fresh, one bite is all you need to become a devotee.

shrimp phad thai

6 servings

4   ounces medium-thick flat rice noodles (see Cook's Note, below)

2   tablespoons plus 1 teaspoon sugar

2   tablespoons plus 1 teaspoon fish sauce (see page 274)

2   tablespoons rice vinegar

¼   cup peanut oil

2   large eggs, beaten with a pinch salt

12   ounces peeled and deveined medium shrimp (see page 275)

¾   teaspoon crushed red pepper flakes

Kosher salt

4   cloves garlic, chopped

2   shallots, thinly sliced

1   cup cubed firm tofu (about 6 ounces)

5   scallions (white and green parts), 3 cut into ½-inch pieces, 2 chopped

1¼   cups mung bean sprouts

⅓   cup salted roasted peanuts, chopped, plus additional for garnish

Lime wedges

Sriracha sauce (see page 274)

1. Put the noodles in a medium bowl and add enough hot water to cover. Soak until tender, about 30 minutes. Drain and set aside. Whisk the sugar with the fish sauce and vinegar in a small bowl.

2. Heat a large skillet over medium heat until hot and add 1 tablespoon of the peanut oil. Pour in the eggs, tilting the skillet as you pour to make a thin, even coating of egg. Cook until just set, about 45 seconds. Invert the eggs onto a cutting board and cut into ½-inch pieces. Set aside.

3. Add another 1 tablespoon peanut oil to the same skillet and heat over high heat. Add shrimp, ½ teaspoon of the pepper flakes, and salt to taste. Stir-fry until shrimp are pink and just cooked through, about 1½ minutes. Transfer to a plate.

4. Heat the remaining 2 tablespoons peanut oil over high heat. Add the garlic, shallots, and remaining ¼ teaspoon red pepper flakes and stir-fry until lightly browned, about 1 minute. Add the tofu and cook about 2 minutes more. Add the noodles and cook, tossing, until lightly coated with the garlic mixture, about 1 minute. Add the fish sauce mixture and large scallion pieces and heat through. Stir in the cooked egg and shrimp, 1 cup of the sprouts, and the ⅓ cup peanuts and toss until hot. Divide the phad Thai among plates and top with the remaining ¼ cup sprouts, additional peanuts, and chopped scallions. Serve immediately with the lime wedges and Sriracha.

COOK'S NOTE Rice noodles for phad Thai are about the same thickness as linguine. They're available in supermarkets and Asian food stores.

chilaquiles with pumpkin & salsa verde 6 servings

Served with tortilla chips, the tomatillo salsa is a nice change of pace from tomato salsa as a party snack.

2 tablespoons extra-virgin olive oil

1½ cups diced, peeled pie pumpkin

2 cups Salsa Verde (see recipe, below)

2 cups chicken broth, homemade (see page 278) or low-sodium canned

2 poblano chiles, roasted, peeled, seeded, and thinly sliced (see page 273)

1½ teaspoons kosher salt

Freshly ground black pepper

1½ cups shredded cooked chicken, turkey, or pork (optional)

4 large handfuls white corn tortilla chips, store-bought (about 48) or homemade (see recipe, below)

¼ cup chopped fresh cilantro

½ cup minced red onion

2 tablespoons crumbled queso fresco

¼ cup Mexican crema, or sour cream thinned with a bit of milk

SALSA

Makes about 3 cups

1 pound tomatillos (about 10)

1 clove garlic

¼ medium onion

¼ jalapeño, with seeds

1 teaspoon kosher salt

Sugar

4 sprigs fresh cilantro

1. Heat olive oil in a large skillet over medium-high heat. Add pumpkin and cook, stirring, until golden brown, about 3 minutes. Add salsa and cook, stirring, until slightly thick, about 3 minutes. Add broth, chiles, salt, and pepper to taste. Bring to a boil, reduce heat, and simmer, uncovered, until squash is tender, about 7 minutes. Stir in chicken, if desired.

2. Stir tortilla chips into sauce and cook over high heat until chips soften slightly but still hold their shape, about 2 minutes. Stir in cilantro. Divide among warmed plates. Scatter some onion and cheese over each serving, then drizzle with crema.

SALSA VERDE

1. Husk and rinse tomatillos. Put in a medium saucepan and add enough water to cover. Bring to a boil and cook, uncovered, until tender, about 7 minutes. Drain.

2. Puree garlic, onion, jalapeño, salt, and sugar to taste in a blender until smooth. Add tomatillos and cilantro sprigs and puree until smooth. Taste, and add another pinch of sugar if salsa is too acidic.

HOMEMADE TORTILLA CHIPS

Line a plate with paper towels. Heat about 1 inch of vegetable oil in a heavy-bottomed skillet over medium heat until quite hot. Cut six white corn tortillas into eight wedges each. Working in batches, fry the tortilla wedges until the edges are crisp and the centers still pliable, 1 to 2 minutes. Using a slotted spoon, transfer the chips to the lined plate to drain.

COOK'S NOTE Chilaquiles should be slightly soupy, not dry. If you make your own tortilla chips, cook the sauce a bit more in Step 1, since they don't absorb as much sauce as store-bought ones do.

baked polenta with broccoli rabe & sausage 6 servings

POLENTA

- 5 cups water
- 1 cup coarse-ground cornmeal (see page 276)
- 1 teaspoon kosher salt
- ½ cup freshly grated Pecorino Romano cheese (2 ounces) (see page 271)

BROCCOLI RABE AND SAUSAGE

- 3 tablespoons extra-virgin olive oil
- 1 pound sweet Italian sausage links
- 2 tablespoons water
- 4 cloves garlic, thinly sliced
- ½ teaspoon crushed red pepper flakes
- 1 pound broccoli rabe, woody stems trimmed
- 1 cup canned crushed tomatoes
- ½ teaspoon kosher salt

1. For the polenta: Preheat the oven to 375°F. Pour the water into a Dutch oven, then whisk in the cornmeal and salt. Bake, uncovered, for 45 minutes. Remove from the oven and whisk. Return the polenta to the oven and bake until it thickens a bit more, about 10 minutes.

2. While the polenta bakes, cook the broccoli rabe and sausages: Heat the olive oil in a large skillet over medium heat. Add the sausages and water, cover, and cook until just firm, about 5 minutes. Uncover the skillet, increase the heat to high, and cook the sausages, turning as necessary, until browned all over and the water evaporates, about 4 minutes. Transfer to a plate and keep warm; leave about 1 tablespoon of drippings in the skillet and discard the rest.

3. Reduce the heat to medium, add the garlic to the drippings, and cook, stirring frequently, until golden brown, about 2 minutes. Stir in the red pepper flakes and cook for 30 seconds. Add the broccoli rabe, crushed tomatoes with juices, and salt; increase the heat to medium-high, cover, and cook, stirring occasionally, until the broccoli rabe is tender, about 4 minutes. Nestle the sausages in the greens, spoon sauce over and around them, and cook until heated through.

4. Just before serving, stir the polenta until smooth, then stir in the cheese. Spoon the polenta onto a serving platter and arrange the greens and sausages over the top.

By getting polenta off the stove and into the oven, you not only eliminate an hour of stirring, you enhance the flavor in a way that lets the creamy texture of the corn really come through.

COOK'S NOTE Broccoli rabe—also called rapini—is more assertive than broccoli and occasionally is downright bitter. Blanching it in salted water before sautéing will mellow it.

We're wise to the world.

Over the past 10 years, we've cooked, tested, and tasted 30,000 recipes derived from 50 cuisines originating in 27 countries from every continent in the world. Each one of those recipes is unique—with one exception. They are all exceptionally delicious.

lemon risotto with shrimp & asparagus 4 servings

8 ounces pencil-thin asparagus

8 ounces large shrimp in their shells

6 teaspoons extra-virgin olive oil

6 cups chicken broth, homemade (see page 278) or low-sodium canned

1 generous sprig fresh thyme or lemon thyme

1 shallot, diced

1½ cups Arborio rice (see ShopSmart, below)

1 teaspoon kosher salt

¼ cup dry vermouth

2 teaspoons finely grated lemon zest

2 tablespoons unsalted butter

2 tablespoons freshly squeezed lemon juice

2 tablespoons chopped fresh flat-leaf parsley

Freshly ground black pepper

SHOPSMART Look for superfina Arborio, vialone nano, or carnaroli rice to make this and other risotto dishes. All have plump, round grains and a high starch content, which creates the creamy quality that makes risotto such a luxurious treat.

1. Cut asparagus just below the tips, then on an angle at ¼-inch intervals, discarding the woody part at the bottom. Set aside.

2. Peel and devein the shrimp, saving the shells, and halve shrimp lengthwise. Heat 2 teaspoons of the olive oil in a large saucepan, add the shells, and cook, stirring, until they turn pink, about 4 minutes. Add broth and thyme. Bring to a simmer over medium-high heat. Reduce heat to keep the broth at a very gentle simmer.

3. Heat the remaining 4 teaspoons olive oil in a Dutch oven or other heavy pot over medium heat. Add the shrimp and cook, stirring occasionally, until just pink but not quite cooked through, about 1½ minutes. Remove the shrimp to a plate.

4. Add shallot to the pot and cook until translucent, about 2 minutes. Add the rice and stir so that it is coated with oil and glossy, about 1 minute. Stir in the salt. Add the vermouth and cook, stirring constantly with a wooden spoon, until it is absorbed by the rice. Ladle in about ½ cup of the simmering broth (leave behind the shrimp shells and thyme sprig) and stir constantly, until the rice again absorbs the liquid, adjusting the heat to maintain a gentle simmer. Continue ladling in about ½ cup of broth at a time, stirring between additions and letting the rice absorb the liquid before adding more. When rice has absorbed about half the broth (about 10 minutes into cooking process), stir in asparagus and lemon zest.

5. When rice is al dente, after 18 or so minutes of cooking time, stop adding broth. Vigorously beat in the butter. Add the shrimp and lemon juice and stir just until heated. Stir in the parsley. Remove from heat. Let risotto rest for a minute or so before serving. Divide among 4 warm bowls, grind a generous amount of pepper over each, and serve.

cholent

6 to 8 servings

1	cup dried chickpeas
¼	cup extra-virgin olive oil
2	medium onions, chopped
4	cloves garlic, chopped
2	teaspoon sweet paprika
2	teaspoons ground coriander
2	teaspoons ground cumin
2	teaspoons ground ginger
1	cinnamon stick
3	cross-cut pieces of beef shin, about 3 pounds
3	carrots, peeled and thickly sliced
½	cup red lentils, picked over
½	cup pearl barley
¾	cup canned whole peeled tomatoes
1	tablespoon kosher salt, plus additional for seasoning
	Freshly ground black pepper

1. Put the chickpeas in a saucepan. Cover with water by a few inches and boil for 5 minutes. Remove from the heat and set aside for 1 hour.

2. Meanwhile, heat olive oil in a large Dutch oven or other heavy pot over medium heat. Add onions and cook until brown and sweet, about 20 minutes. Stir in garlic, paprika, coriander, cumin, ginger, and cinnamon stick and cook until fragrant. Add the beef, carrots, lentils, and barley. Crush the tomatoes by hand as you add them to the pot along with their juices. Drain the chickpeas; add to the pot along with enough water to cover by about 2 inches, about 12 cups. Bring to a boil and simmer, uncovered, for 15 minutes. Skim off any scum that rises to the surface.

3. Preheat the oven to 300°F. Season the cholent with the 1 tablespoon salt and pepper to taste. Transfer the pot to the oven and cook, uncovered, until the meat falls off the bones, the beans are completely soft, and the cholent is stewy, 4 to 5 hours. Taste and season with salt and pepper, as needed. Remove cinnamon stick. Ladle stew into warm bowls.

The equivalent of Jewish baked beans, this slow-cooking Sabbath dish is just right when rest is the order of the day.

sopa seca

4 servings

Sopa seca means "dry soup" in Spanish. This traditional Mexican dish starts out soupy and ends up noodley and delicious.

¼ cup extra-virgin olive oil

12 ounces fideos (bundled vermicelli)

1 medium onion, chopped

3 cloves garlic, minced

1 teaspoon ground coriander

1 teaspoon dried oregano, preferably Mexican

1 teaspoon New Mexican chile powder

1 bay leaf

1½ cups canned whole peeled tomatoes

1 to 2 chipotles in adobo sauce, minced (see page 273)

1½ cups chicken broth, homemade (see recipe 278) or low-sodium canned

1 teaspoon kosher salt

Freshly ground black pepper

2 cups shredded smoked turkey

1 cup coarsely shredded Cheddar cheese (4 ounces)

Mexican crema or sour cream thinned with a bit of milk (optional)

1. Preheat the oven to 375°F. Brush a 9-inch square baking dish with oil. Heat the olive oil in a large skillet over medium heat. Add the fideos and cook, turning them with tongs, until golden brown on both sides, about 5 minutes. Transfer the bundles and any broken pieces to a plate.

2. Add the onion to the skillet and cook over medium heat, stirring occasionally, until golden brown, about 8 minutes. Stir in the garlic, coriander, oregano, chile powder, and bay leaf and cook until fragrant, about 30 seconds. Crush the tomatoes over the pot with your hand and add them to the pot along with their juices. Add the chipotles, increase the heat to high, and cook until thickened, about 2 minutes. Stir in the broth, the toasted fideos, the salt, and pepper to taste. Bring mixture to a boil, reduce heat, and simmer gently, uncovered, breaking up the fideos with a spoon, for about 5 minutes. Stir in the turkey.

3. Remove the bay leaf. Transfer the mixture to the prepared baking dish, sprinkle the grated cheese over the top, and cover loosely with foil. Bake until the cheese melts and the casserole is hot through and through, about 20 minutes. If desired, serve with some crema drizzled over the top.

COOK'S NOTE Chile powder (with an "e") denotes a ground single pepper, such as New Mexican or ancho. Chili powder (with an "i") blends chile with other herbs and spices such as garlic, oregano, cumin, coriander, and clove. We remember it this way; chili powders that end with "i" include other ingredients.

fish & shellfish

grilled striped bass with confit of garlic, lemon & sage 4 servings

2 heads garlic

8 to 12 fresh sage leaves

4 strips lemon zest

2 teaspoons kosher salt, plus
   additional for seasoning

   Pinch crushed red pepper flakes

1/3 cup water

1/4 cup extra-virgin olive oil, plus
   additional for fish

2 tablespoons freshly squeezed
   lemon juice

2 tablespoons honey

1 1/4 pounds wild striped bass fillet,
   preferably a center cut of even
   thickness

   Freshly ground black pepper

1. Separate and peel garlic cloves. Put in a medium saucepan with the sage, lemon zest, the 2 teaspoons salt, red pepper flakes, water, the 1/4 cup olive oil, the lemon juice, and honey. Bring the mixture to a boil, reduce the heat, cover, and simmer, stirring occasionally, until the garlic is very tender, about 25 minutes. Uncover and simmer until the garlic is lightly glazed, about 4 minutes. Set aside.

2. Heat a grill pan over medium-high heat or prepare an outdoor grill. Brush the fillet on both sides with olive oil and season the flesh side with salt and black pepper. Lay the fish flesh side down on the pan and leave it be until you see distinct grill marks and can lift the fish without its sticking to the grill, about 5 minutes. (Test it by gently lifting a corner— if it sticks, cook it a bit longer.) When it lifts cleanly, carefully turn it about 45 degrees from its original position; don't turn it over. Cook for another 3 minutes. Season the skin with salt and black pepper, turn the fillet over, and cook about 5 minutes more or until an instant-read thermometer inserted in the side registers about 135°F. Transfer the fish to a serving platter and let it rest for at least 5 minutes before serving warm or at room temperature.

3. To serve, cut through the natural seam that runs lengthwise down the center of the fillet and then cut across each half to make 4 even pieces. Spoon the garlic confit over and around each piece.

There are a lot of fish in the sea, and we want to keep it that way. That's why we try to stay away from those in short supply. Ask at your fish market about which are most plentiful where you live.

COOK'S NOTE In classic French cooking, a confit is a preparation for preserving meats by slow-cooking them until they become unctuously tender. In modern American kitchens, the method has been adapted to include vegetables such as garlic, tomatoes, onions, and fennel.

halibut steaks with tapenade, tomatoes & herbs 4 servings

FISH

- 1 bunch flat-leaf parsley
- 1/2 bunch fresh thyme, about 20 sprigs
- 2 bay leaves, preferably fresh
- 8 cloves garlic, smashed
- 2 1-pound halibut steaks, 1¼ inch thick

  Kosher salt and freshly ground black pepper
- 3/4 cup dry white vermouth
- 4 tablespoons extra-virgin olive oil
- 12 red and yellow cherry, grape, or pear tomatoes, halved
- 2 teaspoons freshly squeezed lemon juice

TAPENADE

- 1/2 cup kalamata olives, pitted and finely chopped
- 1 tablespoon extra-virgin olive oil
- 1 teaspoon chopped fresh thyme
- 1 teaspoon finely grated lemon zest

  Kosher salt and freshly ground black pepper

KNOW-HOW Fish cooked on the bone is juicier and more full-flavored than filleted.

1. Preheat the oven to 450°F. Set aside 4 sprigs of the parsley. Line a medium gratin or baking dish with the remaining parsley, the thyme, and bay leaves; scatter the garlic on top.

2. For the fish: Season both sides of the halibut steaks with salt and pepper and lay them on the herbs. Pour vermouth around fish and drizzle 2 tablespoons of the olive oil over the steaks. Cover tightly with aluminum foil and bake just until steaks are firm to the touch and opaque, 20 to 25 minutes. Check after 20 minutes—it is best to remove the fish from the oven when it is slightly underdone because it will continue to cook as you make the sauce. While the fish cooks, toss the tomatoes with salt and pepper to taste in a small bowl.

3. For the tapenade: Stir together the olives, the 1 tablespoon olive oil, thyme, and lemon zest in another small bowl. Season with salt and pepper to taste and set aside.

4. After removing the fish from the oven, carefully pour the juices from the pan into a small saucepan. Remove the garlic, thyme, and bay leaves and set aside. Re-cover the fish and set aside. Boil the juices over high heat until reduced by about half and slightly thickened, about 5 minutes. Pull the saucepan from the heat and whisk in the remaining 2 tablespoons olive oil and the lemon juice. Taste and season with salt and pepper.

5. To serve, run the tip of a paring knife between the bone and the flesh and gently lift out the bone to separate each steak into 4 portions (see page 275). Peel the skin from the sides of the steaks. Put 2 pieces on each of 4 plates, top with the tapenade and tomatoes, and drizzle with the sauce.

grilled tuna with artichokes, peppers & tomatoes 6 servings

⅓ cup extra-virgin olive oil

⅓ cup dry white wine

8 baby artichokes

1 lemon, halved

1 yellow bell pepper

2 teaspoons kosher salt, plus additional for fish

1 shallot, sliced

4 cloves garlic, smashed

4 sprigs fresh thyme, plus 1 teaspoon finely chopped

2 sprigs fresh flat-leaf parsley, plus 1 tablespoon chopped

1 bay leaf

¼ teaspoon coriander seeds, cracked

8 Oven-Dried Tomatoes (see page 281)

1 1½-pound center-cut piece tuna, about 2 inches thick

Freshly ground black pepper

1. Put 1 cup water, olive oil, and wine in a medium saucepan. Trim the artichokes' stems, snap off their outer leaves, and halve (see photos, below), rubbing the cut surfaces with lemon as you trim, and add to the pan. Stem, seed, and cut the bell pepper into large squares and add to pan. Add the 2 teaspoons salt, shallot, garlic, herb sprigs, bay leaf, and coriander. Simmer over medium heat until the artichokes are just tender, about 15 minutes. Add the tomatoes and cook 5 minutes longer. Remove vegetables with a slotted spoon and set aside. Increase the heat under the saucepan and simmer the cooking liquid to thicken slightly; set aside. (This can be made up to a day in advance and refrigerated.)

2. Heat a grill pan over medium-high heat or prepare an outdoor grill. Season the tuna generously on both sides with salt and pepper. Grill the tuna until there are distinct grill marks on both sides, turning once, about 5 minutes per side for rare. Remove the tuna from the grill and let it rest for 10 minutes before cutting.

3. Stir the chopped thyme and parsley into the artichoke mixture. Cut the tuna into slices or chunks. Spoon the vegetables into bowls and arrange the tuna on top.

1. Trim the stems of the artichokes with a sharp paring knife.
2. With your fingers, snap off the tough outer leaves.
3. Cut the artichokes in half, rubbing the cut surfaces with half of a cut lemon as you work to keep them from discoloring.

cioppino
4 to 6 servings

¼	cup extra-virgin olive oil
1	medium onion, diced
½	teaspoon fennel seeds
6	cloves garlic, minced
1	tablespoon kosher salt
	Freshly ground black pepper
1	tablespoon tomato paste
½	cup red wine
2½	cups canned plum tomatoes, with their juice
1	cup clam juice
1	cup water
1	bay leaf
½	cup torn fresh basil
1	pound monkfish, preferably on the bone, sliced into 4 steaks
1	medium live Dungeness crab (see Know-How, right, for preparation)
8	ounces cleaned squid, cut into ½-inch pieces
3	tablespoons roughly chopped fresh flat-leaf parsley

1. Heat the olive oil in a large soup pot over medium heat. Add the onion and fennel seeds and cook until golden brown, about 15 minutes. Add the garlic, salt, and pepper to taste and cook 2 minutes more. Stir in the tomato paste and cook for 1 minute. Stir in ¼ cup of the wine and simmer until reduced to a glaze. Add the remaining ¼ cup wine and reduce by half. Crush the tomatoes through your fingers into the pot; stir in their juices, the clam juice, water, and bay leaf, cover, and simmer 30 minutes. (The cioppino may be prepared up to this point and refrigerated overnight in a tightly sealed container.)

2. Adjust the heat so that the cioppino simmers briskly. Stir in the basil and monkfish, cover, and cook 5 minutes. Add the crab and cook 1 minute; finally, add the squid and cook until just firm, about 2 minutes. Remove bay leaf. Transfer the cioppino to a large bowl, scatter the parsley on top, and serve.

KNOW-HOW To prepare the Dungeness crab: Add the crab to a pot of boiling water. Boil for 5 minutes; remove from the pot and cool. Remove the top shell and discard. Remove the gills from the sides of the crab, trim off the face, and scoop out the yellow matter and discard. Cut the body with legs attached into 4 pieces and reserve for the stew.

San Francisco's answer to bouillabaisse, cioppino is distinguished by whatever is fresh off the dock. More tomatoey than its French cousin, our American cioppino is also simpler to make.

tamarind-glazed salmon with citrus salad
4 servings

SALAD

- 1 tablespoon minced red onion
- 2 tablespoons extra-virgin olive oil
- 2 tablespoons freshly squeezed lime juice
- 2 teaspoons honey
- 1/2 teaspoon kosher salt
- 2 blood or navel oranges
- 1 medium grapefruit
- 1 small jalapeño
- 1/4 medium jicama
- 1/2 cup fresh cilantro, chopped

FISH

- 4 6-ounce salmon fillets, with skin
- Olive oil
- 1/4 cup Tamarind Barbecue Sauce, plus additional for serving (see recipe, below)
- Kosher salt

SAUCE

Makes 1 1/2 cups

- 1 ripe medium tomato
- 1/2 cup tamarind concentrate (see page 274)
- 1/3 cup packed dark brown sugar
- 3 chipotle chiles in adobo sauce (see page 273)
- 2 tablespoons sherry vinegar
- 1 clove garlic, smashed
- 1 tablespoon kosher salt

1. Preheat the broiler to high. Line a broiler pan with aluminum foil and set the rack in the pan. Soak the onion in a bowl of very cold water while you prepare the salad.

2. For the citrus salad: Whisk the olive oil, lime juice, honey, and salt in a medium bowl. Working over the bowl, cut the oranges and grapefruit into segments (see page 272) and add to dressing. Stem, seed, and mince jalapeño. Peel and julienne jicama. Stir the jalapeño, jicama, and cilantro into the bowl. Drain the onions, pat dry, and stir them into the salad.

3. To cook the fish: Position the prepared broiler pan about 6 inches from the heat. Lightly brush the salmon flesh first with olive oil and then with some of the tamarind sauce, using about half the sauce for the 4 fillets. Season with salt to taste. Carefully lay fish, skin side down, on the hot broiler pan. Broil the fish until just firm and brown, brushing with more sauce halfway through the cooking, for a total of 7 to 8 minutes. Remove the pan from the oven and set aside for 5 minutes to let the salmon finish cooking. Divide the fish among serving plates, spoon some salad next to each fillet, and pass any remaining tamarind sauce at the table.

TAMARIND BARBECUE SAUCE

1. Preheat the broiler. Line a small pan with aluminum foil and broil the tomato, turning as needed, until the skin chars and splits on all sides. Wrap the tomato in the foil and cool.

2. Core the tomato and chop it roughly, skin and all—it is going to be quite juicy and you want to keep all of it. Puree the tomato with the juices in a food processor or blender with the tamarind concentrate, brown sugar, chipotles, vinegar, garlic, and salt until smooth.

cajun corn-crusted catfish with remoulade 4 servings

FISH

4   6-ounce catfish fillets

2   cups buttermilk

1   teaspoon kosher salt, plus additional for seasoning

1   cup cornmeal

1/2   cup all-purpose flour

2   tablespoons Cajun seasoning (see page 280)

   Vegetable oil for shallow frying

2   ripe large tomatoes, sliced

2   to 3 cups mixed salad greens (optional)

   Freshly ground black pepper

1   cup Remoulade (see recipe, below)

REMOULADE

   Makes 1 cup

3/4   cup mayonnaise

1/4   cup minced sweet pickles

3   tablespoons minced celery

2   tablespoons Creole mustard

1   tablespoon minced fresh flat-leaf parsley

1   scallion (white and green parts), thinly sliced

1/2   teaspoon sweet paprika

1/2   teaspoon kosher salt

1/4   teaspoon finely grated lemon zest

1   dash hot pepper sauce

1. Soak the catfish in the buttermilk with 1 teaspoon salt, cover, and refrigerate for 1 hour. Whisk the cornmeal, flour, and Cajun seasoning together in a shallow bowl.

2. Heat 2 heavy skillets (we like cast-iron) over medium heat with about 1/2 inch of oil. Remove catfish from the buttermilk, shaking slightly so the excess buttermilk drains from the fish. Dredge the fillets in the cornmeal mixture. Lay the catfish rounded side down in the pans and cook until golden brown, about 5 minutes. Flip and cook until the fish feels firm to the touch, about 5 minutes more. Divide the tomatoes and salad greens, if desired, among 4 plates and lay the fish on top. Season with salt and pepper. Spoon a dollop of Remoulade on top. Serve, passing additional sauce at the table.

REMOULADE

Stir together mayonnaise, pickles, celery, mustard, parsley, scallion, paprika, salt, lemon zest, and hot pepper sauce in a medium bowl. Refrigerate for 1 hour before serving.

COOK'S NOTE Coarsely ground Creole mustard has a kick but also enough of a rounded sweet flavor to make it a great all-purpose mustard.

shrimp salad with green goddess dressing 4 to 6 servings

SALAD

- 1½ pounds cooked medium shrimp
- 1 medium cucumber
- 1 rib celery, peeled and diced

  Kosher salt and freshly ground black pepper

  Avocado Green Goddess Dressing (see recipe, below)
- 1 pound asparagus, trimmed and cooked
- 1 ripe medium tomato, cored and cut into 12 wedges
- 1 head Boston or Bibb lettuce, trimmed and washed
- 1 scallion (green part only), very thinly sliced

DRESSING

  Makes about 1 cup
- 1 anchovy fillet
- ⅓ cup mayonnaise
- 1 ripe Hass avocado, seeded, peeled, and cut into chunks (see page 272)
- 1 scallion, thinly sliced
- 1 tablespoon chopped fresh basil
- 1 tablespoon minced flat-leaf parsley
- 1 tablespoon minced fresh tarragon
- 2 teaspoons freshly squeezed lime juice
- 1 teaspoon kosher salt

  Freshly ground black pepper

1. Peel and devein shrimp and cut into ½-inch chunks. Peel and seed cucumber and cut into ¾-inch chunks. Toss the shrimp with the cucumber, celery, and salt and pepper to taste in a medium bowl. Fold in about half the dressing.

2. Arrange the asparagus and tomatoes on individual plates: Fan some asparagus spears on one side of the plate and some tomato wedges across. (If you prefer, you can arrange everything on 1 large serving platter.) Make a bed of lettuce in the center and top with the shrimp salad. Sprinkle the scallion over the salads and serve, passing the remaining dressing at the table.

GREEN GODDESS DRESSING

Soak the anchovy fillet in cold water for 5 minutes. Pat it dry and chop it coarsely. Puree the mayonnaise, anchovy, avocado, scallion, basil, parsley, tarragon, lime juice, and salt and pepper to taste in a blender until smooth. The dressing may be refrigerated in a tightly sealed container for 2 days.

COOK'S NOTE People either love or hate anchovies. If you're in the latter group, skip them in the dressing. But if you're not sure, try the trick of soaking them in cold water first to temper their kick. The little bit used really adds dimension to the flavor of the dressing.

This recipe is worthy of every domestic goddess—from expert to beginner. Offer this alluring salad to your guests and let the adulation begin.

salmon trout stuffed with swiss chard & pine nuts 4 to 6 servings

STUFFING

- 2 pounds Swiss chard, with stems
- 1/4 cup extra-virgin olive oil
- 4 cloves garlic, minced
- 1/2 teaspoon crushed red pepper flakes
- 1/3 cup golden raisins
- 1/4 cup toasted pine nuts
- 1 1/2 teaspoons kosher salt

AIOLI

- 3 cloves garlic
- 1 teaspoon salt, plus a pinch
- 1 large egg yolk
- 2 tablespoons freshly squeezed lemon juice
- 1 tablespoon water
- 1 1/3 cups extra-virgin olive oil (a lighter style preferred)

FISH

- 1 whole book-boned salmon trout (about 3 to 4 pounds), such as arctic char (see ShopSmart, below)

  Kosher salt and freshly ground black pepper

  Extra-virgin olive oil

SHOPSMART A book-boned fish is boneless but attached along the top, so that it opens up like a book. Ask your fishmonger to do it for you.

1. For the stuffing: Strip chard leaves from stems. Chop leaves and set aside. Chop stems to make 1 cup and set aside; discard the rest.

2. Cook and stir the olive oil, garlic, and pepper flakes in a skillet over medium-high heat until fragrant, about 3 minutes. Add chard stems and cook until crisp-tender, about 3 minutes. Add chard leaves, raisins, pine nuts, and salt. Cover; cook until greens are just tender, about 5 minutes. Transfer to a colander and press out any liquid.

3. For the aioli: Bring a few inches of water to a simmer in a medium saucepan. Smash garlic cloves and sprinkle with pinch of salt. With the side of a large knife, mash to a coarse paste. In a heatproof bowl, whisk egg yolk, lemon juice, water, and 1 teaspoon salt until frothy. Place over simmering water and whisk until mixture thickens slightly, about 30 seconds. Remove from heat and add garlic. Whisking constantly, add olive oil, starting with a few drops, then in a steady stream to make a smooth, thick sauce. Refrigerate until ready to serve.

4. For the fish: Open the fish and season with salt and pepper. Spread cooled chard mixture along flesh and close fish. Tie the fish with kitchen twine at about 4-inch intervals.

5. Position a rack 8 inches from broiler and preheat to high. Lay fish on a large pan, brush top with olive oil, and season with salt and pepper. Broil until skin is crispy and golden brown, about 10 minutes. Turn fish over and season with salt and pepper. Broil until skin is crispy and golden brown and an instant-read thermometer inserted into thickest part of flesh registers 135°F to 140°F, about 8 minutes more. Turn broiler off and let fish rest in the hot oven for 10 minutes.

6. Transfer the fish to a serving platter and remove the string. Drizzle each portion with some of the aioli and pass the rest.

grilled mahi tacos with escabeche 6 servings

Add an authentic south-of-the-border relish to a time-honored fish taco and feel your taste buds come alive. Great for the grill or a day at the beach.

SALSA

- 2 ancho chiles, stemmed and seeded
- 3 tablespoons fresh orange juice
- 2 teaspoons honey
- 3/4 teaspoon kosher salt
- 2 tablespoons extra-virgin olive oil

ESCABECHE

- 4 tablespoons extra-virgin olive oil
- 6 cloves garlic, thinly sliced
- 2 to 3 jalapeños, thinly sliced
- 3 carrots, peeled and sliced
- 1 red onion, halved and sliced
- 3 whole cloves
- 2 bay leaves (fresh, if available)
- 1 stick cinnamon
- 2 teaspoons kosher salt
- 1 teaspoon coriander seeds, cracked
- 1/2 teaspoon dried thyme
- 1/2 teaspoon dried Mexican oregano
  Freshly ground black pepper
- 1/2 cup apple cider vinegar

FISH

- 6 5- to 6-ounce mahi-mahi fillets
  Extra-virgin olive oil
  Kosher salt and ground pepper

TACOS

- 12 to 24 corn tortillas
  12 sprigs fresh cilantro

1. For the salsa: Toast the chiles in a dry skillet over medium-high heat, turning and flattening with a spatula, until fragrant, about 1 minute. Put the chiles in a bowl, cover with very hot water, and set aside until soft, about 30 minutes. Drain, roughly chop, and puree the chiles in a blender with the orange juice, honey, salt, and a bit of water, if needed. Blend in olive oil. Set aside.

2. For the escabeche: Heat olive oil in a medium skillet over medium-high heat. Add remaining ingredients except cider vinegar and cook until carrots are crisp-tender, stirring, about 5 minutes. Add 1 cup water and the cider vinegar, bring to a boil, reduce heat, and cook at a gentle simmer until just soft, about 15 minutes. Cool.

3. For the fish: Preheat a grill pan over medium-high heat or prepare an outdoor grill. Brush the fillets all over with a little olive oil and season generously with salt and pepper. Lay the fish on the grill and leave it until you see distinct grill marks and can lift the fish without its sticking to the grill, 5 to 6 minutes. Test it by gently lifting a corner—if it sticks, cook it a bit longer and try again. Carefully turn the fish over and cook until firm to the touch, another 5 to 6 minutes. Brush with some of the salsa and transfer to a platter.

4. To assemble tacos: Grill tortillas until slightly charred but still pliable, about 10 seconds per side. Lay a sprig of cilantro on a single or double tortilla and top first with some of the escabeche and then a piece of fish—half of a fillet per taco will do. Top with sour cream, if desired, and additional salsa.

COOK'S NOTE Escabeche is a spicy pickle popular in Latin America. Use it on any poached, grilled, or fried fish.

pan-seared shrimp
with romesco sauce 4 servings

SAUCE

- 1 small ancho chile, stemmed and seeded (see page 273)
- ¼ cup extra-virgin olive oil
- ¼ cup whole blanched almonds
- ½ medium onion, thinly sliced
- 2 cloves garlic, smashed
- 2 teaspoons kosher salt, plus additional for seasoning

  Freshly ground black pepper
- 2 teaspoons sweet paprika
- ¾ cup roughly chopped jarred, drained piquillo peppers (see page 273)
- ½ slice stale white bread, roughly torn
- 2 tablespoons sherry vinegar

SHRIMP

- 1½ pounds large shrimp, peeled, deveined, and patted dry (see page 275)

  Kosher salt and freshly ground black pepper
- 3 tablespoons extra-virgin olive oil

STYLE If you'd rather grill than pan-sear, skewer the shrimp and serve them on a bed of grilled scallions.

1. For the sauce: Toast the ancho chile in a small dry skillet over medium-high heat, turning and flattening with a spatula, until fragrant, about 1 minute. Put the chile in a medium bowl, cover with very hot water, and set aside until soft, about 10 minutes. Drain, chop roughly, and set aside.

2. Heat the olive oil in a large skillet over medium heat. Add the almonds and cook, stirring, until toasted, about 3 minutes. Transfer the almonds to a plate, leaving the oil in the skillet. Add the softened chile, the onion, garlic, the 2 teaspoons salt, and pepper to taste. Cook, stirring, until onions are lightly browned, about 3 minutes. Add paprika and cook until fragrant, about a minute more. Scrape onion mixture into a sieve set over a bowl; reserve 3 tablespoons strained oil.

3. Pulse the onion mixture, almonds, piquillo peppers, bread, and vinegar in a food processor until coarse. With the motor running, drizzle in the reserved oil. Scrape the sauce into 4 small serving bowls, cover, and set in a warm place while you cook the shrimp.

4. For the shrimp: Spread shrimp on a pan or a piece of aluminum foil. Heat 2 large skillets over medium heat. Sprinkle salt and pepper over the shrimp. Add 1 tablespoon of the olive oil to each skillet and increase the heat to high. Add the shrimp seasoned side down, taking care not to crowd them. (Even with two pans, you may need to cook the shrimp in batches; if you crowd the skillets the shrimp will steam and get soggy.) Cook the shrimp undisturbed until they turn golden brown on the bottom, about 3 minutes. Add a bit more oil to each skillet and season the shrimp with salt and pepper. Turn the heat off and flip the shrimp with tongs. Leave shrimp in the skillets another minute; the residual heat will finish cooking them. Place a bowl of sauce on each of 4 serving plates and arrange some of the shrimp around each bowl.

poultry

our favorite fried chicken

6 to 8 servings

1 quart buttermilk

¹/4 cup kosher salt

2 tablespoons dried thyme

2 tablespoons dried oregano

1 tablespoon hot pepper sauce

2 cloves garlic, smashed

16 pieces chicken, half each white and dark meat, or whatever you prefer (about 6 pounds)

4 cups all-purpose flour

1 tablespoon sweet paprika

1 tablespoon freshly ground black pepper

Solid vegetable shortening or vegetable oil for frying

1. Whisk the buttermilk with salt, thyme, oregano, hot pepper sauce, and garlic in a large nonreactive bowl. Add the chicken pieces, turn to coat, cover the bowl, and refrigerate overnight.

2. Shake the flour, paprika, and pepper in a large, clean plastic or paper bag. Set a large rack over a baking sheet. Drain the chicken in a colander. Shake 2 or 3 pieces at a time in the flour mixture, shake off any excess, and set on the rack.

3. Set another rack over another baking sheet. Fill 2 large heavy skillets with ³/4 inch of shortening. Heat over medium-high heat until a deep-frying thermometer registers 340°F. Working in batches, carefully add the chicken skin side down, with white meat in one skillet and dark in the other. The oil temperature will drop precipitously to about 250°F as you slip in the chicken. Adjust the heat as necessary to keep the temperature right around 250°F—the oil should be bubbling gently around all of the chicken pieces. Fry the chicken until it is a deep golden brown, about 10 minutes. Turn and fry until the other side is a deep golden brown, another 10 minutes for the white meat and 15 minutes for the dark meat. Transfer the cooked chicken to the clean rack. Serve immediately or at room temperature.

COOK'S NOTE The ¼ cup salt serves not only as flavoring but as a brine. Some fried-chicken aficionados claim chicken should be covered while it cooks to stay juicy, but we found that the moisturizing steam also steamed the crispy coating right off our bird. Brining makes the meat juicier. So you have a no-compromise situation on your hands: You get succulent chicken and a crunchy coat.

pan-roasted chicken
with herbs & onions 4 servings

1 whole chicken, (3 to 4 pounds) butterflied (see page 275)

½ teaspoon kosher salt, plus additional for seasoning

Freshly ground black pepper

2 tablespoons extra-virgin olive oil

6 cloves garlic, smashed

2 medium onions, halved and sliced

2 tablespoons chopped fresh sage

1 tablespoon chopped fresh rosemary

1 tablespoon chopped fresh thyme

1 tablespoon all-purpose flour

2 tablespoons whole-grain mustard

1. Preheat the oven to 450°F. Turn the bird skinside up and fold the wing tips back and under. Generously season both sides with some salt and pepper. Heat a large, heavy ovenproof skillet over medium-high heat, add the oil, and heat until shimmering. Add the chicken skin side down and cook until nicely browned on 1 side, about 7 minutes. Transfer the chicken to a plate. Reduce the heat to medium, add the garlic, onions, sage, rosemary, thyme, flour, the ½ teaspoon salt, and some pepper to the drippings and cook until the onions are very soft, about 10 minutes.

2. Lay the chicken on the onions skin side up. Cross the legs so they rest against the breasts. Transfer the skillet to the oven and roast the chicken until an instant-read thermometer inserted in a thigh registers 170°F, 40 to 45 minutes. Let the chicken rest out of the oven for 10 minutes and then carve and put on a serving platter.

3. Stir the mustard into the onions and cook over medium-high heat until slightly thickened, about 4 minutes. The onions will look a bit oily at first but will emulsify once you stir in the mustard and give them a bit of time over the heat. Spoon the onions over and around the chicken and serve at once.

chicken, leek & apple stew

4 servings

8 chicken thighs (2 to 2¹/₂ pounds)

1 teaspoon kosher salt, plus additional for seasoning

Freshly ground black pepper

3 tablespoons unsalted butter, softened

1 tablespoon vegetable oil

2 tablespoons all-purpose flour, plus additional for dredging

3 leeks (white and green parts), halved lengthwise, sliced into thick half circles, and well rinsed (see Know-How, below)

¹/₂ teaspoon celery seeds

¹/₄ cup dry white vermouth

1 cup chicken broth, homemade (see page 278) or low-sodium canned

¹/₂ cup apple cider

4 sprigs fresh thyme

2 firm cooking apples, such as Golden Delicious, cored and diced

Parslied Egg Noodles (see page 279) (optional)

1. Preheat oven to 425°F. Season chicken generously with some salt and pepper. Heat 1 tablespoon of the butter and the oil in a large, deep ovenproof skillet over medium-high heat. Dredge chicken in flour, shaking off any excess, and lay skin side down in the skillet. Cook chicken, turning once, until golden brown on both sides, about 8 minutes. Transfer to a platter.

2. Reduce the heat to medium, add the leeks and celery seeds, and cook until slightly soft, about 4 minutes. Pull the skillet from the heat, add the vermouth, and use a wooden spoon to scrape up any browned bits that cling to the pan. Add broth, apple cider, thyme, and the 1 teaspoon salt and bring to a boil.

3. Meanwhile, use a fork to work the 2 tablespoons flour into the remaining 2 tablespoons butter. Whisk the butter mixture into the skillet until dissolved. Stir in the apples. Return the chicken (now skin side up) along with any collected juices to the pan. Transfer to the oven and bake, uncovered, until the chicken is cooked through, tender, and lightly browned, about 25 minutes. Serve with Parslied Egg Noodles, if desired.

KNOW-HOW Leeks have a well-deserved reputation for being gritty. To clean, split leeks lengthwise, then cut crosswise into half circles. Put cut leeks in a salad spinner with water (or set the basket in a large bowl of water if your spinner doesn't hold water). Swish the leeks to flush out the dirt, then let it settle to the bottom of the bowl. Lift the basket to leave all the grit behind in the water, drain, and spin-dry if needed.

jerk chicken & pineapple kebabs   6 servings

RUB AND CHICKEN

- 1/4   cup firmly packed dark brown sugar
- 1/4   cup dark rum
- 3   tablespoons vegetable oil
- 2   tablespoons apple cider vinegar
- 1   bunch scallions (white and green parts), roughly chopped
- 1   Scotch bonnet chile, stemmed, seeded, and minced (see Cook's Note, below)
- 5   cloves garlic, chopped
- 1   tablespoon freshly grated peeled ginger
- 2   teaspoons ground allspice
- 1   teaspoon pumpkin pie spice
- 4   boneless, skinless chicken breast halves (about 1¼ pounds), cut into large cubes

SKEWERS

- 6   long skewers
- 1   bunch scallions (white and green parts), cut into 2-inch pieces
- 1/2   fresh pineapple, peeled, cored, and cubed
-   Kosher salt

1. For the rub: Pulse the brown sugar, rum, oil, vinegar, scallions, chile, garlic, ginger, allspice, and pumpkin pie spice in a food processor to make a smooth paste. Transfer to a bowl, add the chicken cubes, and toss to coat. Cover and refrigerate the chicken for at least 1 hour or up to 24 hours.

2. For the skewers: Heat a grill pan over medium heat or prepare a grill. Thread the chicken, scallions, and pineapple alternately on skewers (if you use wooden ones, soak them in water for 15 minutes before threading them). Season with salt. (Leave a little space around the meat so the heat gets to all sides.) Grill, turning, until the chicken is cooked through, 10 to 12 minutes.

COOK'S NOTE Heat-seekers won't find a chile much hotter than a Scotch bonnet. If you can't find these tiny yellow, red, or orange chiles, substitute their fiery cousin, the habanero. If you want to experience the Scotch bonnet's heat at full throttle, don't bother removing the seeds.

Cook it fast. Cook it slow. Roast it. Fry it. Stew it. Or put it on a kebab. Everybody loves a great chicken recipe. This is one of them.

chicken with apricots, olives & couscous 4 servings

CHICKEN

8 chicken thighs (2 to 2½ pounds)

   Kosher salt and freshly ground black pepper

3 tablespoons extra-virgin olive oil

2 medium onions, each cut into 6 wedges

4 cloves garlic, smashed

¾ teaspoon dried mint

¼ teaspoon crushed red pepper flakes or to taste

8 ounces dried apricots (about 2 dozen)

¾ cup small green olives, such as picholine (a small, crisp Provençal olive)

COUSCOUS

¾ teaspoon ground cumin

½ teaspoon caraway seeds

3 cups chicken broth, homemade (see page 278) or low-sodium canned

1 teaspoon kosher salt, plus additional for seasoning

   Pinch cayenne pepper

   Freshly ground black pepper

1½ cups uncooked couscous

2 to 3 tablespoons water or chicken broth

1. For the chicken: Position a rack in the middle of the oven and preheat to 450°F. Season chicken thighs generously with salt and pepper. Heat a large ovenproof skillet over medium heat, add oil, and heat until shimmering. Cook chicken skin side down until golden and crispy, about 8 minutes. Turn chicken and brown for another 2 minutes. Transfer chicken to a plate. Pour off 2 tablespoons of the pan drippings and reserve; leave remaining drippings in the skillet.

2. Add the onions, garlic, mint, and red pepper flakes to the skillet and cook until the onions are tender, about 8 minutes. Stir in the apricots and olives. Arrange the chicken, skin side up, on top of the onion mixture and bake, uncovered, until the chicken is cooked through, about 30 minutes.

3. While the chicken bakes, make the couscous: In a small saucepan, toast the cumin and caraway seeds over medium heat, swirling the pan frequently, until fragrant, about 2 minutes. Add the chicken broth, reserved drippings, the 1 teaspoon salt, and cayenne and black peppers to taste and bring to a boil. Stir in the couscous, pull the saucepan off the heat, cover, and set aside until the liquid has been absorbed and the couscous is plump, about 5 minutes.

4. When ready to serve, fluff the couscous with a fork and mound it on a warm serving platter. Arrange the chicken around the couscous. Stir 2 to 3 tablespoons water or broth into the onions so they look glazed. Season with salt, if desired, and spoon onions over the couscous and chicken.

chicken & andouille gumbo

6 to 8 servings

8 cups Roasted Chicken Stock (see page 279)

1 head garlic, unpeeled, halved horizontally

1 heaping tablespoon pickling spice

1 teaspoon crushed red pepper flakes

1 teaspoon anise seeds (optional)

1 bay leaf

1 large strip lemon zest

6 tablespoons vegetable oil or rendered chicken fat

2 medium onions, sliced

2 green or red bell peppers, stemmed, seeded, and cut into thin strips

1 rib celery, chopped

4 cloves garlic, chopped

6 ounces fresh okra, tops trimmed and halved lengthwise

1 15-ounce can peeled whole plum tomatoes, with their juice

4 teaspoons kosher salt, plus additional for seasoning

Freshly ground black pepper

½ cup all-purpose flour, plus additional for dredging

6 whole chicken legs, split into drumsticks and thighs (about 6 pounds)

12 ounces raw andouille sausage, in one piece

3 scallions (white and green parts), thinly sliced on the diagonal

4 cups cooked white rice

1. Put the stock in a medium saucepan along with the garlic head, pickling spice, pepper flakes, anise seeds, if desired, bay leaf, and lemon zest. Bring to a boil over high heat, turn the heat as low as it will go, cover, and let the stock steep.

2. Heat 2 tablespoons of the chicken fat or vegetable oil in a large Dutch oven or heavy pot over medium heat, add onions, and cook until soft, brown, and aromatic, about 20 minutes. Stir in bell peppers, celery, and chopped garlic and cook 10 minutes. Add okra and cook until soft, about 5 minutes. Add tomatoes, crushing them through your fingers into the pot, their juices, the 4 teaspoons salt, and a generous amount of pepper.

3. Meanwhile, pour a good amount of flour into a shallow baking dish. Heat a large heavy skillet over medium-high heat and add 2 tablespoons of the chicken fat. Season the chicken with salt and black pepper to taste and dredge in flour. Cook chicken in batches until brown on both sides but not cooked through, about 15 minutes total, transferring the pieces to a platter as they cook. Then cook the sausage until brown, about 10 minutes. Set the skillet aside with the drippings. Slice the sausage and add it to the vegetables along with the chicken. Strain the chicken broth into the pot and simmer while you make the roux.

4. Add the remaining 2 tablespoons of chicken fat to the skillet and heat until shimmering. Whisk in the ½ cup flour and cook, stirring with a wooden spoon in a figure-eight pattern, until the roux is a dark mahogany brown, about 10 minutes. Pull the pan from the heat and cool slightly. Discard any excess fat that comes to the surface and then whisk the roux into the gumbo. Bring the gumbo to a full boil, then reduce the heat so that it simmers gently for 15 minutes more. Stir in the scallions. Remove bay leaf. Serve the gumbo with rice.

chili-rubbed pan-roasted
chicken with **pico de gallo** 4 servings

CHICKEN

2 tablespoons peanut or corn oil

4 bone-in chicken breast halves (about 10 ounces each), skin on

2 teaspoons chili powder

Kosher salt

PICO DE GALLO

2 cups cherry or grape tomatoes, halved

½ to 1 jalapeño, stemmed and minced with seeds

¼ medium red onion, grated

½ teaspoon kosher salt, plus pinch for garlic

1 clove garlic, peeled

2 tablespoons extra-virgin olive oil

½ cup chopped fresh cilantro

Warm corn tortillas (optional)

1. Preheat the oven to 400°F. Heat a large ovenproof skillet over medium-high heat. Add the oil and heat until shimmering. Season the chicken with chili powder and salt to taste. Lay the chicken in the skillet skin side down and cook until brown, about 4 minutes. Turn the chicken, transfer the pan to the oven, and cook until firm, basting occasionally with the pan drippings, 15 to 20 minutes.

2. While the chicken cooks, make the pico de gallo: Toss the tomatoes with the jalapeño, onion, and the ½ teaspoon salt. Smash the garlic clove, sprinkle with a pinch of salt, and, with the flat side of a large knife, mash and smear the mixture to a coarse paste. Stir the paste into the salsa with the olive oil and the cilantro.

3. To serve, divide the chicken among 4 plates, drizzle with pan drippings, and spoon some salsa over and around. Serve with warm corn tortillas, if desired.

COOK'S NOTE We don't love grape tomatoes because they're cute (though they are), but because they taste like a tomato even in the off-season. They also don't require a lot of chopping because they're already small—and they hold their shape nicely when halved.

Want a midweek meal to feel like a party? Try this quick and easy spicy chicken with salsa. It's a fiesta in a pan.

Provençal

Provençal Roasted Chicken with Honey & Thyme, page 151.

The aroma of a chicken crackling in the oven is pure comfort. With the next four recipes, you'll see how easy it is to bring an international flavor to this worldwide favorite.

Chinese

peanut oil

scallion lengths

soy sauce

ginger coins

five-spice powder

dark sesame oil

honey

nge zest strip

minced garlic

soy sauce

ted orange zest

sliced scallions

grated ginger

rice vinegar

dark sesame oil

Peruvian

diced jalapeño

Cotija cheese

cilantro

olive oil

clove of garlic

red wine vinegar

sugar

water

whole jalapeño

vegetable oil

cumin

 hly ground black pepper

soy sauce

head of garlic

red wine vinegar

kosher salt

garlic paste

Hungarian

garlic paste

kosher salt

ground dried porcini mushrooms

lemon zest

caraway seeds

paprika

shallot

unsalted butter

horseradish

garlic cloves

sour cream

chinese **five-spice** lacquered **chicken** 4 servings

From China to Peru, from Hungary to France, at any given time, anywhere in the world, you can smell the aroma of a chicken roasting in the oven.

CHICKEN

- 1 3- to 4-pound chicken, excess fat trimmed and giblets removed
- 3 scallions (white and green parts), cut in 4 pieces
- 6 coin-sized slices fresh ginger
- 1 1x3-inch strip orange zest
- 2 teaspoons peanut oil
- 2 teaspoons dark sesame oil
- 2 teaspoons honey
- 1 teaspoon soy sauce
- 2 teaspoons five-spice powder (see Cook's Note, below)

SAUCE

- ½ cup soy sauce
- ¼ cup rice vinegar
- 2 teaspoons dark sesame oil
- 1 teaspoon finely grated orange zest
- ½ teaspoon peeled, grated fresh ginger
- 1 small clove garlic, minced
- 1 scallion (white and green parts), thinly sliced

1. For the chicken: Preheat the oven to 425°F. Stuff the chicken cavity with the scallions, ginger coins, and orange zest. Set a v- or regular rack in a roasting pan and brush with 1 teaspoon of the peanut oil. Whisk the remaining 1 teaspoon peanut oil with the sesame oil, honey, and soy sauce. Brush the soy mixture over all of the chicken and sprinkle with five-spice powder.

2. Tuck the wings under the back, cross the legs, and tie them with kitchen twine. Place the chicken breast side down on the rack and roast until the back is golden brown, 35 to 40 minutes. Remove chicken from the oven and turn it breast side up. Cut the string where it holds the legs together and gently open the legs a bit. Baste the chicken with the pan drippings and roast again until the breast is golden brown and a meat thermometer inserted in the thigh registers 170°F, 20 to 25 minutes more. Transfer to a carving board and let it rest for 10 minutes before carving.

3. For the sauce: Whisk the soy sauce with the rice vinegar, sesame oil, orange zest, ginger, garlic, and scallion in a small bowl. Carve the chicken into 8 pieces, serve, and pass the dipping sauce at the table.

COOK'S NOTE Chinese five-spice powder is an aromatic blend of ground cinnamon, cloves, fennel, star anise, and peppercorns or ginger. Asian markets always stock it—and most supermarkets do, too.

peruvian **roast chicken**
with aji verde 4 servings

CHICKEN

- 1 head garlic
- 1 3- to 4-pound chicken, excess fat trimmed and giblets removed
- 2 teaspoons kosher salt, plus additional for seasoning
- ½ teaspoon freshly ground black pepper, plus additional for seasoning
- 1 tablespoon red wine vinegar
- ½ teaspoon ground cumin
- 1 tablespoon light soy sauce
- 1 teaspoon sugar
- 1 teaspoon vegetable oil

SAUCE

- ¾ cup fresh cilantro
- ⅓ cup Cotija cheese (see page 271)
- ⅓ cup extra-virgin olive oil
- ⅓ cup water
- 2 to 3 jalapeños, stemmed, seeded, and diced
- 1 clove garlic
- ½ teaspoon red wine vinegar
- ½ teaspoon kosher salt

1. For the chicken: Preheat the oven to 425°F. Remove 5 cloves from the garlic head, then halve the remaining head horizontally. Season the chicken cavity with salt and pepper to taste, then stuff with the halved garlic. Smash the garlic cloves, sprinkle with the 2 teaspoons salt, and, with the side of a large knife, mash and smear the mixture to a coarse paste. Put the garlic in a bowl and mix with the vinegar, the ½ teaspoon black pepper, and cumin. Rub the garlic mixture on the outside of the chicken. Whisk the soy sauce and sugar together and brush all over the outside of the bird. Tuck the wings under the back, cross the legs, and tie them with kitchen twine. Set a v-rack or regular rack in a roasting pan and brush with the oil.

2. Place the chicken breast side down on the rack and roast until the back is golden brown, 35 to 40 minutes. Remove the pan from the oven and turn the chicken breast side up. Cut the string where it holds the legs together and gently open up the legs a bit. Baste the chicken with the pan drippings and roast again until the breast is golden brown and a meat thermometer inserted in the thigh registers 170°F, 20 to 25 minutes more. Transfer the chicken to a carving board and let it rest for 10 minutes before carving.

3. For the aji verde sauce: Puree the cilantro, cheese, olive oil, water, jalapeños, garlic, vinegar, and salt in a blender until smooth. Carve the chicken and serve drizzled with the sauce.

One of our recipe testers, Santos, phoned home to recreate this family food memory—from Peru to you.

hungarian roast chicken with horseradish sauce 4 servings

CHICKEN

4 cloves garlic

1 teaspoon kosher salt, plus additional for seasoning

3 tablespoons unsalted butter

1 tablespoon Hungarian sweet paprika

1 teaspoon finely ground dried porcini mushrooms (optional) (see Know-How, below)

½ teaspoon caraway seeds, cracked

Freshly ground black pepper

1 3- to 4-pound chicken, excess fat trimmed and giblets removed

1 large shallot, sliced

Zest from half a lemon, peeled in large strips

Parslied Egg Noodles, for serving (see page 279) (optional)

SAUCE

1 to 2 tablespoons drained horseradish

¼ cup sour cream

1. For the chicken: Preheat the oven to 425°F. Smash the garlic cloves, sprinkle with the 1 teaspoon salt, and, with the flat side of a large knife, mash and smear the mixture to a coarse paste. Set half the garlic paste aside. Melt the butter in a small saucepan. Set a v-rack or regular rack in a roasting pan and brush with some of the melted butter. Stir the remaining garlic paste, the paprika, porcini powder, if desired, caraway seeds, and a generous amount of black pepper into the remaining melted butter and cook over medium heat, stirring until fragrant, about 30 seconds. Cool. Smear chicken cavity with reserved garlic paste, then stuff with the shallot and lemon zest. Brush spiced butter over chicken and season with salt.

2. Tuck the wings under the back, cross the legs, and tie them with kitchen twine. Place chicken breast side down on the rack and roast until the back is golden brown, 35 to 40 minutes. Remove the pan from the oven and turn the chicken breast side up. Cut the string where it holds the legs together and gently spread the legs a bit. Baste the chicken with the pan drippings and roast again until the breast is golden brown and a meat thermometer inserted in the thigh registers 170°F, 20 to 25 minutes more. Transfer chicken to a carving board and let it rest for 10 minutes before carving.

3. For the sauce: Whisk the horseradish into the sour cream. Carve the chicken and serve with the sauce and Parslied Egg Noodles, if desired.

KNOW-HOW To make porcini powder, simply grind a few dried porcini mushrooms in a spice or coffee grinder. To crack caraway seeds, use a mortar and pestle or place them in a small plastic bag and roll over them with a rolling pin.

provençal roasted chicken
with honey & thyme 4 servings

CHICKEN

1   3- to 4-pound chicken, excess fat trimmed and giblets removed

Kosher salt and freshly ground black pepper

1   shallot, sliced

1   bunch fresh thyme

Zest from 1 lemon, peeled in large strips

3   tablespoons extra-virgin olive oil

1   tablespoon honey

SAUCE

3   tablespoons water

1   tablespoon freshly squeezed lemon juice

1   tablespoon extra-virgin olive oil

1   tablespoon honey

2   tablespoons minced shallot

2   teaspoons chopped fresh thyme

¼   teaspoon kosher salt

Freshly ground black pepper

1. For the chicken: Preheat the oven to 425°F. Season the chicken cavity with salt and pepper to taste. Stuff the chicken cavity with the shallot, half the thyme, and lemon zest. Set a v-rack or regular rack in a roasting pan and brush with a bit of the olive oil. Whisk the honey and remaining oil in a small bowl. Dip the remaining thyme in the mixture and use it to brush the chicken all over with the honey mixture. Set the thyme aside; you'll use it later as a basting brush. Season bird with salt and pepper to taste.

2. Tuck the wings under the back, cross the legs, and tie them with kitchen twine. Place the chicken breast side down on the rack and roast until the back is golden brown, 35 to 40 minutes. Remove the pan from the oven and turn the chicken breast side up. Cut the string where it holds the legs together and open up the legs a bit. Baste the chicken with the pan drippings, using the thyme sprigs as a brush. Roast the chicken again until the breast is golden brown and a meat thermometer inserted in the thigh registers 170°F, 20 to 25 minutes more. Transfer the chicken to a carving board and let it rest for 10 minutes before carving.

3. For the sauce: Remove the rack from the roasting pan. Put the pan over medium-high heat, add the water, and stir with a wooden spoon to release the brown bits that cling to the pan. Strain the pan drippings into a small bowl and spoon off the fat. Whisk in the lemon juice, olive oil, honey, shallot, thyme, salt, and pepper to taste. Carve the chicken and serve drizzled with the sauce.

Delight yourself with a culinary trip to Provence with the romantic scent of honey and thyme.

chicken-n-biscuits **potpie**

4 to 6 servings

FILLING

4   bone-in chicken breast halves (about 3 pounds)

4   cups chicken broth, homemade (see page 278) or low-sodium canned

4   tablespoons unsalted butter

3   medium carrots, peeled and cut into ½-inch slices

5   button mushrooms, quartered

1   rib celery (with leaves), cut into ½-inch slices

1   tablespoon kosher salt

1   cup frozen pearl onions, thawed

⅓   cup all-purpose flour

1   tablespoon minced fresh flat-leaf parsley

1   tablespoon chopped fresh dill

    Freshly ground black pepper

DOUGH

2   cups all-purpose flour, plus additional for dusting

1   tablespoon baking powder

1   teaspoon sugar

1   teaspoon fine salt

8   tablespoons cold unsalted butter, sliced

1   teaspoon finely grated lemon zest

¾   cup milk, plus additional for brushing

1. For the chicken filling: Put the chicken breasts in a medium saucepan, add the broth (it should just cover the chicken), and bring to a boil. Cover, turn the heat very low, and poach chicken until just firm to the touch, about 20 minutes. Remove chicken from the broth and, when cool enough to handle, shred or dice it into large bite-size pieces, discarding the skin and bones. (If some of the pieces are still a bit pink, they will finish cooking in the pie.) Reserve the broth.

2. Melt the butter in a 9-inch cast-iron or other heavy ovenproof skillet over medium-high heat. Add carrots, mushrooms, celery, and salt and cook until vegetables are light brown, about 4 minutes. Add the onions and cook about 1 minute more. Stir the flour into the vegetables and cook for 1 minute. Pour in the reserved chicken broth and whisk until it comes to a boil. Reduce the heat slightly and simmer, uncovered, until thick, about 3 minutes. Stir in chicken and remove skillet from heat. Stir in parsley, dill, and pepper.

3. For the biscuit dough: Preheat the oven to 450°F. Whisk the flour, baking powder, sugar, and salt in a large bowl. Using your fingers, rub 3 tablespoons of the butter into the flour until the mixture is sandy. Work in the remaining 5 tablespoons butter until it forms pea-size pieces. Stir lemon zest into the milk and stir milk into the flour mixture to make a soft dough. Turn the dough onto a lightly floured work surface and pat into a ½-inch-thick rectangle. Fold the dough in thirds as you would a business letter, then pat into a 10-inch-wide disk. You may leave the dough in one piece or cut into pieces.

4. Bring chicken filling to a simmer. If using the large biscuit round, cut a small hole in the center and lay the biscuit on the hot filling; if using pieces, arrange them on the filling. Brush the biscuit(s) lightly with milk. Put the skillet on a baking sheet and bake until golden brown, about 20 minutes. Let the potpie rest for 5 minutes before serving.

If your concept of chicken potpie involves the frozen food section, think again. This is what you want for supper when it's cold and rainy: comfort food that's familiar but freshened up.

turkey **ropa** viejo

6 servings

Brothy and soupy, this luscious Latin-flavored stew is made in a slow-simmered sauce of succulent spices for an excitingly different turkey taste experience.

TURKEY

2 whole turkey legs (about 6 pounds)

Kosher salt and freshly ground black pepper

2 tablespoons extra-virgin olive oil

1 medium onion, chopped

4 bay leaves

4 cups chicken broth, homemade (see page 278) or low-sodium canned

About 6 cups water

SAUCE

2 tablespoons extra-virgin olive oil

1/2 teaspoon fennel seeds

2 red bell peppers, seeded and chopped

1 medium onion, chopped

6 cloves garlic, minced

2 cups canned crushed tomatoes

1/2 cup white wine

1 tablespoon pimenton (see page 274) or paprika

1 tablespoon dried oregano

1 tablespoon kosher salt

1 teaspoon ground cumin

1 teaspoon freshly ground black pepper

1/2 teaspoon ground coriander

1. For the turkey: Season the turkey legs generously with salt and pepper. Heat a large soup pot or Dutch oven over medium-high heat. Add the oil; when it is shimmering, brown the legs, in batches if needed, turning once, about 10 minutes per leg; transfer to a plate. Add the onion and bay leaves; cook, stirring occasionally, until onion is soft, about 5 minutes. Return the legs to the pot with any collected juices and add the chicken broth and enough water to cover. Bring to a boil, cover, reduce the heat, and simmer gently until the meat is very tender, about 1 1/2 hours.

2. Meanwhile, for the sauce: Heat the olive oil in a large saucepan over medium-high heat. Add the fennel seeds and stir until toasted, about 30 seconds. Stir in the bell peppers, onion, and garlic and cook until soft, about 5 minutes. Stir in the tomatoes, wine, pimenton, oregano, salt, cumin, black pepper, and coriander. Bring the mixture to a boil, reduce the heat, and simmer, uncovered, for 15 minutes.

3. Remove the turkey from the broth and let cool enough to handle. Remove and discard the skin and shred the meat into long, thin, ropy pieces. Add the meat to the sauce with 4 cups of the cooking liquid and simmer, uncovered, for about 15 minutes. Ladle into warm bowls.

COOK'S NOTE Ropa viejo is a Cuban dish that's traditionally made with beef. The term ropa viejo means "old clothes," a reference to the raggy appearance of the pulled meat. Turkey legs are a perfect substitute for beef. They're cheap and flavorful and require long, moist cooking to become tender—and they shred the same way the beef does when it's pulled apart along the grain.

thai green curry game hens

6 servings

1½ teaspoons coriander seeds

1 teaspoon cumin seeds

½ teaspoon white peppercorns

3 serrano chiles, stemmed and chopped

2 cloves garlic

1 large shallot, peeled

1 stalk fresh lemongrass, trimmed and thinly sliced

1 ½-inch piece fresh ginger, peeled and chopped

¼ cup packed roughly chopped cilantro leaves, stems, and roots (see Cook's Note, below)

1 tablespoon fish sauce (see page 274)

1 teaspoon kosher salt

½ teaspoon ground turmeric

3 tablespoons peanut or corn oil

3 Cornish game hens (about 4½ pounds), butterflied (see page 275)

Hot cooked rice

Spicy Carrot Sambal (see page 199) (optional)

1. Preheat the oven to 450°F. Toast the coriander seeds, cumin seeds, and peppercorns in a small dry skillet over medium heat until fragrant, about 8 minutes. Cool and grind in a clean spice or coffee grinder. In a small food processor, pulse the ground spices with the chiles, garlic, shallot, lemongrass, ginger, cilantro, fish sauce, salt, and turmeric. Add the oil and puree to make a smooth paste.

2. Put the hens in a large bowl and rub them all over with the paste. Heat a large roasting pan in the oven until quite hot, about 5 minutes. Arrange the hens, skin side up, in the pan and roast until well browned and crispy and an instant-read thermometer registers 160°F when inserted into a thigh, about 30 minutes. If you prefer the skin very brown and crisp, broil the birds skin side up 4 to 6 inches from the heat for about 4 minutes after roasting. Arrange the hens on a platter as they are or cut into pieces and drizzle with the pan drippings. Serve with hot cooked rice and Spicy Carrot Sambal, if desired.

COOK'S NOTE Yes, you can use the cilantro roots. In fact, Thai cooks prize them for their intensely earthy flavor. Cilantro is not always sold with its roots attached, but when they are, we use them in this fragrant paste or freeze them for later use.

roasted duck with orange-molasses glaze 3 to 4 servings

DUCK

- 1 Pekin (Long Island) duckling (about 5 pounds)

  Kosher salt and freshly ground black pepper

- 3 1x3-inch strips orange zest
- 1 small onion, halved
- 1 cup water

  Sicilian Sweet & Sour Butternut Squash (see page 192) (optional)

GLAZE

- 3 1x3-inch strips orange zest
- 1½ tablespoons dark molasses
- 1½ tablespoons honey
- 2 tablespoons freshly squeezed orange juice
- 2 tablespoons balsamic vinegar
- 2 large garlic cloves, smashed
- 8 whole black peppercorns, lightly crushed
- ¼ teaspoon coriander seeds, lightly crushed

KNOW-HOW We pierce the skin while roasting a duck to let the fat run free. The rendered fat can be saved. It adds fabulous flavor to sautéed greens and a crisp, flavorful crust to fried or roasted potatoes.

1. The day before roasting, remove the giblets and neck from the cavity of the bird and discard. Trim the neck flap and excess fat from around the cavity. Rinse the bird inside and out and pat dry with paper towels. Set the duck on a rack on a baking sheet and refrigerate, uncovered, for 24 hours.

2. The next day, preheat the oven to 300°F. Pierce the duck all over at ½-inch intervals with a skewer or small knife; be sure to pierce the skin on the back. Season the cavity with salt and pepper and stuff it with the orange zest and the onion. Set the duck breast side up on a rack in a roasting pan and pour the water in the pan. Roast 3 hours; remove the duck every hour to again pierce the skin so that the fat drains from the bird. After 3 hours, increase the temperature to 450°F and continue roasting until the skin is crisp and brown, about 30 minutes more.

3. While the duck is roasting, make the glaze: Put orange zest, molasses, honey, orange juice, vinegar, garlic, peppercorns, and coriander in a small saucepan. Heat over medium-high heat until the honey dissolves. Set aside while duck roasts.

4. When the duck is cooked, transfer it to a cutting board and let it rest for 10 minutes before carving. Brush the skin with glaze 4 to 5 five times during the resting period—don't cover it or you will forfeit its lovely crisp skin. Carve the duck and arrange pieces on a warm serving platter. Drizzle a bit more of the glaze over the pieces and pass the rest at the table. Serve with Sicilian Sweet & Sour Butternut Squash, if desired.

mixed grill with chimichurri sauce 6 to 8 servings

SAUCE

- 4 cloves garlic, sliced
- 1 shallot, sliced
- 1 cup fresh flat-leaf parsley
- 2 tablespoons fresh oregano
- 1 tablespoon kosher salt
- $\frac{1}{2}$ teaspoon crushed red pepper flakes
- $\frac{1}{3}$ cup extra-virgin olive oil
- $\frac{1}{3}$ cup red wine vinegar
- 3 tablespoons water

MEAT

- 2 beef blade steaks, each about 6 ounces
- 1 lamb leg steak, $1\frac{1}{4}$ to $1\frac{1}{2}$ pounds
- 1 pork tenderloin, about $1\frac{3}{4}$ pounds
- 1 pound fresh chorizo sausage
- Olive oil for brushing meats
- Kosher salt and freshly ground black pepper

1. For the chimichurri sauce: Pulse the garlic, shallot, parsley, oregano, salt, and red pepper flakes in a small food processor until roughly chopped. Add the oil, vinegar, and water and pulse to make a textured sauce. Transfer to a serving bowl.

2. For the meat: Heat an outdoor grill to medium-high heat. (If you can hold your hand over the fire for 3 seconds, it's medium-high.) About 20 minutes before grilling, bring the meats to room temperature. Preheat the grate for 5 minutes; scrape it clean with a grill brush. Brush the beef, lamb, and pork with olive oil and season generously with salt and pepper. Grill all the meats, turning once, until an instant-read thermometer inserted into the sides of the steaks registers 125°F. For medium-rare, the beef takes about 2 minutes per side, the lamb about 4 minutes. Grill the pork tenderloin until the thermometer registers 145°F, about 15 minutes, and the sausage 160°F, about 10 minutes, turning both as needed to get nice grill marks on all sides. Transfer the meats to a cutting board and let them rest 5 minutes. Slice the beef and lamb steaks across the grain, slice the pork tenderloin, cut the sausage into chunks, and serve all the meats with the chimichurri sauce.

An Argentinean barbecue, or asado, is a meat-lover's paradise with lots of smoky red meat and a spicy herb sauce called chimichurri.

STYLE For the crosshatched marks of a master griller, lay your steaks at an angle across the grill grate and don't move them until they get a good sear. Then rotate them (don't turn them over yet) about 45 degrees from their original spot on the grill. Once you've made your mark, flip and repeat on the other side.

hoisin-glazed beef tenderloin with shiitake mushrooms 6 servings

2	pounds center-cut beef tenderloin roast
1¹/2	teaspoons kosher salt, plus additional for seasoning
	Freshly ground black pepper
2	tablespoons vegetable oil
¹/3	cup hoisin sauce
1	pound fresh shiitake mushrooms, stems removed, caps quartered
3	bunches scallions (white and green parts separate), cut into 2-inch pieces
4	cloves garlic, minced
1	¹/2-inch piece peeled fresh ginger, very thinly sliced
¹/2	teaspoon crushed red pepper flakes
¹/2	cup dry sherry

1. Preheat the oven to 400°F. Heat a large skillet over medium-high heat. Season the beef all over with salt and a generous amount of pepper. Add the oil to the skillet and heat until shimmering, then sear the beef until it is a mahogany brown on all sides, about 8 minutes in all. Transfer the tenderloin to a shallow roasting pan, reserving the skillet. Brush the beef all over with the hoisin sauce and roast until an instant-read thermometer inserted in the center registers 125°F for medium-rare, about 30 minutes. Transfer the roast to a cutting board, tent it very loosely with aluminum foil, and let it rest while you cook the mushrooms.

2. Heat the skillet over medium-high heat. Add the mushrooms, scallion whites, garlic, ginger, the 1¹/2 teaspoons salt, and red pepper flakes and cook until soft, about 8 minutes. Add the scallion greens and sherry and cook until almost all the liquid has evaporated, about 2 minutes. Slice the roast and serve with the vegetables.

COOK'S NOTE We count Chinese hoisin sauce as one of the Condiments We Love. A sweet and spicy blend of fermented soybeans, garlic, chile peppers, and spices, it's fabulous as a glaze for roasted and grilled meats and as a flavoring in sauces.

Go mushroom-hunting at your market. Button mushrooms may abound, but also look for the slightly exotic, dried or fresh: chanterelles, morels, porcini, shiitake, and wood ear.

Ten hours in the oven? Yep, that's right. This is true barbecue— cooking for a long, long time with low indirect heat. The surprise is— we've brought the barbecue indoors.

low & slow oven-barbecued brisket 8 to 10 servings

BRISKET

- 1 tablespoon pimenton (see page 274)
- 1 tablespoon ground coriander
- 1 tablespoon dried oregano
- 1 tablespoon kosher salt
- 2 teaspoons cayenne pepper
- 2 teaspoons ground cumin
- 1 teaspoon ground allspice
- 1 8-pound point-cut brisket (see ShopSmart, below)

SAUCE

- 1/4 medium onion, chopped
- 4 cloves garlic, minced
- 1 tablespoon chile powder, preferably ancho (see page 273)
- 2 cups canned whole peeled tomatoes in puree
- 1/2 cup firmly packed dark brown sugar
- 1/2 cup distilled white vinegar
- 1/4 cup whole-grain mustard
- 1 tablespoon Worcestershire sauce
- 1 tablespoon kosher salt
   Freshly ground black pepper

I. For the brisket: Preheat the oven to 250°F. Combine the spices in a small bowl. Put the brisket in a shallow roasting pan and rub both sides with the spice mixture. Slow-roast until the top is browned and crusty and an instant-read thermometer inserted in the thickest part registers 200°F, about 10 hours. You don't need to baste or turn the brisket— just leave it alone. After a few hours, once a good amount of drippings and crispy bits have pooled in the pan, spoon them off and reserve 1/3 cup—with the bits—for the sauce.

2. For the barbecue sauce: Heat the reserved drippings in a medium saucepan over medium heat. Add the onion, garlic, and chile powder and stir until the onions and garlic are lightly browned, about 5 minutes. Add the tomatoes with the puree, brown sugar, vinegar, mustard, Worcestershire sauce, salt, and pepper to taste and bring to a simmer. Whisk occasionally until the sauce is deep red and a bit thicker, about 5 minutes.

3. Transfer the brisket to a cutting board, cover loosely with foil, and let it rest for 15 minutes. Slice the brisket against the grain and arrange the slices on a serving platter. Serve with the barbecue sauce.

SHOPSMART A full brisket is very big and usually cut into two parts. The first cut is thin and lean; the second cut or point cut is well marbled, making it the perfect choice for slow and gentle cooking. The brisket will have a good layer of fat on one side, about 1/4 inch or so—don't trim it, since it keeps the meat moist. Some will melt off as the brisket cooks. You can trim the remainder before you slice, if you wish, although it sure tastes good.

skirt steak with sweet & sour mushroom compote 2 to 4 servings

8 ounces cremini mushrooms, halved

1 cup red cherry, grape, or pear tomatoes

3 tablespoons extra-virgin olive oil

   Kosher salt and freshly ground black pepper

1/4 cup red wine vinegar

1/4 cup sugar

5 cloves garlic, very thinly sliced

1 sprig fresh rosemary

   Pinch crushed red pepper flakes

1 1/4 pounds skirt steak

COOK'S NOTE Skirt steak—the cut generally used for fajitas and Philly cheese steaks—comes from the inside of the rib cage. It's extremely flavorful but tough if overcooked. So cook it rare and slice very thinly against the grain.

1. Preheat the oven to 500°F. Spread the mushrooms and tomatoes in a single layer on a baking sheet. Toss with 1 tablespoon of the olive oil and salt and pepper to taste. Roast until they are lightly browned and soft, about 10 minutes. Put them in a serving bowl.

2. Mix 1 tablespoon olive oil with all but 2 teaspoons of the vinegar, the sugar, garlic, rosemary, and red pepper flakes in a small saucepan. Bring the mixture to a boil over medium heat, reduce the heat, and simmer, stirring occasionally, until the garlic is tender and mixture syrupy, about 15 minutes. Fold the mixture into the mushrooms and tomatoes, taking care not to smash the tomatoes.

3. Heat a large cast-iron or other heavy skillet over medium heat for 5 minutes. Brush the steak on both sides with the remaining 1 tablespoon olive oil and season generously with salt and pepper. Raise the heat to high, add the steak, and cook, turning once, about 3 minutes on the first side and 1 minute on the second side for medium-rare. Transfer the steak to a cutting board and let it rest for 5 minutes. Slice the steak very thinly on an angle and against the grain and arrange the slices on a serving platter or individual plates. Stir the remaining 2 teaspoons vinegar into the compote and spoon over the steak.

steak frites 2 to 4 servings

STEAK

1½ pounds bone-in rib-eye steak

Kosher salt and freshly ground black pepper

1 tablespoon oil, such as vegetable, soybean, or corn

Spicy Red Pepper Sauce(see page 278)

2 tablespoons minced fresh flat-leaf parsley

FRIES

1 head garlic, loose skin rubbed off, halved horizontally

6 cups vegetable oil

1½ pounds large boiling or baking potatoes, unpeeled, scrubbed

½ cup chopped fresh flat-leaf parsley

Finely grated zest of 1 lemon

½ teaspoon kosher salt, plus additional for seasoning

Lemon wedges, for garnish

COOK'S NOTE A rib-eye steak is from the same cut as a standing rib roast, which is why it is so nicely marbled (a lovely way to say it contains a fair amount of fat). The marbling makes rib-eye butter-knife tender and flavorful. Heads-up: The meat along the giant bone is beyond delicious.

Preheat the oven to 425°F. A half-hour before cooking, remove steak from refrigerator. Heat a large cast-iron skillet over high heat. Pat steak dry and season generously with salt and pepper. Add oil to hot skillet and when it begins to smoke add steak. Reduce heat slightly and cook steak until browned, about 4 minutes. Turn steak and transfer skillet to the oven. Roast until an instant-read thermometer inserted sideways into the steak registers 120°F for medium-rare, about 8 minutes. Transfer steak to a cutting board and let it rest for 10 minutes. Cut steak from the bone and carve meat across the grain. Arrange slices on 2 or 4 plates, drizzle some of the red pepper sauce over and around, and sprinkle with parsley.

GREMOLATA SHOESTRING FRIES

1. Put garlic halves and oil in a deep, heavy-bottomed pot and heat over medium heat until a deep-fry thermometer registers 320°F. Line a pan with paper towels. Use a slotted spoon to transfer garlic to prepared pan and heat oil to 360°F.

2. While oil heats, slice potatoes into shoestring fries with the thin julienne attachment of a mandoline or vegetable slicer. Swish cut potatoes in a bowl of tepid water, then spin them in a salad spinner. Spread on paper towels and blot with more paper towels—you want them bone dry so they don't spatter.

3. Increase heat to medium-high. Working in batches, add the potatoes to the oil, and fry until brown and crispy, about 4 minutes. Scoop fries from oil with a slotted spoon and drain on prepared baking sheet. Repeat with remaining potatoes, making sure oil returns to 360°F before adding each batch.

4. Squeeze cloves from one of the garlic halves and mince; reserve other half for garnish. Toss minced garlic with parsley, lemon zest, and ½ teaspoon salt in a large bowl. Dump fries on top and toss. Mound fries on a platter, season with salt to taste, and serve with reserved garlic and lemon wedges.

deviled short ribs

4 servings

Short ribs start out tough but end up tender after a long, moist roast in the oven.

RIBS

8 pieces English-style beef short ribs, about 6 pounds (see ShopSmart, below)

Kosher salt and freshly ground black pepper

2 medium carrots, peeled and sliced

2 ribs celery, sliced

1 large onion, quartered

6 cloves garlic, smashed

1 bay leaf

1 sprig fresh rosemary

2½ cups chicken broth, homemade (see page 278) or low-sodium canned

⅓ cup red wine vinegar

COATING

⅓ cup dry English-style mustard

⅓ cup honey

1 tablespoon water

1 teaspoon kosher salt

5 ounces sourdough bread, crusts trimmed, and torn into large chunks

2 cloves garlic, minced

3 tablespoons minced fresh flat-leaf parsley

2 tablespoons extra-virgin olive oil

Freshly ground black pepper

1. For the ribs: Preheat the oven to 350°F. Lay the short ribs meaty side up in a large roasting pan and season with salt and pepper. Scatter the carrots, celery, onion, garlic, bay leaf, and rosemary around the ribs. Add the chicken broth and vinegar. Set the pan directly over two burners and bring to a simmer over high heat. Lay a sheet of parchment paper over the ribs and transfer to the oven. Cook until the meat is fork-tender, about 2 hours. Remove from the oven and cool in the liquid, about 30 minutes. (The dish can be prepared up to this point 1 day ahead, covered, and refrigerated.)

2. For the coating: Whisk the mustard with the honey, water, and ½ teaspoon of the salt. Pulse the bread to make coarse bread crumbs in a food processor. Add the garlic, parsley, olive oil, remaining ½ teaspoon salt, and the pepper to taste and pulse briefly to combine. Transfer mixture to a shallow bowl.

3. Preheat the oven to 450°F. Remove the ribs from the braising liquid (reserve liquid for other uses) and pat dry. Brush the meaty side of each rib with some of the mustard mixture, then press it into the bread crumb mixture to coat. Arrange the ribs on a baking sheet and roast until the bread crumbs are brown and crisp, 20 to 25 minutes. Serve the ribs hot or at room temperature.

SHOPSMART English-style short ribs are pieces of individual longish short ribs—not to be confused with flanken, which are thin, short pieces of rib that are connected by meat.

texas-style chili

6 servings

7 ripe medium tomatoes
(about 4 pounds)

2 medium onions, quartered through
the root end

2 poblano chiles

2 jalapeños

8 cloves garlic

1 chipotle chile in adobo sauce,
chopped (see page 273)

1 tablespoon dried oregano,
preferably Mexican

1/2 teaspoon ground cinnamon,
preferably Mexican (see Cook's
Note, page 261)

1/4 teaspoon ground cloves

4 pounds beef chuck, cut into
1/2-inch cubes

1 1/2 tablespoons kosher salt, plus
additional for seasoning

1/3 cup vegetable oil

1/3 cup chili powder, plus 2 teaspoons
(see Know-How, below)

1/4 cup ground cumin, plus 2 teaspoons

1/4 cup all-purpose flour

2 12-ounce bottles Mexican
lager-style beer

2 cups water

Sour cream, shredded Cheddar or
Jack cheese, chopped scallions,
and salsa, for garnishing

1. Position a rack about 6 inches from the broiler and preheat to high. Line a broiler pan with foil. Spread the tomatoes, onions, poblanos, jalapeños, and garlic on the pan and broil, turning until charred on all sides. Cool slightly. Stem the roasted chiles, catching the juices and seeds that run onto the pan, and put them in a food processor with the tomatoes, onions, garlic, and chipotles. Pulse until coarsely textured; add the oregano, cinnamon, and cloves and pulse briefly.

2. Spread the meat out on a sheet of aluminum foil, pat dry, and season it generously with salt to taste. Heat some of the oil in a Dutch oven or other heavy pot over high heat and brown some of the meat well on all sides, taking care not to crowd the pot. Transfer the cooked meat to a plate and repeat until all of the meat is cooked.

3. Whisk the 1/3 cup chili powder, 1/4 cup cumin, and the flour into the meat drippings to make a paste. Whisk in the beer. Return the meat to the pot along with the collected juices, the tomato mixture, the water, and the 1 1/2 tablespoons salt. Bring to a boil, reduce the heat to low, cover, and simmer for 30 minutes. Uncover and simmer, stirring occasionally, until the meat is tender and the sauce is thick, about 1 hour.

4. Just before serving, stir in the remaining 2 teaspoons each of chili powder and cumin. Divide the chili among warm bowls and pass the garnishes.

KNOW-HOW Holding back some of the chili powder and cumin until serving time heightens their flavors in the chili.

Chili just may be the most hotly contested bowl game out there. Beans or no beans? Ground meat or cubed? This is the real deal, Lone Star-style: just cubed chuck steak, spices, and three kinds of chiles.

Don't be afraid to ask for a taste!
Good relationships are the key to
getting good quality ingredients every
time. Get to know your grocer, your
butcher, your baker, your fish guy. Ask
for specific ingredients or about what's
in season. It's the way to get just what
you want—and the very best of it.

roasted fresh ham with cider glaze 8 to 10 servings

BRINE

- 8 quarts water
- 2 cups kosher salt
- 1 cup firmly packed dark brown sugar
- 4 whole cloves
- 2 bay leaves
- 1 tablespoon mustard seeds
- 1 teaspoon crushed red pepper flakes
- 1 cinnamon stick
- 1 8- to 10-pound shank-end fresh ham, bone in and skin on

RUB AND GLAZE

- 1/4 cup extra-virgin olive oil
- 1/4 cup whole-grain mustard
- 1 heaping cup fresh flat-leaf parsley
- 12 fresh sage leaves, chopped
- 9 large cloves garlic, peeled and chopped
- 1/2 teaspoon red pepper flakes
- 1 tablespoon kosher salt
- 1 teaspoon freshly ground black pepper
- 4 large Spanish onions, trimmed and cut into 1-inch wedges
- 1 gallon apple cider
- 2 tablespoons all-purpose flour
- 2 tablespoons unsalted butter, softened

1. One day before roasting: In a plastic container large enough to hold the ham, stir the water with the salt and brown sugar until dissolved. Add the spices. Score ham in a diamond pattern through the skin and fat, taking care not to cut into the meat. Add ham to brine, weight it with a plate to keep it submerged, and refrigerate for at least 4 hours but no more than 8 hours. Drain, rinse, pat the ham dry, and refrigerate.

2. One hour before roasting, remove ham from the refrigerator. Preheat the oven to 450°F. For the rub: Pulse the olive oil, mustard, parsley, sage, garlic, red pepper, salt, and black pepper in a food processor to make a paste. Rub it all over ham. In a large roasting pan, toss the onion wedges with 1 cup of the apple cider and set the ham on top. Roast the ham for 30 minutes, reduce the oven temperature to 325°F, and roast until an instant-read thermometer inserted into the thickest part registers 165° F, about 4 hours. After the first hour, loosely wrap aluminum foil around the bone to keep it from burning.

3. Meanwhile, for the glaze: Boil, then simmer, the remaining apple cider in a saucepan, skimming as needed, until syrupy and reduced to about 2 cups, about 1/2 hours.

4. During the last 1/2 hours of roasting the ham, brush it with the glaze every 30 minutes. Transfer the cooked ham to an ovenproof platter and let it rest in the turned-off oven for 30 minutes. Loosely cover the onions in an ovenproof bowl and put them in the oven as well. Strain the pan juices into a saucepan, skim off any excess fat, and bring to a boil. Make a paste with the flour and butter and whisk a bit at a time into the juices. Boil until thick. Carve the ham and serve with the onions and sauce.

chinese peppered pork chops

4 servings

1/3 cup soy sauce

2 cloves garlic, minced

4 teaspoons sugar

2 teaspoons medium-cracked black pepper

1/2 teaspoon kosher salt

6 1/4-inch-thick loin pork chops (about 1 1/2 pounds)

2 tablespoons vegetable oil

1. Put the soy sauce, garlic, sugar, pepper, and salt in a large self-sealing plastic bag, seal, and shake. Add the pork chops and rub them, through the bag, to work the spices into the meat. Marinate at room temperature for 30 minutes.

2. Heat I tablespoon of the oil in a large skillet over medium-high heat until shimmering. Add half the chops, shaking off excess marinade, and cook, turning once, until just cooked through, about 6 minutes. Repeat with the remaining oil and chops, wiping the skillet clean between batches.

SHOPSMART Thin-sliced pork chops are frequently sold in family packs—plentiful and inexpensive. If you see 'em, buy 'em. Stick them in the freezer and keep this recipe in mind for those busy days when you have no time to shop and little time or inclination to cook. We're betting you have the rest of the ingredients in your pantry.

barbecued spice-rubbed pork spareribs 6 servings

RUB

- 1/4 cup packed dark brown sugar
- 2 tablespoons rubbed dry sage
- 2 tablespoons sweet paprika
- 2 tablespoons kosher salt
- 1 tablespoon ground ginger
- 1 tablespoon ground cumin
- 1 tablespoon ground coriander
- 1 tablespoon garlic powder
- 1 tablespoon freshly ground black pepper
- 2 teaspoons onion powder
- 2 teaspoons dried thyme
- 1 1/2 teaspoons cayenne pepper

RIBS

- 2 racks pork spareribs (6 to 7 pounds total)
- 3 cups mesquite wood chips, soaked in water for 30 minutes

1. For the rub: Whisk all of the ingredients in a small bowl until thoroughly combined. Rub mixture into both sides of the ribs.

2. For the ribs: Place a drip pan on one side of the lower charcoal grill grate. Build a medium-size fire on the other side of the grill. Scatter the soaked mesquite wood chips over the fire. (Or, on a gas grill, set grates for indirect grilling; turn heat to medium and scatter soaked mesquite wood chips over the heating element.) Preheat the cooking grate for 5 minutes; scrape it clean with a grill brush. Lay the ribs on the grate over the drip pan. Cover the grill and open the bottom and top vents. (Make sure the top vents are open on the side away from the fire to allow the smoke to circulate throughout the grill.) Cook the ribs, turning every 30 minutes, until tender but not falling off the bone, about 3 hours. (If the fire dies down, add more coal as needed.) Cut into individual ribs or multiple ribs and serve.

COOK'S NOTE Spice blends are great for rubbing into slow-cooked BBQ ribs and sprinkling over quick-grilling steaks and chops. Blend up a double batch and make it a standard part of a well-prepared cookout kit.

pork rib roast with cranberry-apricot stuffing 4 to 6 servings

3 tablespoons cognac or other brandy

3 tablespoons water

⅓ cup dried cranberries

⅓ cup dried apricots, coarsely chopped

¼ cup whole almonds, toasted and chopped

1 medium shallot, minced

3 tablespoons unsalted butter, softened

1 teaspoon fennel seeds, toasted and crushed

½ teaspoon kosher salt, plus additional for seasoning

Freshly ground black pepper

1 6-rib center-cut pork roast, backbone removed and ribs Frenched (see page 268) (about 4 pounds after trimming)

2 tablespoons vegetable oil

1 cup crème fraîche or sour cream

½ cup Dijon mustard

KNOW-HOW Roasting meat on the bone keeps meat moist and improves its flavor. Pan-searing before roasting is the way to get a great burnished crust on lean meats that would otherwise dry out if left to brown solely in the oven.

1. Warm the cognac and water in a small saucepan, add the cranberries and apricots, and set aside until plump, about 10 minutes. In a small food processor, pulse the fruit and any unabsorbed liquid with the almonds, shallot, butter, fennel seeds, ½ teaspoon salt, and pepper to taste until the fruit and nuts are coarsely chopped.

2. With a boning knife or other long, thin knife, make a cut 3 inches across in the center of one end of the roast. Gently push and work the blade in and straight through the roast to the other end. (If your knife isn't long enough, make a cut at either end and work your way to the center, making sure that the cuts meet.) Insert the narrow end of a wooden spoon into the opening to widen it a bit all the way through. Push the stuffing into the loin, working first from one end and then the other, filling to the center.

3. Preheat the oven to 350°F. Pat the loin dry and season all over with salt and pepper. Heat the oil in a large ovenproof skillet over medium-high heat. Add the roast, holding the bones up so that the bottom gets well browned, then turn the roast to brown the meaty side, about 6 minutes total. Transfer the skillet to the oven and roast the pork meat side down for 30 minutes. Turn the roast over so it sits on the bones and roast until an instant-read thermometer inserted into the center of the meat registers 155°F, about 1 hour more. Transfer the roast to a carving board, tent loosely with foil, and let it rest for 10 minutes before carving.

4. Whisk the crème fraîche or sour cream with the mustard in a small bowl and season with salt and pepper to taste. Slice roast between the bones to make individual chops, arrange them on a platter, and serve, passing the mustard sauce.

The WOW factor comes built into this glorious roast. The fall flavors are fabulous, and so are the Frenched ribs. It's an elegant adventure in home cooking that invites everyone to just dig in.

pork chili verde

6 servings

All the elements of a classic chili verde are made slightly simpler to prepare. If you're up to the challenge, this is the chili for you.

3 pounds trimmed pork shoulder, cut into 1-inch cubes

2 12-ounce bottles Mexican lager-style beer

2 to 3 chipotle chiles in adobo sauce, chopped (see page 273)

1 tablespoon dried oregano, preferably Mexican

6 teaspoons kosher salt

2½ pounds fresh tomatillos (about 24), husks removed and rinsed

2 poblano chiles

2 medium white onions, quartered

5 cloves garlic, peeled

1 bunch cilantro, roots and some stem trimmed, plus sprigs for garnish

2 tablespoons freshly squeezed lime juice, plus wedges for garnish

1 tablespoon ground cumin

Pinch sugar (optional)

¾ cup vegetable oil

1 cup whole unblanched almonds

4 slices sourdough bread, cubed

4 ounces crumbled queso fresco (see page 271) or farmer's cheese

1. Position an oven rack 6 to 8 inches from the broiler and preheat. Put the pork, beer, chipotles, and oregano in a Dutch oven or soup pot and season with 2 teaspoons of the kosher salt. Bring to a simmer, skimming off any foam as it rises to the surface, and cook, uncovered, until the meat is almost tender, about 40 minutes.

2. Meanwhile, spread tomatillos, poblanos, onions, and garlic on a foil-lined broiler pan. Broil the vegetables, turning as needed, until charred on all sides, about 20 minutes. Cool slightly. Transfer about half the tomatillos and onions, and the juices in the pan, to a blender and puree with the garlic, cilantro, lime juice, and cumin until smooth. Roughly chop the remaining tomatillos and onions. Seed and chop the poblanos, skin and all. Stir the vegetables into the puree. Taste, and if the sauce is very acidic, stir in a pinch of sugar.

3. Heat oil in a heavy-bottomed medium skillet over medium-high heat. When oil is hot but not smoking, stir in the almonds and fry until they just begin to brown, about 20 seconds. Transfer with a slotted spoon to a paper-towel-lined plate. Add the bread cubes to the oil and fry, stirring, until golden and crispy, about 30 seconds. Transfer to the plate with nuts and cool. Pull pan from the heat and let the oil cool somewhat.

4. Return the pan to medium heat. Very carefully add the tomatillo sauce to the oil (it will sizzle and can spatter dramatically) and fry, stirring, until thicker, about 5 minutes. Stir the sauce and the 4 teaspoons remaining salt into the pork and simmer until the meat is tender, about 40 minutes.

5. Chop the almonds. Divide the chili among bowls, scatter some of the cheese over each, and top with some of the bread and almonds. Garnish with a sprig of cilantro and a lime wedge and serve.

shanghai potato cakes with pork 4 servings

Pork and potatoes is as American as you can get. Here they are with an Asian twist. Courtesy of the Chinese grandmother of one of our cooks, this recipe is pure comfort food, Shanghai style.

POTATO CAKES

- 2 medium russet or other baking potatoes (about 1 pound), peeled and cut into chunks
- ½ teaspoon kosher salt, plus additional for the potato water
- 2 tablespoons peanut oil, plus additional for frying
- 6 ounces ground pork
- 2 tablespoons soy sauce
- ½ medium onion, chopped
- ½ teaspoon sugar
- 1 large egg, beaten

  All-purpose flour, for dredging
- ½ cup Sweet and Spicy Mustard Sauce (see recipe, below)

MUSTARD SAUCE

  Makes about ¾ cup
- ¼ cup dry English-style mustard
- ¼ cup sugar
- ¼ cup water

1. Put the potatoes with cold water to cover in a medium saucepan, salt the water generously, and bring to a boil. Reduce the heat and simmer until just tender, about 6 minutes; drain. Return the potatoes to the saucepan, mash, and set aside.

2. Heat 1 tablespoon of the oil in a large nonstick skillet over medium-high heat. When the oil is very hot, add the pork and stir-fry until cooked through, about 3 minutes. Stir in 1 tablespoon of the soy sauce. Using a slotted spoon, add the pork to the potatoes. Heat the remaining 1 tablespoon oil in the same skillet, add the onion, and cook, stirring, until lightly browned, about 3 minutes. Turn the heat to medium-low, add the potato mixture, and cook, stirring, to heat through. Stir in the remaining 1 tablespoon soy sauce, the sugar, and ½ teaspoon salt. Transfer the mixture to a bowl and cool slightly, then stir in the egg.

3. Put a baking sheet in the oven and preheat to 200°F. Wipe the skillet clean, add a scant ¼-inch oil, and heat over medium-low heat. Put the flour on a large plate. Form half the potato mixture into 4 cakes about 2½ inches wide and ¾ inch thick. Lightly dredge the cakes in the flour and place them in the hot oil, leaving a few inches between them so that the sides brown. Cook, turning once, until golden brown on both sides, about 4 minutes total; transfer cooked cakes to the oven. Repeat with remaining mixture. Serve cakes with the mustard sauce.

SWEET AND SPICY MUSTARD SAUCE

Whisk the mustard with the sugar and water in a small bowl. Serve at room temperature. The sauce may be refrigerated in a tightly covered container for 1 week.

moussaka

6 to 8 servings

EGGPLANT

- 2 large eggplants, unpeeled
- 1/2 cup extra-virgin olive oil
- Kosher salt and freshly ground black pepper

MEAT SAUCE

- 2 tablespoons extra-virgin olive oil
- 1/2 medium yellow onion, chopped
- 3 cloves garlic, minced
- 1 pound ground beef
- 1/2 teaspoon kosher salt
- 1/2 teaspoon dried oregano
- 1/8 teaspoon ground allspice
- Pinch ground cloves
- 1 cinnamon stick, broken in half
- Freshly ground black pepper
- 1 1/2 cups whole canned tomatoes
- 1 bay leaf

CUSTARD SAUCE

- 5 tablespoons unsalted butter
- 6 tablespoons all-purpose flour
- 3 cups milk, at room temperature
- 1 1/2 teaspoons kosher salt
- Pinch ground nutmeg
- 1 large whole egg
- 2 large egg yolks

MOUSSAKA

- 1/2 cup dried coarse bread crumbs
- 3 tablespoons Pecorino Romano cheese (see page 271)

1. For the eggplant: Preheat the oven to 475° F. Line a baking sheet with aluminum foil. Cut the eggplants lengthwise into 1/2-inch slices. Lay the slices on the baking sheet, brush both sides with oil, and season with salt and pepper. Cover with foil and bake until soft, about 25 minutes. Set aside, covered. Turn the oven down to 350°F.

2. For the meat sauce: Heat the olive oil in a large skillet over medium-high heat. Add the onion and cook, stirring, until lightly browned, about 4 minutes. Stir in the garlic and cook until fragrant, about 1 minute. Add the beef, break it up with a wooden spoon, and stir in the salt, oregano, allspice, cloves, cinnamon, and pepper to taste. Cook, stirring occasionally, until the beef is just slightly pink, about 3 minutes. Crush the tomatoes through your fingers into the pot; stir in their juices and the bay leaf. Bring the sauce to a simmer, cover, and cook until the sauce thickens, about 20 minutes. Discard the cinnamon stick and bay leaf.

3. Meanwhile, for the custard sauce: Melt the butter in a medium saucepan over medium heat. Whisk in the flour and cook, whisking, for 1 minute. Remove the pan from the heat and whisk in the milk, salt, and nutmeg. Return to the heat and bring to a boil, whisking constantly. Reduce heat and simmer 2 minutes. Cool; whisk in the whole egg and yolks.

4. To assemble the moussaka: Brush a 9x13-inch casserole dish with olive oil. Scatter the bread crumbs over the bottom. Lay half the eggplant in the pan, overlapping the slices if needed. Cover with half the meat sauce. Repeat with the remaining eggplant and meat sauce. Pour the custard sauce over the top and smooth. Sprinkle with the cheese and bake, uncovered, until the custard sets and the top browns, about 1 hour. Let the moussaka rest for 10 minutes before cutting.

braised lamb shanks with herbs 4 servings

4 lamb shanks (about 1½ pounds each)

2 teaspoons kosher salt, plus additional for seasoning

   Freshly ground black pepper

   All-purpose flour, for dredging

¼ cup extra-virgin olive oil

2 ribs celery, sliced

1 medium onion, sliced

2 medium carrots, peeled and sliced

8 cloves garlic, smashed

2 tablespoons chopped fresh thyme

2 tablespoons chopped fresh rosemary

1 cup red wine

   About 4 cups chicken broth, homemade (see page 278) or low-sodium canned

1 tablespoon water

1 tablespoon cornstarch

2 tablespoons minced fresh flat-leaf parsley

   Hot cooked polenta (optional)

1. Preheat the oven to 350°F. Season the shanks all over with some salt and pepper to taste. Put the flour in a pie plate and, 2 at a time, dredge the shanks. Heat the olive oil in a large Dutch oven until shimmering. Add the shanks and cook until they are a rich mahogany brown on all sides, about 15 minutes. Transfer the shanks to a plate.

2. Add the celery, onion, carrots, the 2 teaspoons salt, and some pepper to the Dutch oven. Cook until tender and starting to brown, about 20 minutes. Stir in the garlic, thyme, and rosemary and cook until fragrant, about 3 minutes more. Add the wine, increase the heat to high, and with a wooden spoon scrape up any of the browned bits that cling to the pan. Cook until the wine reduces enough to lightly coat the vegetables. Return the shanks to the pan along with enough broth to cover by about two-thirds. Simmer, then transfer the pot to the oven and cook, uncovered, turning the shanks every 30 minutes, until meat is fork-tender, about 2½ hours. Transfer shanks to a foil-lined pan and keep them in the oven while making the sauce.

3. Let the braising liquid stand about 10 minutes, then skim off the fat that comes to the surface. Strain the sauce into a bowl, pressing down on the solids to get as much liquid as possible, and skim again, if needed. Return the sauce to the pot and bring it to a boil over high heat. Whisk the water into the cornstarch until smooth, then whisk into the sauce until thickened, about 1 minute. Taste, and add salt and pepper if desired. Stir in the parsley. Put the shanks in the sauce and turn to coat. To serve, divide the shanks among 4 plates with cooked polenta, if desired, and spoon some of the sauce over; pass the remaining sauce.

masala-yogurt-marinated boneless leg of lamb 6 to 8 servings

5 cloves garlic

1 3-inch piece peeled fresh ginger

2 teaspoons ground turmeric

2 tablespoons water

3 tablespoons vegetable oil

1 3-inch cinnamon stick

1 bay leaf

1 tablespoon ground coriander, plus 2 teaspoons

1 tablespoon ground cumin, plus 1 teaspoon

1 tablespoon curry powder

1 teaspoon cayenne pepper

½ medium onion

1½ cups whole milk yogurt

Grated zest of 1 orange (about 2 tablespoons)

1 butterflied leg of lamb (5 to 6 pounds)

3 teaspoons kosher salt, plus additional for seasoning

Grilled naan or other Indian flat bread (optional)

1. Process the garlic, ginger, turmeric, and water to a paste in a small food processor. Heat the oil in a medium skillet over high heat. Add the cinnamon and bay leaf and stir-fry until the cinnamon unfurls, about 30 seconds. Add the garlic paste, coriander, cumin, curry powder, and cayenne and stir-fry until browned and almost dry, about 1 minute. Scrape the mixture into a large, shallow baking dish and cool slightly. Using the large holes of a box grater, grate the onion into the paste. Whisk in the yogurt and orange zest.

2. Pierce the lamb all over with a fork. Cut the lamb in half following a natural seam that runs across the center of the meat. Put the lamb in the marinade and turn to coat well. Cover with plastic wrap and refrigerate overnight, turning occasionally when possible.

3. About 45 minutes before cooking, take the lamb from the refrigerator. Position an oven rack 4 to 6 inches from the broiler and preheat. Line a broiler pan with aluminum foil. Put the lamb on the prepared broiler pan, smooth side down, and season with 1½ teaspoons of the salt. Broil until just charred, about 15 minutes. Turn the lamb, season with the remaining 1½ teaspoons salt, and broil until an instant-read thermometer inserted into the thickest part of the meat registers 130°F for medium-rare, 5 to 10 minutes more. Transfer the lamb to a cutting board, loosely cover with foil, and let it rest for 10 minutes before slicing. Slice the lamb across the grain, season the slices with salt to taste, and serve with grilled naan or other flat bread, if desired.

COOK'S NOTE Masala means "blend." There are many different kinds of masala, but the term refers to some combination of black pepper, cinnamon, cloves, coriander, cumin, caradamom, dried chiles, fennel, mace, and nutmeg.

kofta kebabs with tzatziki

4 to 6 servings

KEBABS

- 4   cloves garlic
- 1   tablespoon kosher salt, plus a pinch
- 1   pound ground beef chuck or lamb
- 3   tablespoons grated onion
- 3   tablespoons chopped fresh flat-leaf parsley
- 1   tablespoon ground coriander
- 1   teaspoon ground cumin
- 1/2   teaspoon ground cinnamon
- 1/2   teaspoon ground allspice
- 1/4   teaspoon cayenne pepper
- 1/4   teaspoon ground ginger
-     Freshly ground black pepper
-     Olive oil, for brushing the grill
-     Grilled flat bread

YOGURT SAUCE

Makes 1¼ cups

- 2   cups plain whole milk yogurt or 1 cup Middle Eastern-style plain yogurt
- 1   medium cucumber, peeled, halved, and seeded
- 2   teaspoons kosher salt, plus a pinch
- 1/2   clove garlic
- 1   tablespoon extra-virgin olive oil
- 1   teaspoon lemon juice
- 1/2   teaspoon dried mint, crumbled

1. Smash the garlic cloves, sprinkle with a generous pinch of salt, and, with the flat side of a large knife, mash and smear mixture to a coarse paste. Mix the paste and the remaining 1 tablespoon salt with the meat, onion, parsley, and spices.

2. Line a pan with aluminum foil. Divide the meat mixture into 28 rough balls. Mold each piece around the pointed end of a skewer (if you use wooden ones, soak them in water for 15 minutes before threading them), making a 2-inch oval kebab that comes to a point just covering the tip of the skewer. Lay the skewers on the pan, cover, and refrigerate for at least 30 minutes and up to 12 hours.

3. Heat a grill pan over medium heat or prepare a grill. Brush the pan lightly with olive oil. Working in batches, grill the kebabs, turning occasionally, until brown all over and just cooked through, about 6 minutes. Transfer to a serving platter and serve with tzatziki and flat bread.

TZATZIKI (GREEK YOGURT AND CUCUMBER SAUCE)

1. If you're using plain whole milk yogurt, line a small sieve with a coffee filter. Put the yogurt in it, set it over a bowl, and refrigerate 12 hours. Discard the expressed liquid and put yogurt in the bowl.

2. Grate the cucumber on the large holes of a box grater into another bowl. Sprinkle with the 2 teaspoons salt and rub into the cucumber with your hands. Set aside 20 minutes, then squeeze the cucumbers to express as much liquid as possible.

3. Smash the garlic, sprinkle with a generous pinch of salt, and, with the flat side of a large knife, mash and smear the mixture to a coarse paste. Stir the cucumber, garlic, olive oil, lemon juice, and mint into the yogurt. Refrigerate for at least 1 hour before serving.

Whether it's Indonesian satay, French brochette, or Turkish kebab, food on a stick is just plain fun. "Kofta" refers to kebabs made with ground rather than cubed meat.

veal scaloppini with greens & radicchio 2 servings

The perfect date food—romantic, just right for two, and simple to do. Dazzle with wit. Charm with your smile. Then seduce with your scaloppini.

5   slices white bread

3   cloves garlic, minced

2   tablespoons minced fresh flat-leaf parsley

2   teaspoons minced fresh rosemary

2   teaspoons minced fresh thyme

1   teaspoon finely grated lemon zest

    Kosher salt and freshly ground black pepper

2   large eggs, beaten

2   veal scaloppini, top-round center cuts preferred (about 8 ounces each)

1½ cups torn arugula

1½ cups torn frisee

1   cup torn radicchio

2   tablespoons unsalted butter

2   tablespoons extra-virgin olive oil

1   lemon, halved

    Small chunk Parmigiano-Reggiano or Pecorino Romano cheese (see page 271)

1. Pulse the bread into coarse crumbs in a food processor; then spread them on a microwave-safe plate and microwave on high for 1 minute. (Alternately, spread the crumbs on a baking sheet and dry in a 200°F oven for 10 minutes.) Toss the bread crumbs with the garlic, parsley, rosemary, thyme, lemon zest, and salt and pepper to taste.

2. Put the bread crumbs in one shallow dish and the eggs in another. Pat the veal dry and season both sides with salt and pepper. Dip each piece into the egg, shaking off excess, and then press both sides into the breading to coat. Place on a baking sheet, cover, and refrigerate for at least 20 minutes or up to 2 hours to set the breading.

3. Toss the arugula, frisee, and radicchio in a bowl. Heat a medium nonstick skillet over medium heat and add 1 tablespoon each of the butter and olive oil. When the butter stops foaming, add 1 scallopine and cook (press down lightly with a spatula to help keep it from curling), turning once, until golden brown, about 2½ minutes per side. Repeat. After the veal is cooked, add the greens to the skillet, season with salt and pepper, and toss just until they begin to wilt, about 30 seconds. Squeeze the lemon over the greens and toss again. Pile some greens on top of each scallopine and shave the cheese over the greens.

on the side

Nothing rounds
out a meal like
perfect sides.
They bring a
balance of color
and texture and
flavor to the
table like
nothing else can.

roasted pancetta-wrapped radicchio 4 servings

RADICCHIO

3 heads radicchio (about 5 ounces each)

3 tablespoons kosher salt

Extra-virgin olive oil

12 to 18 slices pancetta (about 6 ounces) (see Cook's Note, below)

VINAIGRETTE

1 tablespoon balsamic vinegar

1 tablespoon honey

1 teaspoon Dijon mustard

1 teaspoon chopped fresh thyme

1 teaspoon kosher salt

Freshly ground black pepper

1/4 cup extra-virgin olive oil

1. For the radicchio: Position a rack in the center of the oven and preheat to 450°F. Trim the base of each radicchio head, leaving the core intact, and remove any damaged or brown outer leaves. Quarter each head lengthwise through the core (if the heads are large, cut them into 6 wedges). Stir the salt into a bowl of cold water until dissolved, add the radicchio wedges, and weight them with a small plate to keep them submerged. Soak for 10 minutes; drain and pat dry with paper towels. (This tempers the radicchio's assertive bitterness.)

2. Lightly brush a roasting pan with olive oil. Drape a slice of pancetta over the peak of each radicchio wedge and secure it with a toothpick. Place the radicchio in the pan and roast without turning until the pancetta is crisp and the radicchio soft, about 25 minutes.

3. Meanwhile, for the vinaigrette: Whisk the vinegar, honey, mustard, thyme, salt, and pepper to taste in a bowl. Gradually whisk in the oil, starting with a few drops, then adding the rest in a steady stream to make a smooth, slightly thick vinaigrette.

4. Arrange the radicchio on a serving platter; remove the toothpicks. If serving immediately, drizzle some of the vinaigrette over and pass the remainder. The radicchio may also be served at room temperature; in that case, dress it just before serving.

A perfect accompaniment for antipasti or a roast, this tasty side takes radicchio off those salady sidelines and puts it in the spotlight. It's about time.

COOK'S NOTE Pancetta is an Italian-style bacon that is cured but not smoked. Recognizable by its rolled shape, it can be sliced or diced and often is the foundation for many Italian sauces or stews. When wrapped around vegetables, fish, or roasts, thin discs of pinwheel-patterned pancetta look as distinctive as they taste. Buy it thinly sliced or in a chunk and store it in the refrigerator for a week or in the freezer for up to 2 months.

The fresher, the better.

Fresh herbs are absolutely glorious. Tossed in a crisp salad or roasted with fresh vegetables, their distinctive perfumes and flavors can enhance any food. Basil, oregano, parsley, rosemary, and thyme—a simple windowsill herb garden can provide all the basics. If you don't have a green thumb, pick them from your supermarket's produce section.

sicilian sweet & sour butternut squash 6 servings

Thanksgiving dinner is all about the sides. This sweet-and-sour squash is as much at home on the table at turkey time as is our more traditional oyster dressing.

⅓ cup extra-virgin olive oil

10 cloves garlic, quartered lengthwise

1 large sprig fresh rosemary

1 butternut squash, unpeeled (about 2¼ pounds), washed

Kosher salt and freshly ground black pepper

8 ounces shiitake mushrooms, stemmed and halved

8 ounces red cherry, grape, or pear tomatoes

⅓ cup red wine vinegar

⅓ cup sugar

Pinch crushed red pepper flakes

1. Preheat the oven to 500°F. Heat the olive oil, garlic, and rosemary in a small saucepan over medium heat so it bubbles gently. Cook, stirring occasionally, until the garlic is tender, about 8 minutes. Set aside.

2. Halve the squash lengthwise and scoop out the seeds. Lay the halves cut side down and slice them ½ inch thick. On a large baking sheet brush the slices on both sides with 1 tablespoon of the flavored olive oil, spread them in a single layer, and season with salt and black pepper. Roast until tender but not mushy, about 20 minutes.

3. Toss the shiitake mushrooms with 1½ teaspoons of the flavored olive oil in a medium bowl, and spread them out on one side of a baking sheet. In the same bowl, toss the tomatoes with 1½ teaspoons of the flavored olive oil and spread them out on the other side of the pan; season both vegetables with salt and black pepper. Roast, removing the tomatoes when soft, after about 10 minutes, and the mushrooms when brown and slightly crisp, after another 10 minutes or so. When the vegetables are cool enough to handle, arrange the squash in a gratin or baking dish and strew the mushrooms and tomatoes over the top.

4. Using a slotted spoon, remove the garlic from the oil and scatter it over the roasted vegetables; lay the rosemary sprig on top. Add vinegar, sugar, and red pepper flakes to the oil; bring mixture to a boil, then simmer until slightly syrupy. Pour mixture over vegetables and marinate at room temperature for at least 2 hours. You may refrigerate the dish, covered, overnight, and bring it to room temperature before serving.

cornbread & oyster dressing
4 to 6 servings

OYSTERS

- 20 oysters, shucked, plus their liquor
- 3 cups coarsely crumbled cornbread (see recipe, below)
- 3 slices bacon, cut crosswise into ¼-inch strips
- 6 tablespoons unsalted butter
- 3 medium shallots, thinly sliced
- 2 ribs celery, with leaves, thinly sliced

   Kosher salt and freshly ground black pepper

- 2 tablespoons dry white vermouth
- 3 tablespoons chopped fresh flat-leaf parsley
- 1 tablespoon chopped fresh thyme

CORNBREAD

- 1 cup yellow cornmeal
- 2 tablespoons all-purpose flour
- 1½ teaspoons baking powder
- 1 teaspoon sugar
- ¼ teaspoon fine salt
- 1 large egg
- ½ cup whole milk
- 2 tablespoons unsalted butter, melted

SHOPSMART Try to find already-shucked oysters in their liquor (juice) in small plastic tubs at your grocery store or seafood market.

1. Put the oysters in a strainer over a medium bowl; reserve ¾ cup of the liquor. Toss the oysters with the crumbled cornbread in a large bowl.

2. Bring a small saucepan of water to a boil. Add the bacon and cook 1 minute; drain and pat dry.

3. Melt 5 tablespoons of the butter in a large skillet over medium-high heat. When the foam subsides, add the bacon, shallots, celery, and salt and pepper to taste (remember that the cornbread, the oysters, and their liquor will contribute a good amount of salt). Cook, stirring, until soft, about 10 minutes, and add the reserved oyster liquor, the vermouth, parsley, and thyme and bring to a boil. Toss the bacon mixture with the cornbread mixture, taste, and season as desired. Set aside for 10 minutes. Preheat the oven to 400°F.

4. Lightly butter a shallow 1-quart casserole dish. Add the dressing, mounding it slightly in the center if using an oval dish, and dot with the remaining 1 tablespoon butter. Bake until the top is brown and crusty, about 1 hour. Serve immediately.

CORNBREAD

1. Preheat the oven to 400°F. Butter a 5¾x 3¼x 2-inch loaf pan or 8-inch cast-iron skillet. Whisk the cornmeal, flour, baking powder, sugar, and salt in a medium bowl. In a liquid measuring cup whisk the egg with the milk. Briskly stir the milk mixture into the cornmeal mixture to make a thick batter. Fold in the melted butter until just incorporated.

2. Scrape the batter into the prepared pan and bake until lightly browned and a wooden toothpick inserted in the center comes out clean, about 20 minutes. Cool.

parsley

cilantro

We found this recipe at a location taping in Mexico where we not only had to shop for pottery and pans—but had to build our own stove out of bricks. It was one of our best shoots.

grilled corn with cotija cheese
& cilantro 4 servings

4   ears fresh-picked corn, yellow or white, with husks (each about 8 ounces)

1   tablespoon extra-virgin olive oil

    Kosher salt

1¼ cups crumbled Cotija cheese (see Cook's Note, below)

½   cup chopped fresh cilantro

¼   cup mayonnaise

    Chile powder for sprinkling, preferably ancho (see page 273)

2   limes, cut into wedges

1. Preheat an outdoor grill to medium-high. (If you can hold your hand over the fire for 3 seconds, it's medium-high.) Peel back the husks from the corn, leaving them attached at the ends and twisting to make handles. Strip the silk. Brush each cob with olive oil and season with salt. Arrange the cobs on the grill with the husks dangling over the side so they won't burn. Grill, turning occasionally, until lightly charred all over, about 20 minutes.

2. Spread the cheese on a medium plate and the cilantro on another. When the corn is done, slather the cobs with mayonnaise and then roll them first in the cheese and then in the cilantro. Sprinkle liberally with chile powder and serve with lime wedges and lots of napkins.

COOK'S NOTE Cotija is a pleasantly salty, crumbly, aged Mexican cheese similar to Pecorino Romano (which you can use if you can't find Cotija). It's available in Mexican and specialty food stores.

red, white & blue potato salad

4 to 6 servings

POTATOES

- 4 sprigs fresh thyme
- 3 sprigs fresh flat-leaf parsley
- 1 sprig fresh rosemary
- 1 bay leaf
- 1 cup dry white wine
- 2 cloves garlic, smashed
- 8 ounces small red-skinned waxy potatoes, scrubbed
- 8 ounces small white-skinned waxy potatoes, scrubbed
- 8 ounces small blue-skinned waxy potatoes, scrubbed
- 1 tablespoon kosher salt
- 2 ribs celery, thinly sliced
- 2 scallions (white and green parts), thinly sliced
- 2 tablespoons minced fresh flat-leaf parsley

DRESSING

- 1/4 cup white wine vinegar
- 1 tablespoon whole-grain mustard
- 2 teaspoons kosher salt
  Freshly ground black pepper
- 1/2 cup extra-virgin olive oil

1. For the potatoes: Tie the thyme, parsley, rosemary, and bay leaf together with a piece of kitchen twine and put the bundle in a medium saucepan with the wine and garlic. Slice the potatoes into 1/4-inch-thick rounds and add to the saucepan. Add cold water to cover by about an inch and add the salt. Bring to a boil over medium-high heat and simmer, uncovered, until the potatoes are tender but not mushy, about 5 minutes. Drain; discard the herb bundle.

2. While the potatoes cook, make the dressing: Whisk the vinegar, mustard, salt, and some pepper in a large bowl. Gradually whisk in the oil, starting with a few drops and then adding the rest in a steady stream, to make a smooth, slightly thick dressing.

3. Using a rubber spatula, gently fold the warm potatoes into the dressing, taking care not to break them up. Add the celery and set aside to cool. Just before serving, carefully fold in the scallions and parsley.

KNOW-HOW Smooth-skinned waxy potatoes hold their shape when cooked, making them the spud of choice for salads, crispy pan-fries, or roasting. If you want to show off a potato's colorful skin—a healthier and most stylish choice—cut them before cooking, since the skins slip off if cooked whole and then cut.

oven-baked ratatouille

6 servings

½ cup extra-virgin olive oil

2 medium onions, cut into wedges

6 cloves garlic, smashed

1 tablespoon herbes de Provence
(see Cook's Note, below)

1 bay leaf

2 zucchini (about 10 ounces each),
cut into wedges about 1x3 inches

1 small eggplant (about 1 pound),
unpeeled, cut into wedges about
1x3 inches

1 red bell pepper, seeded and cut into
1-inch-wide strips

1 yellow bell pepper, seeded and cut
into 1-inch-wide strips

10 canned whole peeled tomatoes

1 tablespoon kosher salt

Freshly ground black pepper

1 tablespoon chopped fresh basil

1 tablespoon chopped fresh flat-leaf
parsley

1. Preheat the oven to 400°F. Heat the oil in an ovenproof Dutch oven over medium heat. Add the onions, garlic, herbes de Provence, and bay leaf, cover, and cook, stirring occasionally, until the onions are soft, about 10 minutes.

2. Stir in the zucchini, eggplant, bell peppers, tomatoes, salt, and pepper to taste, breaking the tomatoes into rough chunks with a spoon. Once the vegetables sizzle, put the ratatouille in the oven and bake, stirring occasionally, until the vegetables are tender and browning, up to 1½ hours. (If you prefer your vegetables al dente, you can cut the baking time by as much as half.) Remove from the oven and stir in basil and parsley. Transfer to a bowl and serve warm or at room temperature.

COOK'S NOTE Herbes de Provence is a dried herb blend used in Provençal cooking. It includes dried thyme, savory, fennel, bay leaf, and sometimes lavender.

Imagine. A ratatouille that practically cooks itself. Chop up the best of all those late-summer vegetables; add them to the tomatoes and herbs, and into the oven it goes. One-two-three ratatouille.

taiwanese spicy & sour cucumbers 2 to 4 servings

1 tablespoon dark sesame oil

4 small Thai bird chiles, halved, seeded, and thinly sliced (see page 273)

1 clove garlic, minced

1 tablespoon sugar

3 Kirby cucumbers (about 12 ounces), quartered lengthwise and cut into 1-inch pieces

2 tablespoons rice vinegar

1 teaspoon kosher salt

1. Heat the oil in a small skillet over medium-high heat, add the chiles and garlic, and stir-fry until fragrant, about 30 seconds. Put the chile mixture in a bowl, stir in the sugar, and cool.

2. Add the cucumbers, vinegar, and salt to the chile mixture and mix well. Serve with Chinese Peppered Pork Chops (see page 172) or Shanghai Potato Cakes with Pork (see page 178), if desired, or refrigerate in a tightly sealed container for up to 3 days.

These two flavorful Asian relishes go with so many things. From the oven to the grill, from pork to poultry to a simple bowl of rice, they spice up any meal.

spicy carrot sambal
2 to 4 servings

2 tablespoons vegetable oil

6 whole cloves garlic, peeled

1 jalapeño, minced with seeds

2 tablespoons sugar

1 tablespoon freshly squeezed lime juice

2 teaspoons fish sauce (see page 274)

8 ounces carrots, peeled and grated

1 scallion (white and green parts), thinly sliced

3 tablespoons chopped fresh cilantro

Put the oil, garlic, and jalapeño in a small skillet over medium heat and cook, stirring, until the garlic is lightly browned and fragrant, about 5 minutes. Put the sugar in a bowl and stir in the garlic mixture; cool. Add the lime juice and fish sauce and stir to dissolve the sugar completely. Add the carrots, scallion, and cilantro and toss. Serve with Thai Green Curry Game Hens (see page 155) if desired, or refrigerate in a tightly sealed container for up to 3 days.

drunken beans

6 servings

- 1 pound dried pinto beans, washed and picked over
- 1 large smoked ham hock (about 1 pound)
- 6 cups water
- 1 12-ounce bottle Mexican lager beer
- 1 onion, peeled and halved through the root end
- 1 small head garlic, unpeeled and halved horizontally
- 3 tablespoons unsalted butter
- 1 pound ripe tomatoes, diced
- 1 to 2 jalapeños, sliced into rounds, with seeds
- 2 teaspoons ground coriander
- 2 teaspoons ground cumin
- 1 teaspoon kosher salt, plus additional for seasoning
- Pinch ground cloves
- Freshly ground black pepper
- 3/4 cup chopped fresh cilantro leaves and stems

1. Put the beans in a pot with cold water to cover by a few inches, bring to a boil, and cook for 5 minutes. Remove from the heat, cover, and set aside for 1 hour. Drain. While the beans are soaking, put the ham hock in a saucepan with water to cover and bring to a boil. Drain.

2. Put the beans back into a large pot with the ham hock, 6 cups water, the beer, half of the onion, and the garlic. Bring to a boil, then reduce to a simmer and cook, uncovered, until the beans are almost tender, about 1 hour.

3. Chop the remaining onion half. Melt the butter in a large skillet over medium-high heat. Add the chopped onion, tomatoes, jalapeño, coriander, cumin, the 1 teaspoon salt, cloves, and black pepper to taste and cook, uncovered, stirring occasionally, until slightly thickened, about 8 minutes. Stir in the cilantro. Pour the tomato mixture into the beans and simmer, uncovered, until the beans are tender and the mixture gets thick but is still soupy, about 30 minutes. Discard the garlic and onion halves. Tear or cut meat from the hock and stir it back into the beans—discard the gristle and fat. Taste and season with salt and pepper, if desired. Serve hot.

KNOW-HOW We love the depth of flavor a ham hock adds to a pot of beans, but sometimes its salt cure and heavy smoke can strong-arm other flavors in the mix. By purging the hock—boiling it and discarding the water—you get the best of its rich, deep character without its harsh edge.

summer succotash

4 to 6 servings

4   tablespoons unsalted butter

1   small onion, chopped

3   cloves garlic, minced

¼   jalapeño, stemmed, seeded, and minced

4   teaspoons kosher salt

    Freshly ground black pepper

2   heaping cups fresh corn kernels (from about 4 ears)

1   to 2 teaspoons sugar, depending on the sweetness of the corn (optional)

2   cups cooked lima beans or one 10-ounce package frozen Fordhook lima beans, thawed

1   tablespoon chopped fresh oregano

1   cup grape or cherry tomatoes, quartered

2   tablespoons chopped fresh flat-leaf parsley

1. Melt 2 tablespoons of the butter in a saucepan over medium heat. Add the onion, garlic, jalapeño, 2 teaspoons of the salt, and some pepper; cover and cook, stirring occasionally, until the onion is soft, about 5 minutes. Stir in the corn, sugar, if desired, and the remaining 2 teaspoons salt; cover and cook, stirring occasionally, until soft, about 10 minutes. (If the mixture seems dry, add a splash of water.)

2. Raise the heat to medium-high, add the lima beans and oregano, and cook, stirring occasionally, for 3 minutes. Stir in the remaining 2 tablespoons butter, the tomatoes, the parsley, and a generous grind of pepper and serve.

COOK'S NOTE Fordhook lima beans are bigger and fatter than baby lima beans, as well as a different type—they're not simply grown-up beans. Fresh lima beans can be found at farmers' markets; if you're lucky enough to get your hands on some, shell and boil them in salted water for 10 to 20 minutes until tender.

For protein and flavor, you just can't beat great recipes for beans. Here you have a summer succotash of fresh corn and lima beans and a mix of dried pintos and Mexican spices perfect for the Sunday game on a wintery afternoon.

cauliflower with brown butter & crispy crumbs
4 servings

1 medium head cauliflower (about 2 pounds), cut into bite-size florets

2 cloves garlic, roughly chopped

6 tablespoons unsalted butter

1¼ teaspoons kosher salt

⅓ cup fresh bread crumbs (see Know-How, below)

3 tablespoons minced fresh flat-leaf parsley

Freshly ground black pepper

Lemon wedges

1. Preheat the oven to 450°F. Put the cauliflower on a baking sheet and scatter the garlic on top. Melt the butter in a medium skillet and toss 2 tablespoons with the cauliflower and garlic; set the rest aside in the skillet. Toss the cauliflower with 1 teaspoon of the salt. Roast until the cauliflower is quite tender and the edges are starting to brown, 20 to 25 minutes. Transfer the cauliflower to a serving bowl.

2. Reheat the remaining butter over medium-high heat until brown. Add the bread crumbs and cook, swirling the pan and tossing, until they are brown and crisp—this should take less than 1 minute. Pull the pan from the heat and toss the crumbs with the parsley and the remaining ¼ teaspoon salt. Spoon crumbs over the cauliflower and season with pepper. Serve warm or room temperature with lemon wedges on the side.

KNOW-HOW Sometimes it's the little things that can make the difference in a dish being spectacular or so-so—like using homemade bread crumbs versus store-bought. Crumbs made from quality bread are easy to make. Simply tear up bread, with or without the crusts, and grind it in a food processor—one 2-ounce slice makes about ½ cup of crumbs. If you want moist crumbs—as you do for this crispy topping—start with fresh, not stale, bread. Stale dry bread is better for crumbs used in stuffings or as a binder because the crumbs absorb more liquid.

We're inspired by the magical touch Italians have with vegetables. Keep it simple, and their flavors will sing out like a fine tenor.

scalloped potatoes with
gruyère 4 to 6 servings

Our scalloped potatoes set a new standard for an old tradition while our corn custard serves up an old favorite with a Southern twist. They are both so creamy and comforting, it's hard to choose one. So don't. Make both.

1 large clove garlic, smashed

2 tablespoons unsalted butter

2¼ pounds Yellow Finn or other waxy potatoes (about 6), peeled

2 cups half-and-half

2 teaspoons chopped fresh thyme

2½ teaspoons kosher salt

Freshly ground black pepper

Pinch freshly grated nutmeg

1 cup grated Gruyère cheese (about 2 ounces)

1. Preheat the oven to 350°F. Rub the garlic all over the inside of an 8x8x2-inch casserole dish. Mince what is left of the garlic clove. Smear some of the butter all over the inside of the dish.

2. Using a mandoline or vegetable slicer, slice the potatoes about ⅛ inch thick and put them in a large saucepan with the minced garlic, remaining butter, the half-and-half, thyme, salt, pepper to taste, and nutmeg. Bring to a boil over medium-high heat and cook, stirring, until the mixture has thickened slightly, 1 to 2 minutes. Transfer the mixture to the prepared baking dish and shake the pan to distribute the potatoes evenly. Bake, uncovered, occasionally spooning some of the liquid over the top, until the potatoes are fork-tender, about 50 minutes. Sprinkle the cheese over the top and bake until brown and bubbly, about 15 minutes more. Remove from the oven and let casserole cool 10 minutes before serving.

KNOW-HOW Boiling the potatoes in the cooking liquid before layering them in the baking dish is the key to superior scalloped potatoes. As the half-and-half heats, it draws the starch from potatoes and turns into a satiny sauce. To lighten up this classic, use the same technique with chicken broth.

corn custard with roasted poblano chiles 6 servings

CUSTARD

6   large ears fresh corn, shucked

3   cups half-and-half

5   teaspoons sugar

4   teaspoons kosher salt

    Generous pinch anise seeds, cracked

    Pinch ground nutmeg

3   tablespoons unsalted butter

$1/2$ medium onion, chopped

3   cloves garlic, minced

$1/8$ teaspoon cayenne pepper

    Freshly ground black pepper

    Cornmeal, for dusting the dish

4   large eggs

CHILES

3   poblano chiles, roasted, peeled, and diced (see page 273)

3   tablespoons roughly chopped fresh cilantro

1   tablespoon freshly squeezed lime juice

1   teaspoon kosher salt

1. For the corn custard: Preheat the oven to 325°F. Shear off the corn kernels with a sharp knife over a bowl—you should have about 5 cups of kernels. Working over the bowl, run a knife along the cobs to press out as much of the milky liquid as possible; set aside. Halve 4 of the cobs and put them in a medium saucepan with the half-and-half, 4 teaspoons of the sugar, 2 teaspoons of the salt, the anise seeds, and nutmeg. Bring the mixture to a boil over medium heat. Pull the saucepan from the heat, cover, and set aside.

2. Melt the butter in a medium saucepan over medium heat and add the onion, garlic, the remaining 2 teaspoons salt, and the cayenne pepper. Cover and cook, stirring occasionally, until the onions are soft, about 6 minutes. Add the corn, the remaining 1 teaspoon sugar, and black pepper to taste, cover, and cook, stirring occasionally, until the corn is soft, about 20 minutes. Lightly puree the mixture with a handheld immersion blender (or in a standard blender)—the mixture should be nubbly, not smooth.

3. Butter an 8-cup oval gratin dish and dust with cornmeal. Whisk the eggs in a large bowl, remove the cobs from the half-and-half mixture, then gradually whisk half-and-half mixture into eggs. Stir in the corn mixture and transfer the mixture to the prepared gratin dish. Set the gratin dish in a large, shallow roasting pan and place in the oven. Pour enough hot tap water into the roasting pan to come halfway up the sides of the gratin dish. Bake until the custard is just set around the edges but jiggles slightly in the center when you tap the pan, about 40 minutes. Carefully remove from the oven and cool slightly in the water bath. Serve with Poblano Chiles scattered on top.

POBLANO CHILES

Toss roasted poblano chiles with the cilantro, freshly squeezed lime juice, and salt.

bread basket

Here's a basketful of fresh-from-the-oven breads for breakfast, lunch, and dinner.

sour cream-pecan coffee cake

one 8-inch cake (8 servings)

This is the primal coffeecake. A moment after this shot was taken, all we were left with were a couple of crumbs.

CRUMBS

½ cup granulated sugar

6 tablespoons packed dark brown sugar

1 cup pecans, toasted and chopped

2 tablespoons all-purpose flour

1 tablespoon pure vanilla extract

1 teaspoon ground cinnamon

2 tablespoons unsalted butter, melted

CAKE

2 cups all-purpose flour

1 teaspoon baking soda

1 teaspoon ground cinnamon

½ teaspoon fine salt

Generous pinch freshly grated nutmeg

1 cup sour cream

1½ teaspoons pure vanilla extract

8 tablespoons unsalted butter, softened (1 stick)

1 cup granulated sugar

2 large eggs, at room temperature

1. Preheat the oven to 350°F. Line the bottom of an 8-inch square cake pan with parchment paper; butter the paper and the sides of the pan. For the crumbs: Combine the granulated and brown sugars, the pecans, flour, vanilla, and cinnamon in a small bowl. Add the butter and stir to make moist, coarse crumbs. Set aside.

2. For the cake: Sift the flour, baking soda, cinnamon, salt, and nutmeg into a medium bowl. Mix the sour cream with the vanilla in a small bowl. Beat the butter and sugar in a large bowl with an electric mixer on medium speed until light and fluffy, about 5 minutes. Add the eggs 1 at a time, beating well after each addition. Add the flour mixture in 3 parts, alternating with the sour cream mixture in 2 parts, beginning and ending with the flour.

3. Spread ²/₃ of the batter in the prepared pan and sprinkle half the crumbs over the top. Spoon the remaining batter in mounds on top, then spread it out evenly. Sprinkle the rest of the crumbs over the cake and bake until the top is brown and a toothpick inserted in the center comes out clean, about 1 hour and 10 minutes. Cool the cake in the pan on a rack for 20 minutes, then turn it out of the pan, invert, and cool.

KNOW-HOW A familiar route to light-as-a-feather cakes is to carefully alternate the wet and dry ingredients into the batter's base. This gradual incorporation prevents overmixing the flour. Keeping a light touch when adding flour—be it a cake, muffin, or quick bread—always pays off with a tender crumb.

double-chocolate zucchini bread 2 loaves (about 16 servings)

Sneaking shredded zucchini into a chocolatey bread is a great way to get kids to eat their vegetables. Makes it super-moist, too.

2½ cups all-purpose flour

¼ cup unsweetened natural cocoa (not Dutch-process) (see page 276)

1 teaspoon baking soda

½ teaspoon ground cinnamon

Pinch ground cloves

1 cup unsalted butter, softened (2 sticks)

1½ cups sugar

¼ cup vegetable oil

2 large eggs, at room temperature

1 teaspoon pure vanilla extract

½ cup buttermilk, at room temperature

2 cups shredded unpeeled zucchini (about 8 ounces)

4 ounces bittersweet chocolate, finely chopped

1. Position a rack in the center of the oven and preheat to 350°F. Butter and flour two 9x5x3-inch loaf pans. Whisk the flour with the cocoa, baking soda, cinnamon, and cloves in a medium bowl.

2. Beat the butter and sugar in a medium bowl with an electric mixer on medium-high speed until light and fluffy, about 4 minutes. While mixing, drizzle in the oil and beat until incorporated. Beat in the eggs, one at a time, beating well after each addition.

3. Add the vanilla to the buttermilk. Slowly mix the flour mixture into the beaten butter mixture in 3 additions, alternating with the buttermilk in 2 parts, beginning and ending with the flour. (Scrape the sides of the bowl between additions, if needed.) Fold the zucchini and chocolate into the batter. Divide batter between prepared pans and bake until a toothpick inserted in the center comes out clean, about 55 minutes. Cool in pans on a rack before unmolding and slicing.

STYLE This quick bread can do more than double-duty rounding out a variety of occasions. Serve it toasted for breakfast, wrapped up in a lunch box, alongside a pot of afternoon tea, or with a dollop of ice cream for dessert.

carrot-bran muffins
12 muffins

1 cup whole wheat flour

¾ cup all-purpose flour

¾ cup wheat bran

1½ teaspoons baking soda

1 teaspoon ground cinnamon

¼ teaspoon fine salt

½ cup crushed canned pineapple
(with its juice)

½ cup honey

⅓ cup walnut oil

2 large eggs, lightly beaten

2 cups peeled and grated carrots
(about 2 medium)

¾ cup golden raisins

⅔ cup chopped walnuts

1 heaping tablespoon unsalted
sunflower seeds

1. Position a rack in the center of the oven and preheat to 375°F. Line twelve ½-cup muffin cups with paper liners. Whisk whole wheat and all-purpose flours with the wheat bran, baking soda, cinnamon, and salt in a medium bowl.

2. Stir the pineapple, honey, oil, and eggs into the carrots in a medium bowl. Stir the carrot mixture into the flour mixture just until evenly moist; the batter will be very thick. Fold in the raisins and walnuts. Divide the batter evenly among the muffin cups and sprinkle the sunflower seeds over the tops. Bake until firm when pressed gently, about 20 minutes. Turn the muffins out of the cups and cool on a rack; serve warm.

COOK'S NOTE Nut oils such as walnut, hazelnut, and almond add moistness and a lovely flavor to quick breads. Once opened, store nut oils in the refrigerator to preserve their peak flavor.

blackberry-corn muffins
12 muffins

1½ cups all-purpose flour

1½ cups yellow cornmeal

½ cup sugar, plus additional for sprinkling

1 tablespoon baking powder

½ teaspoon fine salt

1 whole large egg

1 large egg yolk

1¼ cups buttermilk

8 tablespoons unsalted butter, melted (1 stick)

1 teaspoon pure vanilla extract

½ to 1 cup blackberries

1. Preheat the oven to 375°F. Line twelve ½-cup muffin cups with paper liners. Whisk the flour with the cornmeal, sugar, baking powder, and salt in a medium bowl. In another medium bowl lightly whisk the egg and yolk, then whisk in the buttermilk, butter, and vanilla.

2. Quickly fold the buttermilk mixture into the flour mixture with a rubber spatula. Just before the batter comes together, fold in the blackberries. The batter will be slightly lumpy, and that's fine—don't beat it too much or the muffins will be tough. Divide the batter evenly among the muffin cups and sprinkle the tops with sugar. Bake until golden and a wooden toothpick inserted in the centers comes out clean, about 20 minutes. Turn muffins out of the cups and cool on a rack; serve warm.

COOK'S NOTE Muffins invite you to be creative. Change the fruit, add an herb, a chile, or a cheese, and— presto—you've got a muffin with your name on it.

One of the great treats of summer is a visit to a pick-your-own berry patch. There are no better berries than those still warm from the sun when you get them home.

Dive into a sea of biscuits.

So round, so lovely, so flaky and tender. Sweet or savory, split and filled, or simply buttered. The possibilities are endless.

KNOW-HOW Making fabulous biscuits has much to do with how you work the butter into the flour mixture. First, the butter must be very cold. The first bit is worked in thoroughly to help hold the dough together and make the biscuit tender throughout. The second bit is left in pea-size pieces so that when the biscuits bake, the small chunks of butter form flaky layers. As with any quick bread, the less you have to work the dough, the more tender the end result will be.

Biscuits are so easy to whip up, you can have them on the table every day of the week.

cornmeal-buttermilk biscuits
8 biscuits

1⅓ cups all-purpose flour

⅔ cup yellow cornmeal

2½ teaspoons baking powder

1 heaping teaspoon sugar

1 teaspoon fine salt

¼ teaspoon baking soda

6 tablespoons cold unsalted butter, sliced into tablespoon-size pieces

¾ cup buttermilk

1. Position a rack in the center of the oven and preheat to 450°F. Line a baking sheet with parchment paper.

2. Whisk flour, cornmeal, baking powder, sugar, salt, and baking soda in a medium bowl. Rub in 2 tablespoons of the butter with your fingertips until no visible pieces remain. Rub in the remaining 4 tablespoons butter just until it is in even, pea-size pieces. Very gently stir in buttermilk to make a shaggy, loose dough.

3. Turn dough onto a lightly floured work surface and pat into a rectangle about 1/2 inch thick (don't worry if dough doesn't all come together). Fold dough in thirds, like a business letter, and pat lightly into an 8x5-inch rectangle—about 3/4 inch thick. Using a 2- to 3-inch round biscuit cutter, cut 6 biscuits and place on baking sheet. Press dough scraps together and cut 2 more biscuits. Bake until tops are lightly browned, about 15 minutes. Cool slightly on a rack; serve warm.

parmesan, pepper & lemon biscuits 8 biscuits

2 cups all-purpose flour

1 tablespoon sugar

1 tablespoon baking powder

1 tablespoon finely grated lemon zest

1 teaspoon cracked black pepper

½ teaspoon fine salt

6 tablespoons cold unsalted butter

½ cup diced plus ¼ cup finely grated Parmigiano-Reggiano cheese

¾ cup milk

1. Position a rack in the center of the oven and preheat to 450°F. Line a baking sheet with parchment paper.

2. Whisk the flour with the sugar, baking powder, lemon zest, pepper, and salt in a large bowl. Cut butter into tablespoon-size pieces. Work the butter in as directed for Cornmeal-Buttermilk Biscuits (see recipe, above). Scatter grated and diced cheese over the top and toss with a rubber spatula. Using a wooden spoon, stir the milk in to make a loose dough. Fold, cut, and bake as for Cornmeal-Buttermilk Biscuits.

sweet potato biscuits
8 biscuits

1½ cups all-purpose flour, plus additional for dusting

1 tablespoon baking powder

1 tablespoon light brown sugar

½ teaspoon fine salt

¼ teaspoon ground cinnamon

⅛ teaspoon ground allspice

5 tablespoons cold unsalted butter, sliced

¾ cup mashed whole canned sweet potatoes

½ cup milk

1. Position a rack in the center of the oven and preheat to 425°F. Line a baking sheet with a double layer of parchment paper.

2. Whisk the 1½ cups flour, baking powder, brown sugar, salt, cinnamon, and allspice in a medium bowl. Work the butter in as directed for Cornmeal-Buttermilk Biscuits (see recipe, page 216). Combine the sweet potatoes and milk and stir into the flour mixture to make a moist dough.

3. Fold and cut the dough as directed for Cornmeal-Buttermilk Biscuits. Bake until lightly browned, about 12 minutes. Cool briefly before serving.

cream scones with blueberries
8 scones

1¾ cups all-purpose flour

3 tablespoons sugar, plus additional for sprinkling

2½ teaspoons baking powder

½ teaspoon fine salt

6 tablespoons cold unsalted butter, cut into ½-inch cubes

¼ cup dried blueberries

2 teaspoons finely grated orange zest

1 large egg

¼ cup heavy cream, plus additional for brushing

1. Preheat the oven to 425°F. Line a baking sheet with parchment paper. Whisk flour with the 3 tablespoons sugar, baking powder, and salt in a medium bowl. Toss the butter with the flour mixture to coat and, using your fingers, rub in the butter until the mixture resembles coarse meal. Add the blueberries and orange zest and toss.

2. Beat the egg with the ¼ cup cream and stir into flour mixture to make a shaggy, loose dough. Turn dough onto a lightly floured surface and pat into a 6-inch round. Cut into 8 wedges and put on the baking sheet, leaving a few inches between each. Brush tops with heavy cream and sprinkle with sugar. Bake until golden brown, 12 to 15 minutes. Serve warm.

butternut squash, apple & onion galette with stilton 6 servings

DOUGH

1¼ cups all-purpose flour

Pinch salt

8 tablespoons cold unsalted butter, diced (1 stick)

1 large egg, lightly beaten

FILLING

1 large baking apple, such as Rome Beauty or Cortland

1 small or ½ medium butternut squash (about ¾ pound), halved, seeded, and skin on

1 small yellow onion, peeled, root end trimmed but intact

3 tablespoons unsalted butter, melted

2 teaspoons chopped fresh rosemary

2 teaspoons chopped fresh thyme

Kosher salt and freshly ground black pepper

2 tablespoons whole-grain mustard

⅓ cup crumbled Stilton or other blue cheese (about 1½ ounces)

KNOW-HOW Don't be afraid to cook this galette—or any of your pies or tarts, for that matter—until the crust is a rich golden brown. A pastry's buttery taste and flaky crispness really come through when it is fully cooked.

1. For the dough: Pulse the flour and salt together in a food processor. Add the butter and pulse about 10 times until the mixture resembles coarse cornmeal with a few bean-size bits of butter in it. Add the egg and pulse 1 to 2 times more; don't let the dough form a mass around the blade. If the dough seems very dry, add up to 1 tablespoon of cold water, 1 teaspoon at a time, pulsing briefly. Remove the blade and bring the dough together by hand. Shape the dough into a disk, wrap it in plastic wrap, and refrigerate at least 1 hour.

2. For the filling: Halve and core the apple. Cut each half into 8 wedges and put them in a large bowl. Slice the squash and cut the onion into wedges so that both are as thick as the apple wedges and add them to the apples. Add the butter, rosemary, and thyme and toss gently to combine. Season with salt and pepper and toss again.

3. Preheat the oven to 400°F. Roll the dough on a lightly floured surface into a 12-inch disk. Transfer the dough to a baking sheet and brush with mustard. Starting 2 inches from the edge, casually alternate pieces of apple, squash, and onion in overlapping circles—if you have extra pieces of one or another, tuck them in where you can or double them up to use all the filling. Fold and pleat the dough over the edge of the filling. Bake until the crust is brown and the apple, squash, and onion are tender and caramelized, about 55 minutes. Scatter the cheese over the filling and bake until melted, about 5 minutes more. Cool the galette briefly on a wire rack. Cut into wedges and serve.

1. Turn dough onto a clean, unfloured surface and press into a rectangle. Cut dough into 36 pieces. 2. Shape each piece into a ball. 3. Arrange half the balls into 2 layers in pan and sprinkle remaining sugar-bacon mixture over. Arrange remaining balls of dough on top, setting as many as possible in the hollows in the first layer.

maple & bacon **monkey** bread

I large loaf (10 to 12 servings)

6 tablespoons unsalted butter

2 cups milk

¼ cup granulated sugar

1 package active dry yeast
(¼ ounce)

2 large egg yolks, beaten

Vegetable oil

5½ cups all-purpose flour, plus
additional for kneading

1 tablespoon fine salt

12 slices bacon or 10 ounces slab
bacon, diced

1 cup maple sugar (see page 276)

KNOW-HOW Scattering
the yeast over the surface of the
liquid and setting it aside until
bubbly is called proofing the
yeast. It confirms the yeast is
active and can leaven the bread.
If it doesn't foam, check the date
on your package of yeast; it may
have expired.

1. Melt 4 tablespoons of the butter in a medium saucepan over medium-low heat. Add milk and granulated sugar and heat, stirring, until lukewarm (about 110°F). Sprinkle yeast over surface; set aside until foamy, about 10 minutes. Whisk egg yolks into the yeast mixture.

2. Lightly oil a large bowl. Whisk flour and salt in another large bowl. Stir yeast mixture into flour mixture to make a soft dough. Turn dough onto a floured work surface and knead until soft and elastic, about 8 minutes. Shape dough into a ball and put in the oiled bowl. Cover bowl with a clean kitchen towel and let rise at room temperature until doubled in size, about 2 hours.

3. While dough rises, cook bacon in a large skillet over medium-high heat until barely crisp. Drain on paper towels; toss with maple sugar. Butter a 12-cup Bundt pan and sprinkle a bit less than half the sugar-bacon mixture in bottom.

4. Turn dough onto a clean, unfloured surface and press into a rectangle. Cut the dough into 36 equal pieces and shape each piece into a ball. Arrange half the balls of dough in 2 layers in the Bundt pan and sprinkle remaining sugar-bacon mixture over them. Arrange remaining balls of dough on top, setting as many as possible in the hollows of the first layer.

5. Cover with a kitchen towel. Set aside at room temperature until doubled, about 2 hours; or cover with plastic wrap and refrigerate overnight. (If refrigerated, bring to room temperature 1 hour before baking.)

6. Position a rack in the center of the oven and preheat to 400°F. Melt the remaining 2 tablespoons butter and pour over the bread. Bake 15 minutes, tent with aluminum foil, and continue baking until golden brown and an instant-read thermometer inserted in the dough registers 190°F, about 25 minutes. Cool in the pan on a wire rack for 10 minutes; unmold and cool on the rack for 1 hour before serving.

mory's **honey** challah
one 2-pound loaf (24 servings)

1 cup warm water, about 110°F

1 teaspoon sugar

2 teaspoons active dry yeast

4 cups all-purpose flour, plus about
1 cup for kneading

⅓ cup honey

2 whole large eggs

3 large egg yolks

3 tablespoons extra-virgin olive oil

1 tablespoon kosher salt

1 tablespoon poppy seeds

KNOW-HOW Worried about how to tell when this bread is baked? Insert an instant-read thermometer into the middle of the loaf after about 35 minutes in the oven. When it registers 190°F, it's ready to come out.

1. Combine water and sugar in a small bowl. Sprinkle the yeast over the top. Set aside until foamy, about 8 minutes.

2. Put 1 cup of the flour in a large bowl and make a well in the center. Whisk honey with 1 of the whole eggs, the yolks, olive oil, and salt in a small bowl and pour into the well. Stir to combine. Add yeast mixture and remaining 3 cups flour and stir to make a soft, shaggy dough. Knead dough on a lightly floured surface until soft and supple, about 10 minutes.

3. Shape dough into a ball and place in lightly oiled large bowl. Cover with a clean kitchen towel and let rise until doubled in size, about 1 hour. Turn dough onto a lightly floured surface; knead for just a minute, shape into a ball and return to bowl. Cover and let rise again until doubled in size, about 1 hour.

4. Line a baking sheet with parchment paper. Form loaf according to instructions, below. Cover with a clean, dry kitchen towel and set aside to rise until doubled, about 1 hour.

5. Place a rack in the center of the oven and preheat to 375°F. Beat remaining egg. Brush loaf with egg and sprinkle with poppy seeds. Bake until golden brown, about 35 minutes.

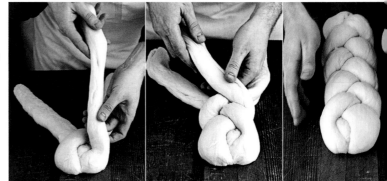

1. Turn dough onto a clean work surface and divide into 3 equal pieces. Roll and stretch each piece into a rope 12 to 15 inches long. Arrange ropes side by side on the work surface.
2. Starting at the far end, braid the ropes. 3. When the braid is finished, tuck both ends under and pinch to seal. Place loaf on prepared baking sheet.

dinner **rolls**

12 rolls

Everything tastes better when there's a basket of warm homemade dinner rolls on the table.

7 tablespoons unsalted butter

2 cups milk, plus 2 tablespoons

3 tablespoons sugar

1 package active dry yeast (¼ ounce)

5 cups unbleached all-purpose flour, plus additional for kneading

1 tablespoon fine salt

Vegetable oil

COOK'S NOTE If you're a novice bread baker, use a thermometer to judge the temperature of the milk in Step 1. If it's too hot, it kills the yeast.

1. Melt 3 tablespoons of the butter in a small saucepan over medium-low heat. Add the milk and sugar and heat, stirring, until lukewarm (about 110°F). Sprinkle the yeast over the surface and set aside until foamy, about 10 minutes.

2. Whisk the flour and salt in a large bowl. Stir the yeast mixture into the flour mixture to make a soft, shaggy dough. Turn the dough onto a floured work surface and knead until it is soft and elastic, about 10 minutes. Lightly oil a large bowl. Shape the dough into a ball and place it in the bowl. Cover with a clean kitchen towel and let rise at room temperature until doubled in size, about 2 hours. (At this point you can also cover the bowl with plastic wrap and refrigerate it overnight. Bring it to room temperature before proceeding.)

3. Butter a 13x9x2-inch baking dish. Turn the dough out of the bowl and gently deflate it. Divide the dough into 12 equal pieces and roll each piece into a ball. Arrange the balls seam side down, in 3 rows of 4, across the length of the prepared baking dish. Cover the dish with a clean kitchen towel and set aside at room temperature until the rolls rise almost to the rim of the baking dish, 2 to 2½ hours.

4. Position a rack in the center of the oven and preheat to 400°F. Melt the remaining 4 tablespoons butter and brush it liberally over the rolls. Bake until golden brown, about 25 minutes. Cool the rolls in the pan briefly before transferring them to a rack to cool completely.

rosemary & sea salt focaccia

one 11x17x1-inch focaccia (8 to 10 servings)

1¾ cups warm water (about 110°F)

4½ cups bread flour, plus additional for kneading

1 package active dry yeast (¼ ounce)

2 teaspoons fine salt

½ cup extra-virgin olive oil

2 tablespoons coarsely chopped fresh rosemary

½ teaspoon coarse sea salt

KNOW-HOW Experienced bread bakers know that the slower a bread rises, the better its taste and texture. (That's why this bread rises twice before forming.) Set breads aside in a warm-but-not-too-hot spot to let them proof gently.

1. Put the water in a medium bowl; whisk in 2 tablespoons of the flour, then sprinkle the yeast over the surface. Set aside until foamy, about 10 minutes.

2. Whisk the remaining flour and the fine salt in a large bowl. Make a well in the center and pour in the yeast mixture and ¼ cup of the olive oil. Gradually stir the liquid into the flour with a wooden spoon to make a shaggy, loose dough. Turn the dough out of the bowl onto a lightly floured work surface. Knead the dough until smooth and elastic, about 10 minutes. (Add just enough flour so the dough is workable but still moist.) Form dough into a ball.

3. Lightly oil a large bowl and place the dough in the bowl; turn the dough around the bowl to coat. Cover bowl with a slightly moist clean kitchen towel and set aside to rise at room temperature for 45 minutes. Turn dough onto a lightly floured work surface, punch it down, and knead briefly before reshaping into a ball. Return to the bowl and set aside to rise for another 45 minutes to 1 hour.

4. Pour remaining ¼ cup olive oil into an 11x17-inch jelly-roll pan. Turn dough onto pan and flatten by hand. Set aside for 10 minutes until dough spreads easily on the pan. Turn dough over so both sides are well coated with oil. Stretch and press dough from center to the edges of the pan. Make indentations in dough with your fingertips and sprinkle with rosemary. Cover with a towel and let rise until puffy, about 1 hour.

5. Preheat the oven to 425°F. Sprinkle the dough with the sea salt. Bake until golden brown, about 20 minutes. Slip the focaccia from the pan and cool on a rack.

grissini

20 breadsticks

¾ cup warm water (about 110°F)

Pinch sugar

1 teaspoon active dry yeast

2 cups all-purpose flour

1 teaspoon fine salt

3 tablespoons extra-virgin olive oil, plus additional for brushing

Coarse sea salt, cumin, caraway, and/or fennel seeds, or cornmeal (optional)

1. Whisk the water and sugar in a small bowl, then sprinkle the yeast over the surface. Set aside until creamy, about 5 minutes.

2. Whisk flour and fine salt in a medium bowl. Make a well in the center and pour the yeast mixture and the 3 tablespoons oil in the center. Gradually mix the liquid into the flour to make a soft, shaggy dough. Turn the dough out onto a floured work surface and knead until smooth and elastic, about 10 minutes. Brush a large bowl with oil. Shape dough into a ball and put it in the bowl, cover with a clean kitchen towel, and set aside at room temperature until tripled in size, 2 to 3 hours.

3. Preheat the oven to 400°F. Line 2 baking sheets with parchment paper. Turn the dough onto a clean work surface and press into a rectangle about 4x14 inches. Use a pizza wheel to cut a plus sign through the dough, dividing it into quarters. Form breadsticks according to instructions below. (If dough snaps back to its original length when rolling, let it rest, covered, for 10 minutes.)

4. Bake grissini until golden brown, rotating the baking sheets once during baking, about 22 minutes. Cool on a rack.

1. Cut each quarter of dough lengthwise into 5 long strips. 2. Roll and stretch each piece with the palms of your hands into very thin strips about 14 inches long.
3. Transfer grissini to 2 parchment-lined baking sheets. Brush each with olive oil and sprinkle with sea salt, seeds, or cornmeal, if desired.

sweets

The perfect punctation to any meal. Double your dessert pleasure with any one of these recipes, which are as easy to prepare as they are delectable to eat.

coconut-ginger layer cake

one 9-inch layer cake (12 servings)

CAKE

- 2 cups cake flour
- 2 teaspoons baking powder
- ½ teaspoon fine salt
- ⅔ cup canned unsweetened coconut milk
- 1 teaspoon pure vanilla extract
- 1½ cups unsalted butter, softened (3 sticks)
- 1½ cups sugar
- 4 large eggs, at room temperature, separated

FROSTING AND COCONUT CRISPS

- 2½ cups sugar
- ¾ cup coconut-flavored white rum
- 1 4-inch piece fresh ginger, sliced
- 2½ cups unsweetened coconut chips (see ShopSmart, page 253)
- 8 large egg whites
- 1 tablespoon freshly squeezed lemon juice
- Pinch fine salt
- 2 cups unsalted butter, cut in egg-sized pieces and softened (4 sticks)

1. For the cake: Preheat the oven to 350°F. Butter two 9-inch cake pans, line them with buttered parchment paper, and dust with flour. Sift flour, baking powder, and salt into a large bowl. Whisk coconut milk with the vanilla in a liquid measuring cup.

2. Beat butter with the paddle attachment of a standing mixer until smooth, about 1 minute. Gradually add sugar while mixing, then beat at high speed until mixture is light and fluffy, about 10 minutes. (Turn mixer off a few times to scrape sides of bowl.) Add egg yolks one at time, making sure each is fully incorporated before adding another. At low speed, add flour mixture to butter mixture in 3 parts, alternating with coconut milk in 2 parts, beginning and ending with flour. Mix briefly at medium speed until batter is smooth; transfer to a large bowl.

3. Thoroughly clean the mixing bowl—if it contains any trace of butter, the egg whites won't whip properly. Whip egg whites on high until they hold stiff peaks. Fold whites into batter in 3 batches. Divide cake batter between prepared pans. Bake until a toothpick inserted in the centers comes out clean and cake shrinks from the sides, about 30 minutes. Cool in the pans on a rack for 5 minutes, then invert onto rack and cool. Leave oven on at 350°F. Thoroughly clean the bowl again.

4. For frosting and crisps: Bring ½ cup of the sugar, rum, and ginger to a boil in a small saucepan, swirling saucepan to dissolve sugar. Set aside 30 minutes; strain, discard ginger.

5. Line a baking sheet with parchment paper. Toss coconut chips with ⅓ cup of the ginger syrup in a large bowl and spread on prepared baking sheet. Bake, stirring occasionally, until golden brown, 12 to 15 minutes; cool.

6. Bring a few inches of water to a boil in a saucepan that can hold the mixer's heatproof bowl above the water. Whisk by

hand in the bowl the remaining 2 cups sugar, the egg whites, lemon juice, and salt. Set the bowl above the boiling water and whisk until the mixture is hot to the touch and the sugar is dissolved. Whip the egg-white-mixture on medium-high speed on the stand mixer fitted with the whisk attachment until egg-white mixture is cool and holds stiff peaks, about 10 minutes. Beat in the butter a few pieces at a time, making sure the pieces are incorporated before adding more. Slowly drizzle in ¼ cup of the ginger syrup while beating until smooth and light. (If the frosting is very soft, refrigerate until set but still spreadable; beat it until light before frosting.)

7. To assemble the cake: Cut each cake layer in half horizontally. Place a layer on a cake stand or flat plate. Using an offset spatula, spread 1 cup of the frosting on top and repeat with the remaining layers to make a 4-layer cake; frost the sides. Press the coconut crisps over the sides and the top to cover completely.

pineapple upside-down cake
one 9-inch cake (8 servings)

Think this one went the way of hula hoops, poodle skirts, and ambrosia? Well, it's back. Fresher and more fabulous than ever.

PINEAPPLE

Half a medium fresh pineapple (halved lengthwise), peeled and cored

5 tablespoons unsalted butter

½ cup firmly packed dark brown sugar

1 tablespoon dark rum

CAKE

1½ cups cake flour

1¼ teaspoons baking powder

½ teaspoon ground cinnamon

¼ teaspoon ground nutmeg

¼ teaspoon fine salt

¾ cup unsalted butter, softened (1½ sticks)

1¼ cups sugar

3 large eggs, at room temperature

½ cup whole milk, at room temperature

COOK'S NOTE The long baking time allows the bottom of the cake (the batter near the very moist pineapple, which will be the top of the finished cake) to cook completely.

1. Position a rack in the middle of the oven and preheat to 350°F. Butter a 9-inch round cake pan, line with parchment paper, and butter the paper.

2. For the pineapple: Cut the pineapple half in half lengthwise and slice it into ¼ -inch-thick fanlike pieces. Cook the butter in a small saucepan over medium-high heat until it is light brown and smells nutty, 2 to 3 minutes. Pull the pan from the heat and whisk in the brown sugar and rum; spread the mixture in the prepared pan. Arrange the pineapple slices in a slightly overlapping spiral, starting in the center and pressing them into the mixture to cover bottomcompletely.

3. For the cake: Sift the flour, baking powder, cinnamon, nutmeg, and salt into a large bowl and whisk. Slowly beat the butter and sugar with a hand-held or standing mixer until just blended. Raise the speed to high and beat until light and fluffy, scraping the sides of the bowl occasionally, about 10 minutes. Beat in the eggs one at a time, allowing each to be fully incorporated before adding the next. At low speed, add the flour mixture in 3 parts, alternating with the milk in 2 parts, beginning and ending with the flour. Mix briefly at medium speed to make a smooth batter. Pour the batter into the prepared pan and bake, rotating the pan once, until cake is dark brown and pulls away from the sides and a wooden toothpick inserted in the center comes out clean, about 1½ hours. Run a knife around the edge of the cake and cool on a rack for 25 minutes, then invert onto a serving platter. Cool before serving.

orange-spice pound cake
one tube cake (8 to 10 servings)

CAKE

- 3½ cups all-purpose flour
- 1 teaspoon ground mace
- ½ teaspoon fine salt
- 8 large eggs, at room temperature
- ¼ cup half-and-half, at room temperature
- 4 teaspoons pure vanilla extract
- 2 cups unsalted butter, softened (4 sticks)
- 2¾ cups granulated sugar
- 2 tablespoons finely grated orange zest
- 2 teaspoons finely grated lemon zest

  Confectioners' sugar for dusting or Orange Glaze (see recipe, below)

GLAZE

  Makes ¾ cup

- 2 to 2½ cups confectioners' sugar
- ¼ cup freshly squeezed orange juice

COOK'S NOTE Most pound cakes are best if allowed to ripen for a day before serving. If you make the cake ahead, wrap it tightly, store it at room temperature, and dust or glaze it before serving. The plain cake will keep at room temperature, tightly wrapped, for 4 days and may be frozen for 1 month.

1. Position a rack in the lower third of the oven and preheat to 325°F. Butter and flour a 12-cup fluted tube pan. (Skip the flour if using a nonstick pan.) Sift the flour, mace, and salt into a medium bowl. Whisk the eggs, half-and-half, and vanilla in a large liquid measuring cup or bowl.

2. Beat butter with the paddle attachment of a standing mixer at medium speed until smooth, about 1 minute. With machine running, very slowly add granulated sugar. Turn the mixer off and scrape down sides of the bowl, then beat on medium speed until light and fluffy, about 4 minutes. Beat in the orange and lemon zests; scrape down the sides of the bowl.

3. While mixing, slowly add flour mixture about ½ cup at a time, stopping mixer frequently to scrape down sides of the bowl. Beat batter very briefly at medium-low speed. Turn mixer to low and slowly dribble in egg mixture. Finish folding batter—which will be thick—by hand with a rubber spatula.

4. Scrape batter into the prepared pan and smooth the top. Bake until a toothpick inserted into cake comes out clean and top springs back when lightly pressed, about 1½ hours. Cool in pan on a rack 10 to 15 minutes, then invert pan to release cake onto rack to cool. Dust the cake with confectioners' sugar, if desired. Or, if you prefer, finish it with Orange Glaze: Set the cake, still on its rack, over a sheet of aluminum foil. Drizzle the glaze over with a large spoon, adding extra in some spots and pushing it a bit so it flows nicely over the sides. If necessary, scrape up any glaze that drips onto the foil and stir it back into the bowl.

ORANGE GLAZE

Sift the sugar. Whisk 2 cups sifted sugar with the orange juice until smooth. If the glaze is thin, whisk in more sugar until you have a smooth but pourable glaze.

Italian pine nut torte

one 10-inch cake (10 to 12 servings)

2 cups pine nuts

6 tablespoons unsalted butter

1½ cups granulated sugar

1 cup all-purpose flour

1 teaspoon finely grated orange zest

9 large egg whites, at room temperature

⅛ teaspoon fine salt

⅛ teaspoon cream of tartar

Confectioners' sugar for dusting

KNOW-HOW Most ovens have hot spots. Ensure that your cakes, breads, pastries, and cookies bake evenly by rotating the pans once during baking time.

1. Position a rack in the middle of the oven and preheat to 350°F. Butter a 10-inch round cake pan and line bottom with parchment paper. Set aside ¾ cup of the pine nuts; spread remaining nuts on a baking sheet and oven-toast, stirring once, until light brown, about 10 minutes. Cool completely.

2. Meanwhile, melt the butter in a small saucepan over medium heat and cook, swirling the pan frequently, until butter is light brown and fragrant, about 6 minutes. Cool. Pulse cooled toasted nuts with ¾ cup of the granulated sugar, the flour, and the orange zest in a food processor until sandy.

3. Whip the egg whites, salt, and cream of tartar in a large bowl with an electric mixer at medium-high speed until foamy. Increase the speed to high, gradually pour in the remaining ¾ cup sugar, and whip until the whites hold soft peaks (see page 276). Stop beating. Sprinkle the flour mixture over the whites; fold the batter together with a rubber spatula until just a few streaks remain. Drizzle in the browned butter, including any toasted bits on the bottom of the pan, and finish folding the batter. Pour batter into the prepared pan and scatter the reserved (untoasted) nuts over the top.

4. Bake the cake until a wooden toothpick inserted into the center comes out clean, about 45 minutes. Rotate the pan halfway through baking so the nuts brown evenly. Cool on a rack for 10 minutes. Run a knife along the inside of the pan to loosen the cake from the edges and invert the cake onto a piece of parchment paper on the rack. Leave the cake nutside down until it is completely cool. When cool, turn the cake nut side up, dust with confectioners' sugar, and serve.

This authentic Sicilian dessert that looks great from all angles and tastes even better with a strong cup of piping-hot espresso.

pear upside-down chocolate cake one 9-inch cake (6 to 8 servings)

PEARS

- 2 tablespoons unsalted butter
- 2 tablespoons firmly packed light brown sugar
- ½ teaspoon finely grated lemon zest
- 1 teaspoon freshly squeezed lemon juice
- 4 Bosc pears, peeled, quartered lengthwise, and cored

CAKE

- ⅓ cup milk
- ¾ cup all-purpose flour
- ½ cup finely ground toasted almonds
- ½ teaspoon baking soda
- ½ teaspoon baking powder
- ½ teaspoon fine salt
- ½ teaspoon ground cinnamon
- ¼ teaspoon ground cloves
- 4 tablespoons unsalted butter, softened
- ¾ cup granulated sugar
- ¼ cup natural unsweetened cocoa (not Dutch-process), plus additional for dusting (see page 276)
- 1 teaspoon pure vanilla extract
- 2 large eggs, at room temperature
- Confectioners' sugar for dusting

1. For the pears: Lightly butter a 9-inch round cake pan, line the bottom with parchment paper, and butter the paper. Put the butter, brown sugar, and lemon zest and juice in a large skillet. Cook over medium heat, stirring, until melted. Add the pears, cover, and simmer, turning once, until the pears are soft and juicy, about 4 minutes. Pour the pears and their syrup into a strainer set over a saucepan. Set the syrup and 1 pear quarter aside. Arrange remaining pears in the prepared pan according to instructions on page 237.

2. For the cake: Set a rack in the middle of the oven and preheat to 350°F. Scald milk in a small saucepan; keep warm. Whisk flour with almonds, baking soda, baking powder, salt, cinnamon, and cloves. Beat butter with an electric mixer at medium speed until smooth, about 2 minutes. Increase speed to medium-high and gradually add granulated sugar; continue beating until mixture is light and fluffy, about 4 minutes, scraping down sides of bowl. Add cocoa powder and vanilla and beat 1 minute. While mixing at medium-low speed, add eggs one at a time, beating well after each addition.

3. While mixing slowly, add the flour mixture in 4 additions; turn off the mixer and fold in the hot milk with a rubber spatula. Spread the batter over the pears, taking care not to disturb them. Tap the pan lightly on the counter to settle the batter. Bake until a toothpick inserted in the center comes out clean, about 50 minutes. Cool cake in the pan on a rack for 20 minutes, then invert the cake onto a serving plate. Cool briefly, carefully peel the parchment paper from the top, and then cool completely.

4. To finish the cake: Boil the reserved pear syrup until slightly thick and lightly brush the top of the cake with syrup. Whisk a few tablespoons of cocoa powder with an equal amount of confectioners' sugar, and sift over the cake; serve.

1. Peel, quarter, and core the pears.
2. Arrange pears in pan, stem ends toward center, rounded sides down, and ¼ inch from the side. Chop reserved pear and use just enough to fill center.
3. Spread cake batter over the pears, taking care not to disturb them.

little devil's food cakes

12 cupcakes

CUPCAKES

- 1 cup all-purpose flour
- 6 tablespoons natural unsweetened cocoa (not Dutch-process) (see page 276)
- ½ teaspoon baking soda
- ¼ teaspoon baking powder
- ¼ teaspoon salt
- 8 tablespoons unsalted butter, softened (1 stick)
- 1 cup sugar
- 2 large whole eggs, at room temperature
- 1 large egg yolk, at room temperature
- 1 teaspoon pure vanilla extract
- ½ cup water

FROSTING

- 8 ounces semisweet chocolate, finely chopped
- ¾ cup heavy cream

  Optional flavorings for 1 batch frosting: 2 tablespoons coffee liqueur, eau de vie (fruit brandy—such as framboise, a raspberry-flavored brandy), or dark rum; or ½ teaspoon mint extract or orange extract

  Fresh raspberries, colorful candies, or chopped pistachios (optional)

1. For the cupcakes: Position a rack in the middle of the oven and preheat to 350°F. Line twelve ½-cup muffin cups with paper liners. Whisk the flour with the cocoa powder, baking soda, baking powder, and salt.

2. Beat the butter with an electric mixer at medium speed until smooth, about 2 minutes. Increase the speed to medium-high and gradually add the sugar. Beat until light and smooth, about 5 minutes. Reduce the speed to medium-low and beat in the whole eggs and yolk one at a time, incorporating each fully before adding the next. Beat in the vanilla. Scrape down the sides of the bowl.

3. Bring water just to a boil in a small saucepan and remove from the heat. With the mixer at low speed, beat the flour mixture into the butter mixture in 4 additions. Drizzle in the hot water, about 2 tablespoons at a time, and mix briefly to make a smooth batter. Divide the batter among the muffin cups, filling them $^2/_3$ full. Bake until the centers of the cupcakes spring back when pressed gently, about 20 minutes. Cool cupcakes in the tin on a rack for 10 minutes, then remove from the tin and cool completely before frosting.

4. For the frosting: Put chocolate in a medium heatproof bowl. In a small saucepan, bring cream to a boil. Pour cream over chocolate and shake bowl gently so cream settles around the chocolate. Set mixture aside until the chocolate is soft, about 5 minutes. Whisk gently until smooth, taking care not to incorporate too many air bubbles. Stir in one of the flavorings, if desired. Dip the tops of the cooled cupcakes into the frosting. (Frosting can also be chilled and whipped, then piped or spread onto the cupcakes.) Set them upright and let stand a minute or two, until frosting is slightly set, then decorate with fresh berries, candies, or chopped pistachios, if desired. Let cakes stand on rack until frosting is completely set.

Your own personal chocolate cake. Whipped or dipped, topped with candy or one perfect raspberry, these little devils are always irresistible.

baked apples with maple-cream sauce
6 servings

APPLES

- 2 tablespoons unsalted butter, softened
- 1 tablespoon maple syrup
- 2 teaspoons finely grated lemon zest
- 2 nut biscotti, crumbled (not chocolate)
- 3 tablespoons dried currants
- 6 large red baking apples, like Rome Beauty
- 1/4 cup lemon juice
- 6 cinnamon sticks
- 2 cups apple cider or juice

SAUCE

- 7 tablespoons maple syrup
- 6 tablespoons bourbon
- 1 cinnamon stick
- 1 cup heavy cream

1. For the apples: Preheat the oven to 375°F. Using a fork, blend the butter, maple syrup, and lemon zest in a small bowl. Work in the crumbled biscotti and the currants.

2. Slice about 1/4 inch from the top of each apple. Use a melon baller to scoop out the seeds and cores, but don't cut through to the bottom of the apples. Remove a 1/2-inch band of peel from around the holes with a vegetable peeler. Stand the apples in a baking dish just large enough to hold them. Brush the peeled flesh and the insides of the apples with some of the lemon juice. Spoon some of the butter mixture into each apple and place a cinnamon stick in the center to make a "stem." Pour the cider around the apples and bake until tender, basting occasionally with the cider, 35 to 40 minutes.

3. While the apples bake, make the sauce: Put the maple syrup, bourbon, and the cinnamon stick in a small saucepan. Bring to a boil, reduce the heat, and simmer, uncovered, until the sauce is thick and syrupy. Whisk in the heavy cream, bring to a boil, and cook until just thickened, about 3 minutes. Serve the apples in small bowls with the warm sauce spooned over and around them.

SHOPSMART Some apples are best for baking, others for eating out of hand. For cooking apples, look for Rome Beauty, Braeburn, and York Imperial. If you want the best of both worlds, look for Granny Smith, Newtown pippin, and Winesap, all good all-purpose apples. For pies, use a mix of apples to get the benefit of the fruits' different qualities.

apple & nut crumb pie

one 9-inch pie (8 servings)

DOUGH

1¼ cups all-purpose flour

2 teaspoons sugar

½ teaspoon fine salt

8 tablespoons cold unsalted butter

1 large egg, lightly beaten

1 teaspoon pure vanilla extract

FILLING

1 cup sugar

1 teaspoon ground cinnamon

½ teaspoon ground allspice

¼ teaspoon ground nutmeg

½ teaspoon kosher salt

3½ pounds baking apples

8 tablespoons unsalted butter

2 teaspoons pure vanilla extract

1 tablespoon all-purpose flour

TOPPING

1¾ cups all-purpose flour

¾ cup sugar

½ cup pecan pieces

1½ teaspoons ground cinnamon

¾ teaspoon ground allspice

Pinch nutmeg

¼ teaspoon fine salt

10 tablespoons unsalted butter, melted

1½ teaspoons pure vanilla extract

1. For the dough: Pulse flour, sugar, and salt in a food processor briefly. Cut butter into dice. Sprinkle butter over and pulse until mixture resembles coarse cornmeal but a few bean-size bits of butter remain. Drizzle egg and vanilla over and pulse once or twice; don't let dough form a mass around blade. Remove blade and bring dough together by hand. Shape dough into a disk, wrap in plastic wrap, and refrigerate 1 hour.

2. Dust work surface with flour. Roll dough into a 12-inch circle; center in pie plate. Trim overhang to 1 inch and fold it under to create a double-thick rim for crust; flute. Pierce bottom of dough 5 or 6 times with a fork and freeze for 20 minutes.

3. Position a rack in the lower third of the oven and preheat to 425°F. Line crust with parchment paper and fill with dried beans. Bake until firm and just set, about 18 minutes. Reduce temperature to 375°F. Remove paper with beans. Return crust to oven and bake until golden and dry, about 10 minutes.

4. For the filling: Whisk sugar, spices, and salt in a large bowl. Peel, core, and cut apples into ½-inch chunks; toss with sugar mixture. In a large skillet, melt half the butter over medium-high heat. Add half the apples, tossing to coat. Cover and cook until apples are tender, 6 to 8 minutes. Transfer to a colander set over a bowl. Repeat with remaining butter and apples.

5. Pour juices into skillet and simmer until thick and beginning to caramelize, about 4 minutes. Put apples in large bowl and fold in thickened juices; sprinkle vanilla and flour over and toss. Pour filling into pie shell, mounding slightly in the center.

6. For topping: Whisk flour with sugar, pecans, spices, and salt. Drizzle butter and vanilla over and toss. Squeeze mixture to make crumbs. Some should be large, some small. Sprinkle over filling and bake until juices are bubbling and crust is golden brown, about 35 minutes. Cool until warm and serve.

Nothing takes you to another place and time like the smell of a warm, spicy apple pie in the oven.

241

lattice-top peach pie
one 10-inch pie (8 servings)

CRUST

2½ cups all-purpose flour

2 tablespoons sugar

½ teaspoon fine salt

1 cup cold unsalted butter, sliced into 16 even pieces (2 sticks)

⅓ cup very cold water

2 teaspoons white or cider vinegar

FILLING

3 pounds ripe peaches (6 to 7)

¾ cup packed light brown sugar

¼ cup instant tapioca

1 teaspoon freshly squeezed lemon juice

½ teaspoon pure vanilla extract

⅛ teaspoon ground mace

1 large egg, beaten with a pinch salt

1. For the crust: Whisk the flour with the sugar and salt in a large bowl. Toss 4 pieces of butter with the mixture to coat and then use your fingers to rub the butter into the flour until the mixture is powdery and pale yellow. You should not see any obvious bits of butter, and the mixture should feel cool and dry to the touch. Work in the remaining butter in the same manner, but this time just until pieces are the size of large beans. Combine the water and vinegar in a liquid measure and drizzle it evenly over the flour mixture. Toss and stir the mixture with a rubber spatula until it comes together in a loose, shaggy dough. A large handful of dough should hold together when you squeeze it in your palm; if it does not, add another tablespoon or so of cold water and toss again.

2. Turn dough onto a clean surface and shape into a rectangle with a short end toward you. Starting at the far end, press the heel of your hand into the dough and smear it away from you with short strokes. Continue pressing and smearing, working to the edge close to you. When all the dough has been worked, scrape and press it together in a mass and divide into 2 equal pieces. Shape pieces into disks and wrap each in plastic wrap. Refrigerate at least 1 hour or up to 2 days.

1. Line a baking sheet with parchment paper. Roll the remaining dough into a 14-inch circle. Using a pastry wheel or fluted pastry cutter, make 18 ½-inch-wide strips. 2. Lay half the strips ½ inch apart on the parchment. Gently fold every other strip back on itself at the middle. Lay the longest of the remaining strips perpendicular to the

others and just below the folds. Unfold the folded strips—they should now lie across/on top of the single strip. Fold back the strips that were not folded the first time and place another strip about ½ inch from the single strip; unfold the strips. Repeat with 2 more strips to complete lattice on one side. Repeat the process on the other side.

3. Roll one piece of dough into a 14-inch circle and center it in a 10-inch pie plate; trim the overhang to 1 inch and refrigerate. Weave the lattice top according to instructions, opposite. Freeze until firm, about 20 minutes.

4. For the filling: Peel, halve, and pit the peaches (see page 273). Slice each half into 6 wedges and halve them crosswise. Toss fruit with the sugar, tapioca, lemon juice, vanilla, and mace in a large bowl. Set aside until the peaches get juicy, about 15 minutes.

5. Brush the rim of the bottom crust with some of the egg. Pour the fruit into the crust. Brush the lattice with the egg wash, taking care not to drip over the sides, and gently slide it on top of the fruit. Adjust the lattice, if needed, and trim the overhang flush with the edge of the pie plate. Fold overhang of bottom crust up and over lattice's edge; crimp and flute the edges as desired (see third how-to photo, opposite). Refrigerate pie for 30 minutes.

6. Position a rack as low as possible in the oven and preheat to 400°F. Bake the pie on an aluminum foil-lined baking sheet until the crust is deep golden brown and the filling is bubbly, about 1 hour and 25 minutes. About halfway through baking, loosely crimp foil around the edges of the pie to protect the crust from burning and rotate the baking sheet. Cool the pie on a rack before cutting.

individual deep-dish berry pies 4 small pies

Don't tell anyone, but this is one of our simplest recipes—and one of our most impressive. Just mix up this medley of peak summer berries topped with pastry and ice cream, and listen to the oohs and ahhs.

4 cups mixed berries, such as raspberries, blueberries, blackberries, or stemmed and halved strawberries

⅓ cup sugar, plus additional for sprinkling

2 tablespoons instant tapioca

1 teaspoon pure vanilla extract

2 tablespoons unsalted butter

1 sheet frozen puff pastry (8 ounces), thawed

   Whipped cream or vanilla ice cream, for serving

1. Position a rack in the center of the oven and preheat to 400°F. Toss the berries with the ⅓ cup sugar, tapioca, and vanilla extract in a large bowl. Divide the fruit among four 6-ounce ramekins and dot each with some butter.

2. Using a pizza wheel or very sharp knife, divide the puff pastry sheet into 4 squares. Brush the outsides and rims of the ramekins with water. Lay a puff pastry square over the top of each ramekin and gently press the points that drape over the sides against the ramekins to seal. Lightly brush the tops with water and sprinkle with sugar.

3. Bake the pies on a baking sheet until the pastry is puffed and golden brown, 25 to 30 minutes. Cool at least 20 minutes before serving with a dollop of whipped cream or a scoop of vanilla ice cream.

COOK'S NOTE These little pies are best if served the day they're made. If you're not serving them right away, keep them at room temperature before reheating—don't refrigerate them or the crust will get soggy.

strawberry-rhubarb tart

one 13x5-inch tart (4 to 6 servings)

TART

- 1 sheet frozen puff pastry (8 ounces), thawed
- 1 tablespoon milk
- 2 cups strawberries, stemmed
- 1 cup sliced rhubarb (1 large rib, trimmed but not peeled)
- ¼ cup sugar
- 1 teaspoon pure vanilla extract
- 2 tablespoons unsalted butter

GLAZE

- 1 tablespoon currant jelly
- 1 tablespoon very hot water

Confectioners' sugar, for dusting

Lightly sweetened whipped cream, for serving

SHOPSMART Buy strawberries of roughly the same size so that when they're "shingled" on the tart, they fit together nicely.

1. Position a rack in the center of the oven and preheat to 375°F. Line a baking sheet with parchment paper. Roll the pastry into a rectangle about ⅛ inch thick. Cut two ¾-inch-wide strips from a long side. Cut remaining pastry into a 13x5-inch rectangle and place on the prepared baking sheet. Brush a ¾-inch border down one long side with water and lay one narrow strip on top, pressing gently. Repeat on the other side. (The filling should be thick enough so you don't need pastry strips on the short sides of the tart to keep the filling from spilling out when the tart is assembled.) Trim any overhang, if necessary. Very lightly roll a pizza wheel along the inside of the strips to score halfway through the base. Brush the top of the strips with milk, taking care not to drip down the sides. Pierce the base all over with a fork, line it with a piece of aluminum foil that extends along the sides of the strips but not over, and weigh foil down with pie weights or dried beans. Use a paring knife to flute the outer edges of the tart by making small cuts an inch apart. Bake until set, about 15 minutes. Remove the foil and weights and bake until light golden brown, about 15 minutes more. Cool on a rack.

2. Trim the strawberries' broad tops and put the trimmings in a small saucepan with the rhubarb, sugar, and vanilla extract. Simmer over medium heat, stirring frequently, until fruit is thick and jamlike, about 15 minutes. Add butter and puree with an immersion blender or in a food processor until smooth. Cool. Halve the remainder of the strawberries lengthwise.

3. To assemble the tart: Spread cooked mixture in the shell. Arrange strawberries in shingled rows down length of the tart.

4. For the glaze: Stir together jelly and hot water. Brush warm glaze over strawberries. Dust the sides lightly with confectioners' sugar, slice, and serve with whipped cream.

Welcome to Cookie Central.

Homemade cookies are the one gift everyone loves to receive. For the holidays, when a friend is home sick, for any kind of special celebration, we go into cookie-baking mode. Make large batches and small, giving each cookie your personal touch. There's no better way to say, "I'm thinking of you."

lemon sugar cookies

about 24 cookies

I cup granulated sugar

3 tablespoons finely grated lemon zest

2 cups all-purpose flour

¼ teaspoon fine salt

I cup unsalted butter, softened (2 sticks)

2 tablespoons confectioners' sugar

2 large egg yolks

1½ teaspoons pure vanilla extract

I large egg white, lightly beaten

1. Process ½ cup of the granulated sugar with 2 tablespoons of the lemon zest in a small food processor. Whisk the flour with the salt in a medium bowl.

2. Beat the butter with the remaining ½ cup granulated sugar and the confectioners' sugar in a large bowl with an electric mixer until light and fluffy, about 3 minutes. Beat in the yolks, vanilla, and the remaining I tablespoon lemon zest. Slowly beat in the flour mixture. Roll dough by hand into several I-inch-wide logs. Wrap in plastic wrap and refrigerate for at least 2 hours.

3. Preheat the oven to 325°F. Line 2 baking sheets with parchment paper. Spread the lemon-sugar down the center of another piece of parchment or waxed paper the length of the logs of dough. Brush a log of dough with some of the egg white, then lay it in the lemon-sugar. Lift the sides of the paper and roll the dough back and forth to coat it with the sugar. (If the sugar clumps up, brush off excess with a pastry brush.) Repeat with the other logs. Cut the logs into I-inch-thick cookies and lay them on the prepared baking sheets, leaving about I inch between cookies. Freeze for IO minutes.

4. Bake the cookies until the edges are golden and the centers set, about 25 minutes. Transfer cookies to a rack to cool. Serve or store in a tightly sealed container for up to 5 days.

snickerdoodles

about 20 cookies

2¾	cups all-purpose flour
1	teaspoon baking soda
½	teaspoon fine salt
½	cup shortening
8	tablespoons unsalted butter, softened (1 stick)
1½	cups sugar, plus 3 tablespoons
2	large eggs
1	tablespoon cinnamon

1. Preheat the oven to 350°F. Sift the flour, baking soda, and salt into a bowl.

2. With a handheld or standing mixer beat together the shortening and butter. Add the 1½ cups sugar and continue beating until light and fluffy, about 5 minutes. Add the eggs, one at a time, beating well after each addition. Add the flour mixture and blend until smooth.

3. Mix the 3 tablespoons sugar with the cinnamon in a small bowl. Roll the dough, by hand, into 1½-inch balls. Roll the balls in the cinnamon sugar. Flatten the balls into ½-inch thick discs, spacing them evenly on unlined cookie sheets. Bake until light brown, but still moist in the center, about 12 minutes. Cool on a rack.

What's in a name? Sweet memories. We can taste the cinnamon and sugar at just the mention of this cookie.

COOK'S NOTE Everyone's oven is a little different. To make sure that cookies and cakes cook evenly, rotate the pans about halfway through cooking, from top to bottom shelves, as well as right to left.

Add a glass of milk and you've got an instant peanut-butter-cookie playdate.

peanut butter cookies
about 50 cookies

1⅓ cups all-purpose flour

½ teaspoon baking soda

Pinch fine salt

8 tablespoons unsalted butter, softened (1 stick)

½ cup firmly packed dark brown sugar

1 large egg, at room temperature

¾ cup smooth peanut butter

Granulated sugar, for rolling

1. Whisk the flour with the baking soda and salt in a small bowl. Slowly beat the butter with the brown sugar in a medium bowl with an electric mixer until just blended. Then beat on high until light and fluffy, scraping the sides of the bowl as needed, about 10 minutes. Beat in the egg and peanut butter.

2. Turn the mixer to low and beat in the flour mixture to make a smooth dough. Scrape the dough onto a piece of plastic wrap, flatten into a disk, wrap, and refrigerate until firm, about 2 hours.

3. Preheat the oven to 375°F. Line 2 baking sheets with parchment paper. Put the granulated sugar on a pie plate. Using about 2 teaspoons per cookie, shape the dough into balls, then roll them in the sugar and space them an inch apart on the prepared baking sheets. Press a crosshatch on top of each cookie with the tines of a fork, flattening slightly as you do. Bake, turning the pans once, until lightly browned, about 9 minutes. Briefly cool the cookies on the baking sheets, then transfer to racks to cool.

KNOW-HOW These cookies are small and sandy, not thin and chewy. If the dough sticks to your hands as you roll it into balls, wet your hands slightly with cool water.

almond snowball cookies

about 30 cookies

¾ cup sliced almonds

¾ cup sugar

¾ cup unsalted butter, sliced and softened (1½ sticks)

½ teaspoon pure vanilla extract

⅛ teaspoon almond extract

1⅔ cups all-purpose flour

½ teaspoon fine salt

1 cup confectioners' sugar

1. Pulse the almonds and sugar in a food processor until very finely ground. Add the butter and process until smooth, about 1 minute. Scrape the dough off the inside of the bowl, if needed. Add the vanilla and almond extracts and pulse to combine. Add the flour and salt and pulse to make a soft dough. Turn the dough out onto a large piece of waxed paper and roll into a log about 15 inches long and 1½ inches wide. Wrap and refrigerate for 30 minutes.

2. Preheat the oven to 325°F. Line 2 baking sheets with parchment paper. Cut the chilled dough into ½-inch pieces and roll by hand into balls. Space the cookies evenly on the prepared baking sheets and bake until slightly golden, rotating the sheets once, 15 to 20 minutes. Put the confectioners' sugar in a pie plate. Briefly cool the cookies on a rack, then gently toss in the confectioners' sugar until evenly coated. Return to rack, cool to room temperature, and then toss again in the confectioners' sugar.

coconut brownies

24 brownies

BROWNIES

- 10 ounces semisweet chocolate, finely chopped
- 2 ounces unsweetened chocolate, finely chopped
- 8 tablespoons unsalted butter, cut into pieces (1 stick)
- 1½ cups all-purpose flour
- 1½ teaspoons baking powder
- ¼ teaspoon fine salt
- 2 cups sugar
- 4 large eggs
- 1 teaspoon pure vanilla extract

GLAZE

- 6 ounces semisweet chocolate, finely chopped
- ½ cup canned unsweetened coconut milk
- 1 cup unsweetened coconut chips (see ShopSmart, below), toasted

1. For the brownies: Position a rack in the middle of the oven and preheat to 350°F. Line a 13x9x2-inch baking pan with parchment or waxed paper so the edges of the paper come up the sides all around the pan. Press paper into the corners, but don't worry if it isn't absolutely smooth. Lightly butter paper.

2. Put the semisweet and unsweetened chocolates and the butter in a heatproof bowl. Bring a saucepan filled with an inch or so of water to a very slow simmer; set the bowl on the pan (without touching the water). Stir occasionally until melted and smooth.

3. Whisk flour, baking powder, and salt in a medium bowl. Whisk sugar, eggs, and vanilla in a large bowl. Gradually stir the chocolate mixture into the egg mixture until blended. Add the flour mixture to the chocolate mixture and stir again until just blended. Scrape the batter into the prepared pan. Bake until a wooden toothpick inserted into the center of the brownies comes out coated with fudgy crumbs, about 35 minutes. Cool on a rack.

4. For the glaze: Put chocolate in a medium bowl. Bring coconut milk to a boil, stirring constantly, and pour it over the chocolate. Let the mixture stand for 10 minutes, then stir until smooth. Spread the warm glaze evenly over the brownies, then scatter the coconut over the top. Refrigerate, loosely covered, until glaze sets, about 2 hours. Lift the paper to remove brownies from the pan, fold back the sides, and use a warm knife to cut the brownies into 24 squares.

SHOPSMART Coconut chips are large-flake, slightly crisp, unsweetened coconut. We find them in Middle Eastern stores and in specialty and natural-food stores. If you can't find them, use unsweetened shredded or flaked coconut.

mixed-berry summer pudding

4 to 6 servings

8 cups mixed berries, such as blackberries, blueberries, raspberries, and/or trimmed and quartered strawberries

½ cup honey

2 teaspoons finely grated lemon zest

I tablespoon freshly squeezed lemon juice

1½ pounds prepared pound cake

Whipped cream or vanilla ice cream, for serving

I. Toss half the berries in a medium saucepan with the honey and the lemon zest and juice. Bring to a boil over medium heat, then simmer gently, uncovered, until the berries burst and get juicy, about 8 minutes. Pull the saucepan from the heat, stir in the remaining berries, and cool.

2. Trim the crust from the pound cake; chop the trimmings and set aside. Slice the cake into ⅜-inch-thick pieces. Use the slices to line the bottom and sides of a 2-quart bowl or soufflé dish, trimming the cake as needed to cover the bowl completely and reserving enough to cover the pudding. Gently fold the cake trimmings into the cooled berries, pour the mixture into the lined bowl, and cover completely with the remaining cake slices. Cover the pudding loosely with plastic wrap, set a small plate directly on top, and weigh it down with a heavy can or cans, making sure the entire surface is evenly weighted. Refrigerate for at least 6 hours or overnight.

3. To serve, remove the plastic wrap and run a thin-bladed knife between the cake and the bowl. Set a flat serving plate or stand on top of the bowl and invert; lift off the bowl. Serve wedges of pudding with whipped cream or vanilla ice cream.

SHOPSMART Summer pudding is all about the berries—make it when they're juicy and in season. Look for strawberries that are red from tip to stem, blackberries that are almost bursting, and raspberries and blueberries that are fully fragrant.

cherry-blueberry cornmeal buckles 6 servings

FRUIT

Softened unsalted butter

¼ cup sugar, plus additional for dusting

2 cups sweet or sour cherries, fresh or frozen, pitted

1 cup fresh blueberries

BATTER

1 cup all-purpose flour

⅓ cup polenta-style cornmeal

⅓ cup granulated sugar

2 teaspoons baking powder

½ teaspoon fine salt

2 teaspoons grated lemon or orange zest

¾ cup plus 2 tablespoons milk

4 tablespoons cold unsalted butter, thinly sliced

Confectioners' sugar

Whipped cream

1. For the fruit: Position a rack in the center of the oven and preheat to 375°F. Lightly butter the insides of six 1-cup (3-inch) ramekins, dust with sugar, and space them evenly on a baking sheet. Toss the cherries and blueberries with the ¼ cup sugar in a medium bowl.

2. For the cornmeal batter: Whisk the flour with the cornmeal, granulated sugar, baking powder, and salt in a medium bowl. Stir the zest into the milk. Rub the butter into the flour mixture with your fingers until the mixture is powdery. Fold and stir the milk mixture in with a rubber spatula just until the flour mixture is moistened. Divide the batter among the molds and spoon the fruit on top. Bake until the cornmeal batter puffs and browns, 25 to 30 minutes. Cool for at least 20 minutes. Dust with confectioners' sugar and serve with a dollop of whipped cream.

chocolate mixed-nut brittle

1½ pounds brittle (24 servings)

2 cups mixed nuts, such as pecan and walnut halves, plus whole cashews and blanched almonds

1 teaspoon unsalted butter, softened

⅓ cup Dutch-process unsweetened cocoa (see page 276)

½ teaspoon baking soda

1½ cups sugar

¾ cup water

½ cup light corn syrup

1. Preheat the oven to 350°F. Spread the nuts on a baking sheet and oven-toast, stirring once, until golden brown, about 10 minutes; keep warm.

2. Lay a reusable flexible nonstick sheet liner on an overturned baking sheet (or use buttered aluminum foil). Spread the softened butter on the underside of a large offset spatula. Whisk the cocoa with the baking soda.

3. Put the sugar, water, and corn syrup in a medium heavy-bottomed saucepan. Cook over medium heat, stirring gently with a wooden spoon, just until the sugar dissolves. Increase the heat to high and boil the mixture until a candy thermometer registers 310°F (the hard-crack stage). (A reminder: Hot sugar is HOT, so be very careful.) Immediately pull the saucepan from heat and whisk in the cocoa mixture. Stir in the nuts with a wooden spoon. Working quickly but carefully, pour the hot brittle onto the nonstick liner or buttered foil and spread it as thin as possible with the buttered spatula. Cool for 5 minutes, then slip the spatula under the brittle to release it from the liner. Cool completely and break into jagged pieces. Keep the brittle at room temperature in an airtight container for up to 5 days.

At FN Kitchens, we love to make the ultimate version of everything. Here we've bumped up the memory-filled flavor of peanut brittle by adding chocolate and lots and lots of different kinds of nuts.

KNOW-HOW That crunchy candy that's so terrific to eat is not as fun to clean out of the saucepan—unless you know this trick: Fill the pot with water and bring to a boil (and dip the thermometer in, too). The encrusted sugar mixture will melt, and you'll be able to wash up the pan easily.

raspberry & fig gratin

4 servings

Unsalted butter, softened

8 to 12 fresh black Mission or green figs, stemmed and halved

1 cup raspberries

4 large egg yolks

⅓ cup sugar

1 teaspoon finely grated orange zest

½ cup freshly squeezed orange juice

2 tablespoons Chambord (raspberry-flavored liqueur)

1. Position a rack in the top of the oven and preheat the broiler to high. Lightly brush a 4-cup gratin dish with butter. Spread the figs and raspberries evenly in the dish.

2. Put about 1 inch of water in a saucepan and bring to a simmer over medium heat. In a heatproof bowl that can rest in the saucepan without touching the water, beat the egg yolks, sugar, orange zest, orange juice, and Chambord until foamy and light, about 30 seconds. Set the bowl over the water and whip with an electric mixer or whisk, moving in a circular motion around the bowl, until the eggs thicken, about 2 minutes.

3. Pour the egg mixture over the fruit, place under the broiler, and cook until nicely browned, about 3 minutes. Serve warm.

KNOW-HOW If the eggs start to thicken up too quickly, simply lift the bowl off the pot and continue beating off the heat for a bit. The eggs are cooked and foamy enough if, when you lift the whisk over the mixture, they slowly fall back into the bowl in a thick, round stream.

Strikingly out of the ordinary, this early summer or early fall custard is as sensual and sensational as you can get.

mexican-style chocolate fondue 4 servings

1 cup heavy cream

4 cinnamon sticks, preferably Mexican canela (see Cook's Note, below)

6 ounces chopped semisweet chocolate

Generous pinch ancho chile powder (see page 273)

SUGGESTED DIPPERS

Cubed pound cake

Dried apricots

Mini bananas

Fresh or dried orange slices

Fresh or dried pear slices

Almond cookies

Coconut strips

Strawberries

Sliced mango

1. Heat the cream and cinnamon in a small saucepan over medium heat just until it begins to boil. Pull off the heat, cover, and steep for 15 minutes. Remove and discard the cinnamon.

2. Put the chocolate and ancho powder in a medium bowl. Return the cream to a simmer, pour it over the chocolate, and let stand for 5 minutes. Stir the chocolate mixture until melted and smooth. Transfer the chocolate mixture to a fondue pot and keep warm over a low Sterno flame. Serve with a selection of the dippers.

COOK'S NOTE Mexican cinnamon, or canela, isn't called so because it's grown there, but rather because it's preferred there. The type of cinnamon most commonly sold in the United States is cassia cinnamon. Mexican cinnamon, or Ceylon cinnamon, is considered to be the "true" cinnamon. It has a softer, slightly sweeter taste than cassia. Look for it in Mexican markets and specialty food stores.

What goes around may come around. But it's never out of style to gather around the table.

Silky and simple, this is a dessert to be slowly savored.

flan
8 servings

1¼ cups sugar

2 tablespoons water

1 teaspoon freshly squeezed lemon juice

4 cups milk

6 large eggs

2 teaspoons pure vanilla extract

1. Position a rack in the middle of the oven and preheat to 350°F. Set an 8x8x2-inch glass baking dish next to the stove. Stir ¾ cup of the sugar, the water, and lemon juice in a small saucepan. Bring to a boil over medium-high heat and cook, swirling the pan but not stirring, until the sugar is amber-colored caramel. Pull pan from the heat and pour the caramel into baking dish. Working quickly so caramel doesn't harden, tilt and rotate the dish to coat the bottom and sides. Set aside.

2. Put milk in a medium saucepan and bring to a simmer over medium heat, stirring occasionally. Whisk eggs with the remaining ½ cup sugar. Gradually whisk milk into egg mixture. Add vanilla. (Don't beat mixture too much or flan will have air bubbles.) Strain mixture into a large degreasing or glass measuring cup or heatproof pitcher. Pour mixture into caramel-lined dish. Skim foam or bubbles from the surface.

3. Put a roasting pan in the oven and set flan in the center. Pour enough hot water into the pan to reach halfway up the sides of the baking dish. Tent loosely with aluminum foil and bake about 1 hour and 10 minutes, until flan is set around the edges but still wobbles a bit in the center when you give the dish a gentle shake. Cool flan in the water bath on a rack until water is room temperature. Remove the flan from the water and cool. Stretch and seal plastic wrap across the top of the dish but not on the surface of the flan and refrigerate until thoroughly chilled, at least 4 hours or up to 2 days.

4. Gently pull the edges of the flan away from dish with your fingertips. Invert a large, deep serving platter over the baking dish and flip; the flan should fall gently onto the platter and caramel will flow over it. Cut into squares and serve with a spoonful of caramel drizzled around each piece.

grapefruit campari sorbet

4 to 6 servings

1¼ cups sugar

1 cup water

2 teaspoons egg white powder

2½ cups ruby red grapefruit juice, with pulp (2 large grapefruit)

¼ cup Campari (a bittersweet Italian apéritif)

1. Bring the sugar and water to a boil in a small saucepan and cook until all the sugar is dissolved. Put the egg white powder in a large bowl and slowly whisk in the hot sugar syrup. Let cool until just room temperature. Whisk in the grapefruit juice and Campari, cover with plastic wrap, and refrigerate until completely cooled.

2. Put the mixture into an ice cream freezer and freeze according to the manufacturer's directions.

STYLE If serving sorbet to a crowd, try this: Warm up your ice cream scoop in water and then scoop balls onto plastic-lined pans and set them in the freezer until you are ready to serve. When dessert time arrives, drop this pretty-in-pink ice into a delicate dish and set it off with a cookie of your choice.

The last temptation is light, icy, and refreshing. Like all sorbets, it cleanses the palate—and the conscience—after an indulgent meal.

eight

essentials

Good technique
is the key to
great cooking.
Here are some
basic skills,
definitions, and
recipes you'll
find useful in
preparing the
recipes in the
rest of the book.

Tools of our trade.

Though our cooks can work wonders with a chef's knife, a few handy gadgets make our jobs much easier. Take a peek inside our tool box.

Most ingredients are cut into smaller pieces before being used in a recipe. Sometimes you want the pieces uniform in shape and size, sometimes it doesn't matter.

Chopping: To chop something is simply to cut it into smaller pieces. It's a larger cut than a dice or a mince and doesn't have to be uniform. To chop vegetables, keep the tip of the chef's knife on the cutting board and cut uniformly down through the vegetable with a rocking motion, all of the way down the blade. Carefully feed the item being chopped toward the blade, keeping your fingers curled in tight.

Dicing: A dice is a cube that is usually ¼- to ¾-inch square. To cut something—usually a vegetable—in a dice, first trim the vegetable so that its sides are straight and at right angles. Next, cut the vegetable in panels in the thickness you want your dice to be. Stack the panels and cut uniform matchsticks in the width you want your dice to be. Then,

finally, line up your sticks and cut them into uniform dice.

Mincing: A mince is a very tiny cut of food—usually an herb or vegetable. To mince something, first chop it roughly on a cutting board. Gather up the pieces in a pile. Position your knife above the pile. Keeping the tip touching the cutting board, repeatedly raise and lower the length of the blade down through whatever you're mincing. Move blade in an arc, chopping until the food is the desired fineness.

Grating: Grating gives food a very fine texture. Commonly grated foods include nutmeg, hard cheeses, and citrus peel. Grate on a mandoline, a box grater, or a microplane.

French: To remove the cartilage and fat between rib bones on a rack of lamb, pork roast, or chops so that the clean bones are exposed. It makes for a striking and elegant presentation. Your butcher can French bone-in meats with a few quick cuts.

food mill

salad spinner

immersion blender

whisk

cast-iron skillet

kitchen shears

paring knife

tongs

spatula

chef's knife

instant-read thermometer

microplane

knife sharpener

Japanese-style
ginger grater

vegetable peeler

nutmeg grater

mandoline

spider

baking mats

offset spatula

box grater

dough scraper

Graham
KERR

The produce section.

Taking time to store fresh produce properly prolongs its taste, nutrients, and aesthetic quality. Here are the ideal storage conditions for some of the most common fruits and vegetables.

Potatoes, sweet potatoes: Store unwashed, in a cool, dark, dry, well-ventilated place—not the refrigerator.

Onions, shallots, garlic: Store at room temperature in a dark, dry, well-ventilated space—though not with tubers. Each emits a natural gas that causes the other to rot.

Stem vegetables (rhubarb, celery, asparagus): Store in the crisper section of the refrigerator in sealed plastic bags.

Buds and flowers (broccoli, cabbage, Brussels sprouts, artichokes): Store in perforated plastic bags in the refrigerator crisper.

Tomatoes: Store at room temperature on the countertop—never in the refrigerator.

Lettuces, herbs, salad and cooking greens: Soak separated leaves in cool water, then spin dry in a salad spinner. Store loosely packed in a container with a damp paper towel over the top, then covered with plastic wrap.

Mushrooms: Store, unwashed, in a single layer on a plate, covered with a slightly damp paper towel on an upper refrigerator shelf.

Berries: Store unwashed and covered with plastic wrap in a single layer on a paper towel-lined plate in the refrigerator.

Apples, lemons, limes, oranges: Store in plastic bags in the crisper section of the refrigerator.

Peaches, melon: Let sit at room temperature for a few days to soften, then store in the refrigerator for 3 to 5 days.

cheese course

Whether it's used in a recipe or eaten alone on its own merit, we love cheese: sharp, mild, soft, firm, blue, yellow, or white. Here are a few of our favorites.

Cotija: Though it's often called the Parmesan of Mexico because of the way it's used, this semi-firm, semi-sharp cheese more closely resembles feta. Crumble it over warm refried beans or on top of other Mexican-style dishes.

Farmhouse Cheddar: This is not your childhood Cheddar. This creamy and sharp artisanal cheese once produced farm-by-farm in England is experiencing a renaissance. Though the best ones still come from England, we also love some of those coming out of Vermont and Wisconsin.

Manchego: Made from sheep's milk in the rocky region of central Spain, manchego has a firm, somewhat dry texture and an assertive flavor. It has nuances of the wild herbs that grow on the land where the Manchego sheep graze.

Mascarpone: The dairy-rich region of Lombardy in Italy created this super-rich cream cheese.

Parmigiano-Reggiano: There's Parmesan, and then there's Parmigiano-Reggiano. While domestic Parmesans are aged for about 14 months, Parmigiano-Reggiano is aged for at least 2 years, which accounts for its intense, nutty flavor and granular texture. You'll know it's the real deal if you see "Parmigiano-Reggiano" stamped on the rind, and if the cheese has been cut from a large, straw-colored wheel. If a recipe calls for Parmigiano-Reggiano, it's worth the price tag. If it calls for Parmesan, a domestic version will do.

Pecorino Romano: While Parmigiano-Reggiano is the most famous Italian grating cheese made from cow's milk, this is its sharp-flavored sheep's-milk parallel. Pecorino Romano can be used the same way Parmesan is used.

Queso fresco: Literally "fresh cheese" in Spanish, this Mexican cheese has a slightly grainy texture and mild flavor.

Saga blue: This delicately veined blue cheese from Denmark has the texture of a firm cream cheese and a mellower flavor than many other blue cheeses.

Chop, chop.

With a few simple tricks, preparing fresh fruits and vegetables for cooking is fast and easy. Once you learn the tricks, you'll use them again and again.

SECTIONING CITRUS
1. Cut the ends off of the fruit. Remove remaining peel by cutting down fruit from one end to the other.
2. Cut between a section and the membrane to the center of the fruit. Turn the knife and slide it alongside the membrane up the other side of the section.
3. Repeat with remaining sections.

ZESTING CITRUS
To make long, wide pieces of peel, use a vegetable peeler to remove just the top layer of peel (the white pith underneath is bitter). To make finely grated citrus peel, use a microplane—again, avoiding the pith.

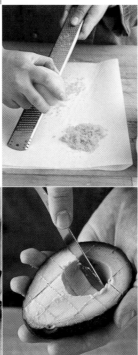

CUTTING AN ONION
A lot of our recipes call for onion wedges. When you cut an onion into wedges, remove the stem end, but leave the root end intact so that the onion doesn't fall apart as it cooks.

SEEDING, DICING AVOCADO
1. Cut to the seed around the midsection of the avocado. Hold avocado in both hands and twist gently to separate. Tap seed with a knife. When blade catches, rotate knife and lift out seed.
2. Make cuts down the length of the avocado. Make cuts across the avocado.
3. Scoop dice into a bowl.

FRESH GINGER: Fresh gingerroot doesn't need to be peeled if it is being poached in a sauce and then removed (as in Red Fruit Salad, page II). If you do need it peeled, cut off one end of the root, then peel with a vegetable peeler, moving down the root. To grate, use the fine side of a box grater. Mince ginger by hand. If you use a food processor, you'll get unappetizing strings and fibers.

GARLIC: Press the pointy side of the head of garlic gently down onto a hard surface with the heel of your hand until it breaks apart into individual cloves. To peel the cloves, press down on them with a knife until the peel cracks, then simply remove it.

ROASTING PEPPERS: Fire-roasted peppers—sweet or hot—can be prepared anywhere there's an open flame or very high heat. To use a gas burner, hold the pepper over the flame with tongs or a long fork and turn to roast it evenly. Or place the whole pepper (or peppers) on a grill, turning occasionally. To roast under a broiler, halve them and remove the stem and seeds. Place halves, cut side down, on a foil-lined baking sheet. When skins are evenly charred and blistered, place peppers under an inverted bowl and let cool for about 20 minutes. The steam that builds will make it easy to remove the skin with a paring knife. Discard skin.

PEELING PEACHES & TOMATOES: Bring a medium saucepan of water to a boil over high heat. Set a bowl of ice water next to the stove. Slice an "X" in the skin on the bottom of each peach or tomato with a knife. Drop the fruit into boiling water for about IO seconds, then immediately plunge it into the ice water. Drain and slip the skins off the fruit, using the loosened skin at the "X" to get started.

FRESH HERBS: Herbs with tender stems such as cilantro, parsley, basil, and mint can simply be snipped—stems and all—with clean kitchen shears or minced with a chef's knife on a cutting board. Only the leaves of those herbs with woodier stems such as rosemary, thyme, and oregano should be used. To remove the leaves from the stem of these types of herbs, hold the stem in one hand and, starting at the top, strip the leaves by running the fingers of your other hand down the stem.

CHILES
If you are working with very hot chiles, such as jalapeños, Scotch bonnets, or habañeros, you might want to wear plastic gloves. Chile oils are potent and not easily washed away. The seeds, ribs, and blossom ends of a chile hold much of its heat. Use them—or don't—depending on how hot you like your food. To seed and chop a chile, cut off each end, then cut it vertically from top to bottom. Open it up and lay it flat. Remove the seeds and ribs, if you like. Cut into narrow strips, then chop or mince.

Ancho chiles: The dried form of the poblano chile. The heat meter of the ancho can range from slightly warm to downright lip-tingling. This slightly fruity chile also appears in the market ground into a powder.

Chipotle chiles: These dried, smoked jalapeños lend a little heat and a rich, chocolatey flavor to foods. The curing process mellows their heat a bit, compared to the fresh chile. In addition to the dried form, they also come packed in adobo sauce, a concoction of chiles, herbs, and vinegar.

Piquillo peppers: A fire-engine red pepper from Spain that's slowly roasted over a wood fire, then peeled and packed in its own juices. One of our favorite finds, they add sweetness and a little heat to sauces and salad dressings.

Poblano chiles: If you've ever enjoyed the cheese-stuffed and deep-fried dish called chiles rellenos, you've likely had a poblano. Generally, the darker green they are, the more heat they have—though poblanos are one of the milder chiles. In their dried form, they're called ancho chiles.

Thai bird chiles: Despite their name, these tiny firecracker chiles are originally from South America but have been eagerly embraced by Asian cooks. They come in red or green, but either way, they're extremely hot.

SHOPSMART Organize your shopping list by sections of your market—and pick your produce last. Although produce is often right up front in a large market, choose it last so it doesn't get squished at the bottom of your cart.

SHOPSMART Use all of your senses—smell the tomatoes, pinch the peaches, listen to the artichokes (they should squeak when squeezed), and taste when you can.

The main event: meat, poultry, fish.

Your butcher or fish market may do the big jobs, but the details are best left to the cook. Here are the basics.

SHOPSMART Be open to the best your fish market has to offer. It's better to think about buying a type of fish rather than having your heart set on a specific species: Look for a white-fleshed fish or a good grilling fish. That way, if the snapper is better than the sole, you serve what's freshest. Look for moist pristine-looking filets, with no gaps between the muscles. Whole fish should look shiny, with clear vibrant eyes, as if it just came from the sea. All fish should smell sweet and fresh—not fishy.

SHOPSMART Red meats should have a rosy bloom and poultry should look plump and moist. Meat packages should be firmly wrapped, with no leaking or excess moisture. Check expiration dates and package labeling to make sure that the meat is fresh and has been handled properly. Refrigerate meats directly after purchasing.

SHOPSMART Price is not always a reflection of quality. Don't assume the most expensive is the best. For example, low-cost cuts of meat handled properly can be as sublime as top-of-the-line cuts. Try new products to find what tastes best to you.

spices & condiments

Curry, Madras-style: The city of Madras on the southeastern coast of India spawned two classics: its famous namesake fabric and this moderately hot curry powder. At its most basic, Madras-style curry includes ground coriander, turmeric, chiles, cumin, and fennel.

Fish sauce: This pungent sauce made from the liquid from salted and fermented fish is what distinguishes much Southeast Asian cooking from other Asian cuisines.

Harissa: Look in Middle Eastern markets for this fiery Tunisian sauce. A blend of hot chiles, garlic, cumin, coriander, caraway, and olive oil, it's *de rigueur* with couscous but just as delicious with grilled meats, and stirred into soups and stews.

Pimenton: This smoked Spanish paprika comes either hot or sweet. We absolutely love it for the depth of flavor and warmth it adds to foods. Try it on mashed potatoes or sprinkled on deviled eggs.

Sambal oelek: Fiery but sweet, this paste made with chiles, brown sugar or molasses, and salt accompanies many curry and rice dishes in Indonesia, Malaysia, and Southeast Asia. It also adds a little sweet heat to sauces.

Sriracha sauce: This is the red-orange sauce you see in those squeeze bottles on the tables of Thai restaurants. A moderately hot chili sauce, it's used widely in Thai cooking as a condiment.

Tamarind concentrate: An intensely sour sauce made from the fruit of a tree native to India and North Africa. The concentrate is used widely as a flavoring in Southeast Asian, Middle Eastern, and Latin cuisines. It's a terrific addition to barbecue sauce.

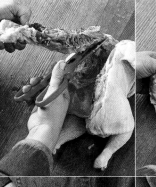

BUTTERFLYING POULTRY

1, 2. Cut out the backbone with shears or a knife, taking care not to cut into thighs. 3. Turn bird around so legs face away from you. Lay bird open and make a small notch in the white cartilage at tip of the breastbone with the tip of a knife. Run fingers along breastbone to loosen, then grip and lift out.

DEVEINING SHRIMP

1. Shrimp can be deveined in the shell or out. To devein through the shell, make a cut along the back of the shrimp just deep enough to expose the vein. 2. Gently remove the vein with the tip of the knife or your fingers. 3. Peel the shells off, starting at the head end.

BONING HALIBUT

1. After the halibut is cooked, cut off the skin with a small, sharp knife. 2. Cut alongside either side of the backbone. 3. Gently lift out the backbone at its center.

CUTTING MEAT

After the meat has rested for the proper amount of time (5 minutes for a steak and up to 30 minutes for a roast) to avoid shredding it and losing its precious juices, cut it across the grain with a sharp carving knife on a cutting board.

FOR VIDEO demonstrations of a whole host of cooking techniques, visit www.foodnetwork.com. Click on the "Cooking" tab at the top of the page, then go to "Cooking Demos."

let the baking begin

Baking is pure pleasure, especially when your ingredients are the freshest and best you can buy. Sift through a few of our baking-day imperatives.

Baking powder: This leavener will only make your biscuits and quick breads light as air if it's fresh. Check the date on the box or can before you start mixing and stirring to be sure your baking powder will work.

Cocoa: Unsweetened cocoa powder comes in two forms. Dutch-process cocoa is treated with alkali, which softens cocoa's acidity and mellows the intensity of the cocoa flavor. We've used the natural form of cocoa because we love the intense chocolate flavor it gives to our sweets.

Cornmeal: Cornmeal comes in three textures: fine, medium, and coarsely ground. Although the three are generally interchangeable in recipes and can be used according to your own preference, polenta is traditionally made with a coarser grind.

Maple sugar: Twice as sweet as granulated white sugar, maple sugar is a New England specialty made by continuing to boil maple syrup until all of the liquid evaporates. Look for it in the baking section of your supermarket.

Vanilla extract: Nothing but true vanilla extract—or the actual bean itself—will give your foods that aroma and flavor that is so sweet and seductive. Always use real vanilla extract.

Soft-peak egg whites

MEASURING

In some kinds of cooking, you can play a little loose with the measurement of some ingredients. In baking, accuracy is critical. How you measure your flour affects the final recipe. We spoon flour into a dry measuring cup and then level it off with a spoon handle or knife.

TOASTING NUTS OR SEEDS

1. Spread the nuts or seeds in a single layer on a baking sheet. 2. Bake at 350°F for 7 to 10 minutes, shaking occasionally to brown all of the nuts or seeds evenly.
3. Remove from the oven and place the pan on a wire rack to allow the nuts to get crisp as they cool.

CHOPPING CHOCOLATE

Place chocolate bar or block on a cutting board and press down on it in several places with a large, sharp knife to break it up. For more finely chopped chocolate, hold the tip of the knife in place with your free hand and move the the knife in an arc, making small chops as you go.

CREAMING BUTTER

Creaming the butter for cakes and cookies is crucial. Beating the butter—often with sugar—before other ingredients are added creates air bubbles that make your baked goods high, light, and tender. Have butter at room temperature before creaming.

KNEADING DOUGH

1. Push and stretch the dough in front of you.
2. Fold the dough into a ball and repeat the first step over and over again, until dough is no longer sticky. 3. Push and stretch the dough with the heels of both hands, folding it into a ball, until dough is satiny and smooth, usually about 10 minutes.

WHIPPING EGG WHITES

1. Begin with egg whites at room temperature and a bowl that is absolutely clean and free of any fats or oils. 2. Beat egg whites at moderate speed with a wire whisk or an electric mixer. When foamy, increase the speed.
3. Beat until whites form stiff, stable peaks but are still moist and glossy.

WHIPPING CREAM

Chill a metal bowl and the beaters for your electric mixer in the freezer at least 15 minutes before you begin. Pour cold whipping cream into the chilled bowl and beat on medium-high speed until medium-firm peaks form. Don't overbeat, or you'll wind up with butter.

chicken broth
about 3 quarts of broth, plus 3 to 4 cups poached chicken

1 4-pound whole chicken

1 onion, peeled and quartered

2 carrots, quartered

2 ribs celery, quartered

1 to 2 dark green leek tops (optional)

1 medium parsnip, quartered (optional)

3 generous sprigs fresh thyme or 1 teaspoon dried

3 generous sprigs fresh flat-leaf parsley

5 black peppercorns

1 bay leaf

   About 4 quarts water

1. Combine chicken, vegetables, fresh herbs, peppercorns, and bay leaf in a stockpot. Pour in enough water to cover chicken completely. Heat water to just under a boil over medium-high heat. Reduce heat to a very low simmer. Skim any fat and scum from the surface with a ladle or large spoon. Cook until chicken is cooked through but not dry, about 1 hour.

2. Remove chicken from the pot and cool. Continue to simmer the broth while you cut the chicken meat from the bone. Use the meat for salad, soups, or other recipes. Return the bones to the pot and simmer for another hour.

3. Strain the broth into another pot, a large bowl, or plastic container. Fill the sink up with ice water to come about halfway up the sides of the container. Nestle the broth in the ice bath and stir it periodically to cool it down. Cover and refrigerate for up to five days or freeze up to 3 months.

spicy red pepper sauce
about 1 cup

½ cup piquillo peppers (see page 273)

¼ cup fresh flat-leaf parsley leaves

3 tablespoons mayonnaise

3 tablespoons extra-virgin olive oil

1½ teaspoons hot pepper sauce, or to taste

1 teaspoon Dijon mustard

1 clove garlic, peeled

½ teaspoon kosher salt

Puree peppers, parsley, mayonnaise, olive oil, hot pepper sauce, mustard, garlic, and salt in a blender until smooth. Pour sauce into a bowl and set aside. Cover and refrigerate if storing, up to 2 days. Bring sauce to room temperature before serving.

roasted chicken stock

about 3 quarts

5 pounds mixed chicken bones and wings, backs, and/or necks

2 tablespoons vegetable oil or chicken fat

3 medium carrots, quartered

2 medium onions, unpeeled, quartered

2 ribs celery, quartered

1 to 2 dark green leek tops (optional)

3 cloves garlic, unpeeled

1 large tomato, chopped

3 generous sprigs flat-leaf parsley

2 sprigs fresh thyme or 1 teaspoon dried

2 bay leaves

¼ teaspoon black peppercorns

2 cloves

1. Preheat the oven to 450°F. Spread the bones out in a large roasting pan. Roast until golden brown, about 1½ hours. Drain and discard any liquid the bones give off as they roast.

2. While the bones roast, heat the oil in a stockpot over medium-high heat. Add the vegetables and cook, stirring occasionally, until brown, about 30 minutes.

3. When bones are cooked, transfer them to the stockpot; add a splash of water to the roasting pan, stir to scrape up any brown bits, and pour the liquid into the stockpot. Add parsley, thyme, bay leaves, peppercorns, and cloves and enough cold water to cover the bones. Bring to a boil over high heat, then reduce heat to keep stock at a gentle simmer for 4 to 5 hours. Skim any fat or foamy scum that rises to the surface.

4. Strain stock through a fine-meshed strainer into 1 large or several smaller containers. Cool stock by placing container(s) in an ice-water bath or in very cold water in the sink. Stir stock occasionally to cool it as quickly as possible. Cover containers tightly and refrigerate up to 5 days or freeze up to 3 months.

Homemade chicken stock in the freezer is like gold in the bank.

parslied egg noodles

6 servings

Kosher salt

1 12-ounce package wide egg noodles

4 to 6 tablespoons cold unsalted butter, cut into bits

3 tablespoons chopped fresh flat-leaf parsley

Freshly ground black pepper

Bring a large pot of cold water to a boil over high heat and salt it generously. Add the noodles and cook, stirring occasionally, until al dente, about 5 minutes. Ladle ¼ cup of the noodle cooking water into a medium skillet. Whisk in the butter bit by bit over low heat, letting each piece melt completely before adding the next, to make a creamy sauce. Stir in the parsley and season with salt and pepper. Drain the noodles, toss with the sauce, and serve immediately.

Sometimes there's time to make a classic with all of its steps, and sometimes you just want something that tastes great—fast.

béchamel sauce
about 4 cups

4 tablespoons unsalted butter

1 shallot, chopped

½ medium carrot, peeled and chopped

½ rib celery, chopped

6 tablespoons all-purpose flour

4 cups milk

3 sprigs fresh flat-leaf parsley

1 sprig fresh thyme

1 small bay leaf

1½ teaspoons kosher salt

Pinch freshly grated nutmeg

Freshly ground black pepper

Melt the butter in a medium saucepan over medium heat. Add the shallot, carrot, and celery and cook, covered, until softened, about 5 minutes. Stir in the flour with a wooden spoon and cook until it lightens in color, about 2 minutes. Slowly whisk in the milk and bring to a boil. Add the parsley, thyme, and bay leaf. Reduce the heat to maintain a gentle simmer and cook, whisking occasionally, until the sauce is thick, about 15 minutes. Strain the sauce into a bowl and season with the salt, nutmeg, and pepper. Press plastic wrap on the surface of the sauce until ready to use.

cajun seasoning
about ⅓ cup

1 tablespoon dried oregano

1 tablespoon dried thyme

1 tablespoon sweet paprika

1 tablespoon kosher salt

2 teaspoons garlic powder

1 teaspoon onion powder

1 teaspoon cayenne pepper

1 teaspoon English-style dry mustard

½ teaspoon freshly ground black pepper

Combine oregano, thyme, paprika, salt, garlic powder, onion powder, cayenne pepper, dry mustard, and black pepper thoroughly in a small bowl. Store in an airtight container.

streamlined béchamel
about 4 cups

2   tablespoons unsalted butter

¼   cup all-purpose flour

4   cups milk

I   sprig fresh flat-leaf parsley

I   sprig fresh thyme

½   bay leaf

½   onion studded with I clove

½   teaspoon kosher salt

   Pinch freshly grated nutmeg

   Freshly ground black pepper

Melt the butter in a medium saucepan over medium heat. Stir in the flour with a wooden spoon and cook until it lightens in color, about 2 minutes. Slowly whisk in the milk and bring to a boil. Add the parsley, thyme, bay leaf, and onion. Reduce the heat to maintain a gentle simmer and cook, whisking occasionally, until the sauce is thick, about 15 minutes. Remove the herbs and onion and season with salt, nutmeg, and pepper.

KNOW-HOW When time is short, make this version of this essential sauce. It's quicker than the classic, left, because you use an onion studded with a clove to flavor the sauce rather than the chopped vegetables.

A well-stocked pantry and a dash of inspiration mean a delicious dinner is on the table in no time.

oven-dried tomatoes
about 2 cups

2   pounds ripe plum tomatoes, cored and halved lengthwise

I   teaspoon kosher salt

   Fresh herb sprigs, such as thyme, rosemary, or sage (optional)

   Extra-virgin olive oil (optional)

I. Preheat the oven to 250°F. Arrange the tomatoes, cut side up, in a single layer on a parchment or foil-lined baking sheet. Sprinkle with the salt. Bake until slightly shriveled but still plump, about 5 hours.

2. If not using immediately, refrigerate the dried tomatoes in a sealed container for up to 4 days. Or layer them with the herb sprigs, if desired. Add olive oil to cover, seal tightly, and refrigerate for up to 2 weeks.

index

index

index

index